Longman Archaeology Series

Science-based dating in archaeology

Longman Archaeology Series

Advisory editor:
Barry Cunliffe,
Professor of European Archaeology, University of Oxford

Each volume in this important new series will tackle a major theme currently in need of synthesis or reassessment. The books are designed for professional archaeologists, students and the serious amateur enthusiast, and cover a range of levels as well as topics. A common feature of the series is the application to archaeology of ideas and techniques derived from anthropology, ethnology and other related disciplines.

★Already published

M. J. Aitken

Science-based dating in archaeology

Longman
London and New York

Addison Wesley Longman Limited,
Edinburgh Gate,
Harlow, Essex CM20 2JE, England
and Associated Companies throughout the world.

*Published in the United States of America
by Addison Wesley Longman, New York*

First published 1990
Third impression 1997

British Library Cataloguing in Publication Data
Aitken, M. J. (Martin Jim)
  Science-based dating in archaeology. – (Longman
  archaeology series)
  1. Archaeology. Scientific techniques
  I. Title
  930'.1028
  ISBN 0-582-05498-2 CSD
  ISBN 0-582-49309-9 PPR

Library of Congress Cataloging-in-Publication Data
Aitken, M. J. (Martin Jim)
  Science-based dating in archaeology/M. J. Aitken.
    – (Longman archaeology series)
    Includes bibliographies and index.
    ISBN 0–582–49309–9 ppr
    ISBN 0–582–05498–2
    1. Archaeological dating. I. Title. II. Series.
  CC78.A39   1990
  930.1'028'5–dc19   89–2380
                                                                         CIP

Transferred to digital print on demand 2001

Printed and bound by Antony Rowe Ltd. Eastbourne

Contents

List of figures

List of tables

Preface

In writing this book my primary aim has been to provide an *entrée* to dating methods provided by the physical sciences, having in mind archaeologists, general scientific readers and specialists interested in techniques not their own. I have employed a two-tier system. On the one hand there is the main text in which each chapter starts off at an elementary level and continues as far as possible in plain English with a minimum of equations; on the other hand there are end-notes for each chapter which go more deeply into various points and which in general presume on a basic mathematical background. There has not been room to attempt a definitive assessment of the techniques or to give a proper account of the contribution to archaeology so far made.

This latter, already substantial, will continue to increase in volume – and also in scope as technological advances make new things possible. Archaeology grows in complexity too, and the time when one person could be expert both in archaeology and in laboratory science is long past. Hence the growing importance of the interface between the two disciplines. Not only does this serve the utilitarian purpose of maximizing the benefit derived from laboratory effort; also, there can be much stimulation of ideas, in both directions, through informed dialogue. I hope this book will improve the efficacy of the interface in both its aspects.

My involvement in science-based dating is through my work, mainly in luminescence and magnetic techniques, at the Oxford University Research Laboratory for Archaeology and the History of Art. I willingly record my debt to its director, Professor E. T. Hall, as well as to past and present members of the laboratory as a whole and particularly to my research students. For my own enthusiasm in this field I owe much to the privilege of early guidance from Professor C. F. C. Hawkes who, together with the late Viscount Cherwell, provided the initiative for the formation of the laboratory in 1955.

Specifically for this book I have been fortunate in having advice and suggestions from: Adrian Allsop, Jeffrey Bada, Mike Baillie, David Bowen, Sheridan Bowman, Rex Galbraith, Richard Gillespie, John Gowlett,

Rainer Grün, Ernie Hailwood, Robert Hedges, Rupert Housley, Miro Ivanovich, Ian Law, Foss Leach, Stephen Moorbath, Gordon Pearson, Mervyn Popham, Helen Rendell, Stephen Robinson, Nick Shackleton, Pete Smart, Barnaby Smith, Stephen Stokes, Chris Stringer, Gerald Sykes, Henrik Tauber and John Westgate. I am grateful to all of them as well as to those who assisted in its preparation: Judith Takacs – illustrations; Katherine Manville, along with Jane Simcox, Mona Winter, June Gibbard and Adrian Allsop – word processing; Natalie Garton and Gill Spencer – library search. Without their help the book never would have seen the light of day.

Martin Aitken

The Ofslang, Islip
November 1988

Acknowledgements

Among the books I have consulted I would particularly like to acknowledge the help I obtained from: *The Ice Ages* by J. and K. P. Imbrie; *Tree-ring Dating and Archaeology* by M. G. L. Baillie; *Reconstructing Quaternary Environments* by J. J. Lowe and M. J. C. Walker; and *Die ESR-Altersbestimmungsmethode* by R. Grün; publication details will be found in the references.

For their specific permission to reproduce figures which appear in the text, I am grateful to the following: Academic Press (Orlando), *Thermoluminescence Dating* (Figs. 6.1–6.20); Academic Press Inc. (London) Ltd. and Dr. A. J. Clark, *Journal of Archaeological Science*, Vol 15 (Fig. 9.10); © 1982 by the American Association for the Advancement of Science and Dr. W. G. Mook, *Science* Vol 215, p. 159, 8 January 1982, G. M. Woillard and W. G. Mook, "Carbon-14 Dates at Grande Pile: Correlation of Land and Sea Chronologies" (Fig. 2.12); Antiquity Publications Ltd., *Antiquity*, Vol 61 (Fig. 4.11) and Dr. Gordon Pearson, Vol 61 (Fig. 4.6); Blackwell Scientific Publications Ltd., *Geophysical Journal of the Royal Astronomical Society*, Vol 70 (Fig. 9.11); Canberra Archaeological Society, *Archaeology at ANZAAS 1984* (Fig. 8.4); Croom Helm and Dr. M. Baillie, *Tree Ring Dating and Archaeology* (Figs. 2.15 and 2.17); Harvard University Press, *Ice Ages*, (c) 1979 by John Imbrie and Katherine Palmer Imbrie (Data from C. Emiliani, "Pleistocene Temperatures", Journ. Geol., 63, 1955) (Fig. 2.2); Kluwer Academic Publishers, *Milankovitch and Climate*, ed. Berger, 1984 (Fig. 2.4); Macmillan Magazines Ltd., *Nature* Vol 328, p. 518, 1987 (Figs. 2.9 and 2.10), Vol 315, p. 318, 1985 (Fig. 2.19), Vol 304, p. 264, 1983 (Fig. 5.2); National Research Council of Canada, *Canadian Journal of Earth Science*, Vol 24 (Figs. 7.3 and 7.5); Pergamon Press PLC, *Nuclear Tracks*, Vol 10, R. Grun and C. Invernati, 'Uranium Accumulation in Teeth and its effect on ESR Dating – a detailed study of a mammoth tooth', 1985, (Fig. 7.4); *Philosophical Transactions of the Royal Society of London* D. Q. Bowen and G. Sykes, Vol B318 (Fig. 8.2) and Dr. R. E. M. Hedges, Vol A323 (Fig. 4.13); University of Washington, *Quaternary Research* Vol 3 (Fig. 2.3) and Vol 27 (Fig. 2.8).

1 Generalities

1.1 THE IMPACT OF SCIENTIFIC TECHNIQUES

A fragment of Bronze Age pottery found in Greece will be dated by matching its form and decoration to a phase of the ceramic chronology established for the region. The basic framework to which that chronology is related – by archaeological cross-linkages – is the Egyptian calendar. This begins around 3000 BC, at the start of the First Dynasty, and it is fixed in calendar years through the recorded observation, more than 1000 years later, of a datable astronomical event[1] in the ninth year of the reign of Sesostris III; this recording ties down the floating chronology provided by fragmentary lists of kings and their reign lengths. On account of the astronomical anchoring the framework is essentially science-based, but the usual meaning of scientific techniques is exemplified by radiocarbon dating which from the early 1950s provided a time-scale extending into the Neolithic and beyond; the impact was dramatic, upsetting previous conjectures about the pace of man's development – what had been thought to have taken man one or two millennia to achieve was now seen to have taken four or five. Far beyond the Neolithic in the early stages of hominid development more than a million years ago it is potassium–argon dating that provides the time-scale and allows a proper understanding of the origins of early modern man to be developed. The stages by which *Homo sapiens sapiens* emerged from his forebears, and particularly the role of the Neanderthal branch, are increasingly datable by a number of other techniques, filling what used to be the gap between potassium–argon and radiocarbon – recent technical developments in the former are closing it anyway.

Subsequent to 3000 BC there has been impact too. For regions more remote from Egypt than Greece chronological schemes had been developed on the hypothesis that there would have been diffusion of technical and cultural developments outwards from the Near East towards western Europe. Here too radiocarbon (when calibrated) stimulated a reappraisal, showing the hypothesis to be untenable and that independent invention had occurred. Thus scientific dating is not just a boring necessity that tidies things up by providing numbers, it is vital for valid interpretation.

1.2 ABSOLUTE DATING AND DERIVATIVE DATING

There is a tendency to regard all scientific techniques as being 'absolute'. The proper meaning of absolute dating is that it is independent of any other chronology or dating technique, that it is based only on currently measurable quantities. Most of the techniques discussed in this book are indeed absolute, but not all, e.g. archaeomagnetic dating requires a reference curve having a time-scale provided by archaeological or other chronology. Radiocarbon is absolute only to within limits; for high accuracy, calibration by means of tree-ring dating (dendrochronology) is required. Some techniques can be applied in either absolute or derivative mode, e.g. amino acid dating and obsidian hydration dating.

1.3 THE EVENT BEING DATED

An obvious requirement in a dating technique is that there is a measurable time-dependent quantity that forms the 'clock'. It is also necessary that there must be an event that starts the clock and that this event must be relatable to the archaeology of interest. Some techniques automatically relate to the archaeology, e.g. the thermoluminescence clock in pottery is set to zero by ancient man's firing of a kiln. In others the association may only be approximate, e.g. the radiocarbon clock in wood starts when the wood forms, not when the tree was felled nor when man utilized it; hence the emphasis on 'short-lived' samples such as grain and twigs.

1.4 REASONS FOR DATING

Scientific dating is expensive,[2] both in equipment and personal effort; it may also be destructive of highly prized archaeological material. Therefore the archaeological questions that will be answered need to be carefully considered before the process is set in motion. It also needs to be established that the likely error limits are good enough; although this book attempts to give indication of these for the various techniques, direct discussion with the dating laboratory enables the likely performance of the technique on the site concerned to be properly assessed.

There is a hierarchy of reasons for dating. At the top there are dates which have world-wide significance, e.g. the relationship of early modern man to Neanderthal Man. Then there are dates that establish or strengthen the basic chronological framework of a region. Another reason is the need to date a site when there is doubt about its relationship to the region's chronological framework. Finally there may be the need to test a new technique or to assess the performance of an established one in particular circumstances.

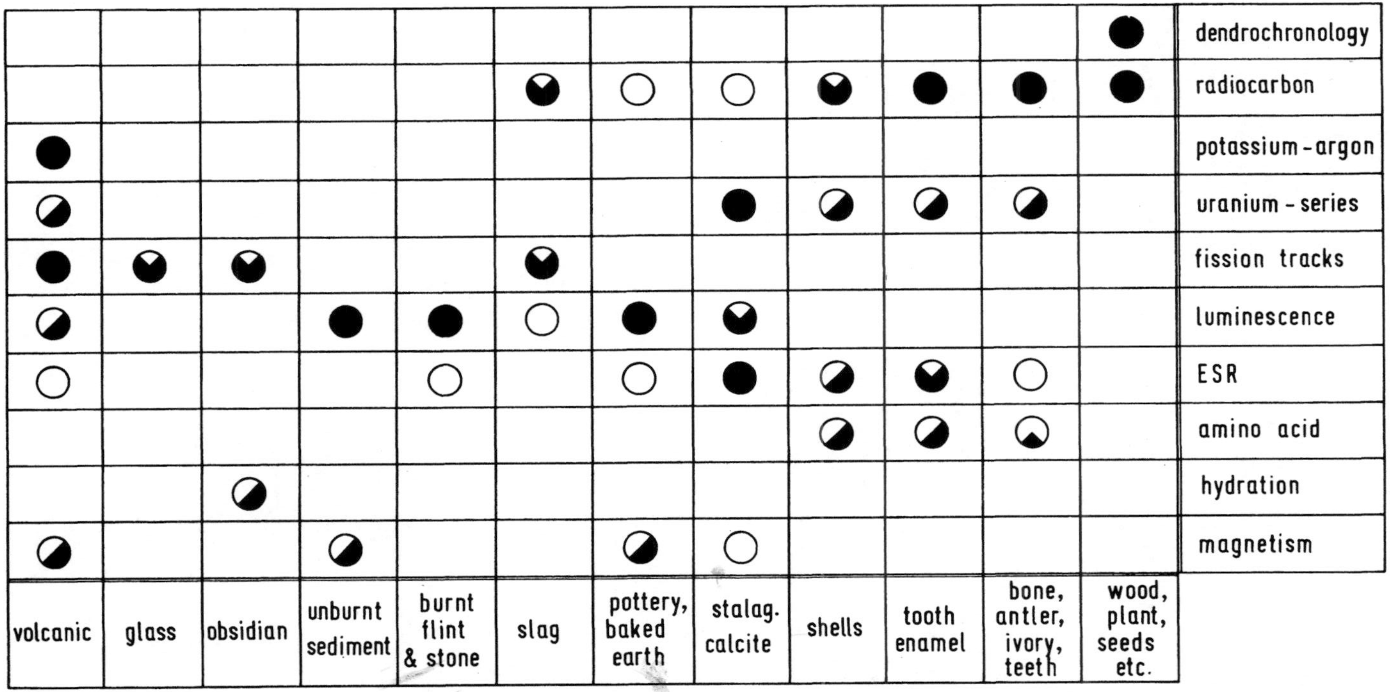

	dendrochronology	radiocarbon	potassium–argon	uranium–series	fission tracks	luminescence	ESR	amino acid	hydration	magnetism
wood, plant, seeds etc.	●	●								
bone, antler, ivory, teeth		●		◐			○	◐		
tooth enamel		●		◐			◐	◐		
shells		◐		◐			◐	◐		
stalag. calcite		○		●		◐	●		○	
pottery, baked earth		○		○		●	○			◐
slag		◐			◐	○				
burnt flint & stone						●	○			
unburnt sediment						●				◐
obsidian					◐				◐	
glass					◐					
volcanic			●	◐	●	◐	○			◐

Fig. 1.1 Applicability chart. Given a closed circle and an appropriate age range there are good prospects of a reliable date; less than closed circles indicate there are qualifications to be made, perhaps about reliability or perhaps about limitations in applicability. The chart is comparative in either direction; it is intended as a guide to further reading rather than a definitive judgement.

1.5 WHICH TECHNIQUE?

Figures 1.1 and 1.2 provide overviews which may be useful to archaeologists in considering which techniques might be useful on their various sites. Inevitably there are many qualifications in regard to applicability, and having read the appropriate chapter the archaeologist should consult a relevant laboratory for assessment of likely error limits and reliability in the particular circumstances concerned; essential data in this assessment are the state of preservation of the available samples and the precision of the association between the event which the technique would date and the event of archaeological significance.

1.6 DATING TERMINOLOGY

The pre-eminent technique, radiocarbon, produces an age in 'radiocarbon years' and these are not quite the same as calendar years; conversion to the latter requires reference to a calibration curve, as discussed in section 4.4. In general the other techniques produce an age directly in calendar years (though often with error limits that encompass the difference between radiocarbon age and calendar age).

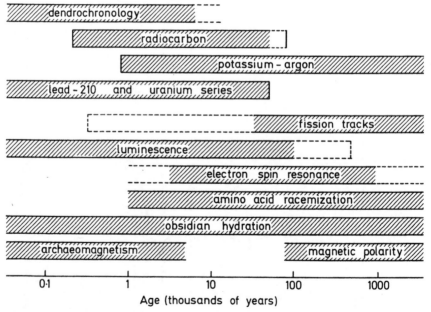

Fig. 1.2 Age ranges of techniques. Actual limits are dependent on circumstances, e.g. state of sample preservation; also, they are liable to widen with continued technical development.

To avoid continued confusion the 1985 International Radiocarbon Conference at Trondheim recommended the use of *cal* AD, *cal* BC, and *cal* BP for calibrated dates and ages; BP means 'years before present', the latter being defined as AD 1950. Omission of 'cal' implies use of radiocarbon years.

While this convention may deal with the problem as far as radiocarbon is concerned there is the difficulty that for other techniques AD, BC and BP imply calendar years, a usage established for the two former over many centuries. *In this book* the traditional meaning is retained for AD and BC, i.e. calendar years with respect to the birth of Christ; BP means 'radiocarbon years before AD 1950' as recommended at the conference, though it is used sparingly, substitution of 'radiocarbon age' usually being made; simple 'years ago' implies calendar years before the date of determination. A convention adopted by the journal *Antiquity* is the use of *ad, bc* and *bp* for uncalibrated dates and ages, and corresponding capital letters after calibration. Though highly convenient it has not been generally adopted, its use being restricted mainly to Britain; it has not been followed in this book.

Although used sparingly in this book, common terminologies for 'thousand years' are *kiloyear* (kyr) and *kiloan* (ka), the latter being French; similarly Myr and Ma for million years.

NOTES

1. The event was the heliacal rising of the bright star Sothis (Sirius). This star rises during daylight for a major portion of the year but its rising gets progressively earlier; hence there comes a day on which it is just enough in advance to be visible. Because there were only 365 days in the Egyptian calendar and no adjustment for leap year, the event moved forward by 1 day every 4 years, completing a full Sothic cycle in 1453 years. The cycle is tied into the Christian calendar by the recording in AD 139 of a heliacal rising on New Year's Day in the Egyptian calendar. The recording of a heliacal rising on the sixteenth day of the eighth month of the seventh year of Sesostris III allows dating of that day to 1870 ($\pm$6) BC. Historical records are complete enough to give Egyptian history a firmly based chronology back to 2000 BC. Earlier than this the chronology is extrapolated by means of the Turin canon and the incomplete fragments of the Palermo stone. Most interpretations place the start of the First Dynasty within a century of 3000 BC.

   Other regions, e.g. Mesopotamia, have astronomically based calendars too, though none reaching earlier than 3000 BC. The Mayan calendar of the Aztecs is another example.

2. A major part of science-based dating is carried out through collaborative programmes between laboratories and archaeologists, funded by national research councils. As a direct service, laboratories are increasingly under obligation to recover the full cost and the following current estimates, in US dollars, give a rough guide as to what to expect: radiocarbon, 200–600; uranium series, 700–1500; thermoluminescence date, 100–500; thermoluminscence authenticity test, 250; obsidian hydration, 25–500. Addresses of laboratories that provide a service are usually obtainable from national archaeology associations, etc.

2 Climatic clocks and frameworks

2.1 INTRODUCTION

In the present chapter we outline some climate-based approaches to dating which, with one notable exception, evolved essentially from visual observation of archaeological/geological material; these are in contrast to the main content of the book which is concerned with laboratory-derived techniques which were taken into the field. We may regard the former as natural ways of dating in the sense that observation of the changing seasons and the motions of sun, moon and stars are natural ways of telling the time as opposed to using intricate technical devices known as clocks.

Particularly for Palaeolithic archaeology, climatic variation provides a chronological framework; it is the task of more quantitative techniques to provide absolute dates for this framework. For more recent archaeology it is the annual growth rings of a tree and the annual layers in sediment from melting glaciers that are relevant and in themselves precisely quantitative; these annual clocks have been of critical importance in providing absolute calibration of the radiocarbon time-scale.

In outlining the dating connotations of climatic change we are seeing only the tip of the iceberg of the much larger topic of palaeoclimate reconstruction. For the latter the reader should consult other texts such as those by Lowe and Walker (1984) and by Bradley (1985).

2.2 CLIMATE-BASED FRAMEWORKS

Successive glaciations and deglaciations define a period of recent geological time known as the Quaternary (roughly the last 2 million years). The Pleistocene is the first epoch of the Quaternary and this follows the Pliocene, the last epoch of the Tertiary period. The beginning of the Pleistocene is indicated in the fossil record by an abrupt change from warm to cold conditions, though there is also evidence for glaciations during the late Pliocene. The present epoch, the Holocene or Postglacial starts about 10,000 years ago at the termination of the last glaciation.

Evidence that the glaciers of the Alps, Scandinavia, North America and China had formerly been more extensive came from observation of erratic boulders (ie. out of geological context) and scratch marks on rocks, and from recognition of raised beaches, glacial drift deposits and glaciated landscapes. This led to the notion of four major ice ages which in the Alpine chronology were named *Günz, Mindel, Riss* and *Würm*, the latter being the most recent; in North America the identifying names were *Nebraskan, Kansan, Illinoian* and *Wisconsinan*; in the Lushan terminology of China the names are *Poyang, Da Gu, Lushan* and *Dali*. Subsequently, indicators of climate such as flora and fauna, and soil conditions, have been studied and the framework is now much more complex than a

Table 2.1 Some terminologies used in the northern hemisphere for glacial and interglacial [a] stages of the Quaternary

European Alps	Northern Europe[b]	Britain	Central North America	China[c]
Postglacial	Holocene	Flandrian	Holocene	Postglacial
Würm	Weichselian	Devensian	Wisconsinan	Dali
Riss-Würm	Eemian	Ipswichian	Sangamon	Lushan-Dali
Riss	Saalian	Wolstonian (?)	Illinoian	Lushan
Mindel-Riss	Holsteinian	Hoxnian	Yarmouthian	—
Mindel	Elsterian	Anglian	Kansan	Da Gu
Günz-Mindel	Cromerian	Cromerian	Aftonian	—
Günz	Menapian	Beestonian	Nebraskan	Poyang
Donau	Waalian	Pastonian		
Biber	Eburonian	Pre-Pastonian		
	Tiglian	Bramertonian		
	Pretiglian	Baventian		
		Antian		
		Thurnian		
		Ludhamian		
	Reuverian	Reuverian		

[a] Interglacials are shown in italics. Except for China this table is derived from Lowe and Walker (1984) who warn against assuming correlation between columns except in respect of the first two lines.

[b] Development of these stratigraphic frameworks is a continuing process: for instance it was proposed by Woillard (1978) that following the *Eemian* there were additional interglacial stages, *St–Germain I*, and *II*, before the Weichselian was reached; subsequently these have usually been regarded as interstadials – see section 2.4.3.

[c] An account of glacial stratigraphy in China has been given by Derbyshire (1987) who advises against continued use of the traditional terminology given here. In the extensive loess deposits of central China there are four major formations: *Wucheng, Lower Lishi, Upper Lishi* and *Malan*, the latter corresponding to the last glacial stage (see Kukla 1987).

succession of four *glacials* with intervening *interglacials*: within a glacial there are warmish short-lived episodes termed *interstadials*, contrasting with adjacent colder *stadials*.

Although the Alpine framework has been widely used in palaeolithic archaeology, particularly in the southerly parts of Europe, its transference to non-Alpine regions raises problems of correlation, arising essentially from the discontinuous nature of the record; there are comparable difficulties with other frameworks; not only is the record made up from components in different locations of a region but it may be that in some regions evidence of particular phases may be totally lacking – in some cases due to eradication by a later glaciation of the region. Table 2.1 indicates some of the main terminologies in use for glacials and interglacials. However, it is only for the first two lines that correlation between regions can be assumed; further back in time there is uncertainty about correlation, not only because of the possibility of missing phases but also because what is recognized as an interglacial in one region may be regarded only as an interstadial elsewhere. Another dimension is the archaeological record based on hominid development and stone-tool technology, which interlocks with the climatic record. Figure 2.1 indicates some of the terms used in describing the archaeology of the Middle and Upper Pleistocene epoch; the age scale is that for Europe and increasingly the techniques of the following chapters are giving indication

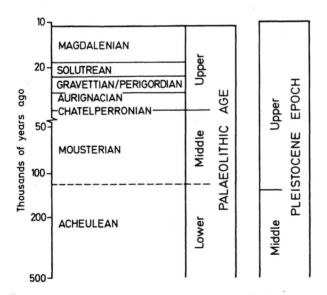

Fig. 2.1 Some archaeological subdivisions of the Palaeolithic lying within the Middle and Upper Pleistocene. Although the names derive from sites in Europe (as also the age scale), they tend to be used for similar cultural assemblages elsewhere.

of the extent to which this is applicable to similar industries elsewhere, as well as throwing light on the question of inter-regional correlation between climatic phases.

Subdivisions: loess deposits

The simplicity of the initial concept of four ice ages was soon lost when stadials and interstadials began to be identified. As an example of the complication that is liable to develop through intensive work, Table 2.2 lists some of the type sites that have been used to label interstadials of the Weichselian of north-west Europe; there is also division of this glacial stage into broad *substages* of *Early-glacial*, *Pleniglacial* and *Late-glacial*; correspondingly (though not necessarily with an exact relationship in time) in the Alpine chronology there are substages Würm-I, Würm-II, and Würm-III; the Devensian and the Wisconsin are similarly divided into *Early*, *Middle*, and *Late*, with *Main Wisconsin* alternatively being used for the latter.

Table 2.2 Interstadials of the Weichselian glacial stage

Substage	Interstadials	Stadials
Late-glacial		Younger Dryas
	Allerød	
		Older Dryas
	Bølling	
		Oldest Dryas
Pleniglacial	*Denekamp*	
	Hengelo	
	Moerschoofd	
Early-glacial	*Odderade*	
	Brörup	
	Amersfoort	

Note: The interstadials extend back from about 12,000 years ago to 70,000 years or beyond (but not beyond about 110,000). They represent the system of classification developed in The Netherlands; around the world there is a multitude of other classifications for the last glacial stage (see Nilsson 1982; Sibrava *et al.* 1986), but the Dutch system is quite widely used in Europe.

For other regions and other glaciations the number of identified interstadials is usually less; this does not necessarily mean they do not exist because it may be that the record is more fragmentary or the research not as yet sufficiently comprehensive, e.g. exposures on separate sites are taken to represent the same interglacial, whereas they actually represent different ones. However, more or less continuous records are provided by the thick *loess* deposits of windblown sediment which cover large areas in the middle latitudes of the Northern Hemisphere, as well as occurring in South America and New Zealand. Loess is indicative of cold, windy conditions, one source being the silt produced by moving glaciers as they grind up rocks; for some deposits the sediment comes from adjacent desert regions. Interglacials are indicated by soil formation, giving *palaeosol horizons*, and usually there are distinct boundaries, *marklines*, indicative of change from cold to warm conditions. In central China the deposits, which have a thickness of 100 m or more, provide a virtually complete record of climatic change throughout the Quaternary; dating is primarily by means of geomagnetic polarity changes recorded in the sediment with interpolation by rate of deposition (see Fig. 2.4); luminescence dating is applicable too.

Another form of continuous record is provided by the occasional long pollen sequence that reaches back to the beginning of the last interglacial – see section 2.4.3 – and much further back in some cases (see Flenley, 1984). But of dominating importance are the remarkable recordings in deep-sea sediments and polar ice – see section 2.3.

Late-glacial and Postglacial subdivisions

The terminology used for the rapid changes of climate that occurred in north-west Europe subsequent to recession of the ice at the end of the last glaciation is given in Table 2.3. The successive zones were originated on the basis of palaeoclimatic indications found in Scandinavia, but subsequently they were redefined as *chronozones* in terms of radiocarbon years. The climatic zones found in peripheral regions, e.g Britain, have only approximately the same age scale, tending to be 'time-transgressive' to some extent; this is discussed further in section 2.4.3 (see also Lowe and Gray 1980).

There are many more terminologies and frameworks in use around the world than the Euro-centric ones given here. However, it is hoped that the reader involved with other regions will have been given some forewarning of what to expect – and take the precaution of learning the terminology as an essential for following continuing revision of frameworks as new evidence comes to light. For a comprehensive account of world-wide terminologies and correlations, see Nilsson (1982) and Sibrava *et al.* (1986).

Global climate

As discussed in the next section, oxygen-isotope variations on the floor of the deep ocean provide a stratigraphic record of global climate. There are some regions in which this spans the Quaternary without interruption, and furthermore its dating is reliable and absolute; initially this was by magnetic polarity changes and radiometric techniques, but subsequently an astronomically based time-scale has been developed. While it is not to

Table 2.3 Subdivisions[a] of the Late-glacial and Postglacial phases of NW Europe

			Chronozone	Radiocarbon years [b] before present	Calendar years [c] BC
Postglacial	Holocene (Flandrian)	Late	Sub–Atlantic		
				2,500	550–800
		Middle	Sub–Boreal		
				5,000	3,800
			Atlantic		
				8,000	c.7,000
		Early	Boreal		
				9,000	c.8,000
			Pre–Boreal		
				10,000	c.9,000
Late-glacial			Younger Dryas		
		Late		11,000	c.10,000
	Weichselian		Allerød		
				11,800	
			Older Dryas		
				12,000	
			Bølling		
				13,000	c.12,000

[a] The terminology for the Holocene is that proposed by Blytt and Sernarder on the basis of plant remains in Scandinavian peat bogs. Climatic descriptions: Pre-Boreal: Sub-Arctic; Boreal: warmer and dry; Atlantic: warm and wet; Sub-Boreal: warm and dry; Sub-Atlantic: cool and wet. The climatic optimum was reached at the boundary of the Atlantic and Sub-Boreal.

[b] The ages, in conventional radiocarbon years, are those used by Mangerud *et al.* (1974) to define chronozones (see section 2.4.3) which in the Holocene approximate to the Blytt and Sernarder climatic zones. In the Late Weichselian the Allerød and Bølling are interstadials (warm); the Bølling chronozone comprises both the Bølling interstadial and the Oldest Dryas cold zone preceding it. For a review of these phases see Turner and Hannon (1988).

[c] Calendar years BC are derived as indicated in section 4.4; beyond 7000 BC they are tentative.

be expected that continental climate will mimic the global one in every detail, the isotope variations do provide a dated framework to which climatic changes on land can eventually be related.

2.3 THE OXYGEN-ISOTOPE TIME-SCALE

2.3.1 DEEP-SEA CORES

On the floor of the ocean there is a mixture of terrigeneous sediment and biogenic ooze, the latter being primarily made up of calcareous and siliceous skeletons *(tests)* of marine microfauna; these may have been *planktonic* (near surface) or *benthic* (adapted to living in deep water). *Foraminifera* and *coccoliths* form calcareous tests; *radiolaria, zooplankton* and *diatoms* (algae) form siliceous tests. Temperature information is obtained from such parameters as the relative abundance of different species and the morphology of a particular species; there are others. Although the oxygen–isotope ratio found in calcareous tests was initially regarded as an indicator of the temperature of the water in which the shell carbonate formed, it is now generally agreed that the predominant influence is the amount of water locked up in glaciers, so that the ratio reflects global climate.

Samples are obtained by means of long coring tubes, of the order of 10 cm in diameter and 10 m in length; the deposition rate in the regions used is typically of the order of a few millimetres per century. The stratigraphic column so obtained carries, in addition, a magnetic polarity record which allows direct location of the climatic variations on the magnetic time-scale discussed in section 9.5. The magnetic record is carried by the terrigeneous sediment because it acquires a weak but permanent magnetization at deposition, hence indicating successive reversals of the earth's magnetic field.

2.3.2 ISOTOPIC FRACTIONATION

In addition to its principal isotope, ^{16}O, oxygen has two other stable isotopes: ^{17}O and ^{18}O. The latter is the more abundant of these, its percentage with respect to ^{16}O lying in the range 0.19–0.21% for natural materials. The atoms of the three isotopes are identical except in respect of the number of neutrons in their nuclei, these being eight, nine and ten respectively. Although almost similar in their chemical behaviour there are some processes which give preference to the heavier isotopes and some which discriminate against them, the degree of fractionation being dependent on temperature.

As a net result of these processes glaciers are isotopically 'lighter' than sea-water. The consequence is that in glacial times the increase in the amount of water locked up in glaciers leads to an enrichment of the heavier isotopes in the oceans. There is further fractionation during formation of shell carbonate: the lower the temperature the heavier is the isotopic composition of the shell.

The enhancements are slight, but accurately measurable with a high-precision mass spectrometer. Attention is restricted to the more abundant of the heavier isotopes oxygen-18 and for shell formed at the most intense part of an ice age the ratio ($^{18}O/^{16}O$) is about 0.1% higher than the value at the peak of an interglacial;[1] variations in the ratio are usually expressed *per mil*, a difference of 0.1% being written as 1 ‰. The value of the ratio for a sample is given as the difference from the value for a certain standard,[2] also on the per mil scale; this difference is denoted by $\delta^{18}O$.

Another consequence of glaciation is a fall in sea-level, leaving behind shorelines which are now submerged; conversely, interglacials are evidenced by *raised beaches*, though crustal deformation also plays a part. In so far as sea-level change is due to changes in ice volume it is estimated that a decrease by 10 m corresponds to $\delta^{18}O$ becoming less negative by about 0.1 ‰ – just detectable. The influence of water temperature during shell formation is approximately 0.2 ‰ per ° C change; there are other more complex influences too.

2.3.3 RECORDS OF ISOTOPIC VARIATIONS

Figure 2.2 shows one of the first records obtained from Quaternary deep-sea cores. This was published by Emiliani (1955) while working at the University of Chicago; it was there that the idea of temperature-sensitive isotopic composition had been originated by Urey (1948) and for some years the variations were interpreted as primarily reflecting the temperature of the water in which the shell was formed, the effect of ice volume being considered as being a lesser influence. Subsequently other workers (e.g. Olausson 1965; Shackleton 1967; Dansgaard and Tauber 1969) argued that the influence of ice volume was dominant and that the isotope variations could be considered as a palaeoglaciation record.

One of the indications confirming this interpretation was the agreement found in a Pacific core examined by Shackleton and Opdyke (1973) between the isotope variations exhibited by planktonic shells formed in near-surface water with those exhibited by foraminifera which had lived on the ocean floor; the assumption was made that water on the bottom being always

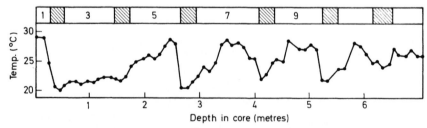

Fig. 2.2 Temperature variation for surface water of the Caribbean inferred by Emiliani (1955) from measurement of the oxygen–isotope ratio in planktonic foraminifera obtained from a core of sea-bottom sediment. Subsequently it was concluded that the major influence on the ratio was global ice-volume rather than water temperature. Hence the variation shown here is an overestimate. The stage numbers given at the top continue in use today; as will be seen warm stages have odd numbers and cold ones have even numbers (redrawn from Imbrie and Imbrie 1986).

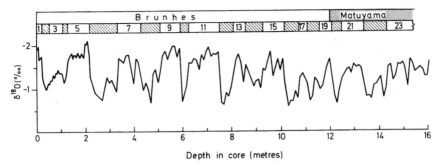

Fig. 2.3 Oxygen–isotope variation in core V28–238 from the Pacific (Shackleton and Opdyke 1973, 1976). During the isotope stage 19 the magnetization of the sediment changed from reverse polarity (Matuyama chron) to normal polarity (Brunhes chron); the accepted age for this change was 700,000 years at the time the core was measured (subsequently revised to 730,000 years). The time-scale for the isotope variations was obtained by using this age and assuming a constant sedimentation rate, with radiocarbon dating for the upper part of the core (redrawn from Shackleton and Opdyke 1973).

close to freezing, there would have been no influence there of temperature of formation.[3] The core concerned was the first to provide a time-scale for the isotope variations. This was by means of magnetic measurements; these indicated that a major reversal of geomagnetic polarity had occurred at the same time as Stage 19 (see Fig. 2.3). Through its recording in volcanic rocks dated by the potassium–argon method this reversal was known to have occurred about 700,000 years ago. The upper part of the core, roughly the top 1 m, was dated by radiocarbon and the time-scale for intervening stages was estimated on the assumption of a constant sedimentation rate, an assumption confirmed as approximately valid by later chronological assessments (see Table 2.4).

Analyses of deep-sea cores from different parts of the world, both in respect of oxygen-isotope ratio and temperature-sensitive species, etc. have confirmed the isotope ratio as a record of palaeoglaciation and the general synchroneity of climatic variation between the Northern and Southern Hemispheres.

Correlation of continental climate
Being continuous, deep-sea cores provide a more satisfactory record of global climate than is generally available on land except in regions of thick loess deposition, as mentioned earlier. In central Europe such deposits show a comparable number of interglacials to the deep-sea record (Fink and Kukla 1977) and in China the correspondence is remarkable[4] – as illustrated in Fig. 2.4. Of course the climate in other land regions does not necessarily follow that in the loess regions; however, data from long pollen sequences (see section 2.4.3) show a similar pattern, at least from the last interglacial

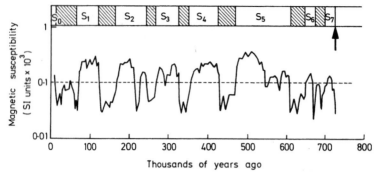

Fig. 2.4 Magnetic susceptibility profile in Chinese loess at Xifeng; also shown is the alternation of loess layers and palaeosols (S_0, S_1, S_2, etc.), corresponding to cold and warm periods respectively. For various reasons (see section 9.3.3) palaeosols have an enhanced magnetic susceptibility and this latter gives a more detailed record of climate than is otherwise available, high susceptibility being indicative of warmth (see Heller and Liu 1982, 1984, 1986). The pattern of variation synchronizes well with that of the deep-sea oxygen isotope but this is not necessarily true of other land regions (see, for example, Winograd *et al.* 1988).

The age scale has been derived by interpolation between the Brunhes–Matuyama magnetic polarity boundary (indicated by arrow) and the Holocene soil, S_0, dated by radiocarbon; the interpolation is on the basis that whereas the rate of loess deposition was uniform the time interval represented by a palaeosol layer was greater than that corresponding to its thickness by a factor dependent on magnetic susceptibility (Kukla *et al.* 1988). The above diagram, which is redrawn from Kukla (1987) is based on magnetic data by Liu *et al.* (1985). Magnetic susceptibility variations in loess profiles have also been reported from Alaska but in these the palaeosols are characterized by low values (Begét and Hawkins, 1989).

onwards; also, in the range in which there is dating by radiocarbon, there is concordance with the isotope record. Hence correlation is assumed as a working hypothesis and Palaeolithic levels for which the soil conditions and the residual flora and fauna, etc. indicate a warm climate are attributed to one of the warm (odd number) isotope stages; which particular one is determined by indications such as stratigraphy, particular types of flora and fauna occurring, and developmental stage of any hominid remains; also, the dating techniques of the following chapters are increasingly utilized (e.g. Stringer *et al.* 1986).

Direct and unambiguous data about correlation can be obtained for some regions not too distant from the ocean when pollen is found in a deep-sea core that carries a good record of the global isotope variations (e.g. Turon 1984); similarly the magnetic parameters of the sediment in a core may relate to the climate on land (e.g. Robinson 1986).

Lake sediments and shoreline deposits have also been used for correlation studies (see Lowe and Walker 1984); of course, long continuous sequences occur only beyond the limits of glaciation.

Labelling of stages and substages

The stage numbers allocated by Emiliani (see Fig. 2.2) continue in use but have been developed so as to include substages. This is by letters, e.g. the warm substages of Stage 5 were named 5a, 5c and 5e, with the intervening cold troughs being named 5b and 5d. More recently a decimal system has been used so as to give more flexibility in dealing with the complexities of the isotope curve (see Pisias *et al.* 1984); thus the peak of substage 5e is labelled 5.5 with further subdivision into 5.51, 5.52 and 5.53 where it appears to bifurcate. Substage 5e is usually considered to be correlative with the last interglacial (in European terminology the Eemian – see Table 2.1), the warm phase Stage 3 representing only an interstadial.

Terminations

Besides discussion in terms of stages there is also use of *terminations*; the way in which these relate to the stages is indicated in Table 2.4. These terminations were allocated by Broecker and van Donk (1970), being based on the observation that the isotopic variations in a core from the Caribbean showed a marked sawtooth pattern; this pattern is consonant with interpretation in terms of a slowly increasing glaciation being terminated by the rapid onset of a warm phase. Note that a termination number has been given to only some of the cold phase conclusions.

2.3.4 THE MILANKOVITCH ASTRONOMICAL THEORY OF CLIMATE

Historical résumé

Speculation that the ice ages were triggered by variation in the amount, and distribution, of solar radiant energy falling on the earth *(insolation)* has been current since the middle of the nineteenth century, the variation being due to changes in the earth's orbital parameters. This speculation began soon after the recognition, at the beginning of the nineteenth century, first that Alpine glaciers had formerly extended well beyond their present limits, and, secondly, that there had been a succession of such glacial advances (and retreats). An explanation based on the precession of the equinoxes was proposed by Adhemar in Paris and this was developed by Croll in Edinburgh who included consideration of the effects arising from changes in the eccentricity of the orbit. The first publication by the Yugoslav astronomer, Milankovitch, was in 1920 and his work culminated with a publication (Milankovitch 1941) giving detailed insolation curves for various latitudes during the past 600,000 years; two of these are shown in Fig. 2.5.

The theory that orbital variations control climate has had its vicissitudes both before and after the work of Milankovitch. There was growing acceptance following the publication just mentioned, notably by Zeuner

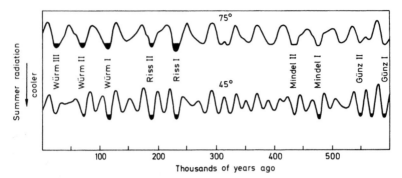

Fig. 2.5   Milankovitch insolation curves for latitudes 75°N and 45°N. Low
points are identified with substages of the ice ages as recognized in the European
Alps (adapted from Milankovitch 1941). The variation is more rapid for the lower
latitude because of the greater influence of the 22,000-year precessional cycle.

(1946) in London who used it as a basis for palaeolithic dating. However,
when radiocarbon dating became available in the early 1950s, although initial
geological application (to the last phase of the Wisconsin glaciation) gave
results in agreement with the theory, subsequent applications going further
back in time, perhaps beyond the time range for which the technique was
then reliable, gave a picture that was more complex than predicted by the
insolation curves. There was then general rejection of the theory, except
by a few.

Reinstatement did not begin until the mid-1960s, one important factor
being improvements in the uranium-series technique so as to give reliable
results beyond the effective 40,000-year limit of radiocarbon. Application of
this technique (Broecker *et al.* 1968; Mesolella *et al.* 1969) to the raised coral
terraces at Barbados (and elsewhere) – indicative of high sea-levels and hence
of minima in ice volume – gave good correlation with maxima in the 45 °N
insolation curve at 125,000, 105,000 and 80,000 years ago (see Fig. 2.5). At
the same time analyses of the growing body of deep-sea climatic data were
leading increasingly to speculation of correlation with insolation and, once
a firm time-scale became available from magnetic stratigraphy, correlation
was put on a sound basis (see Hays *et al.* 1976; Emiliani 1978). A highly
readable account of this reinstatement of the astronomical theory has been
given by Imbrie and Imbrie (1986), who also trace developments since the
earliest recognition of glacial variation. More recently, remarkably precise
uranium-series dating of coral became possible, allowing a more critical
test of correlation (Edwards *et al.* 1987).

With the validity of the theory firmly established the emphasis was
then on the inverse process, i.e. using the astronomical data to give
more accurate dating for the global climatic variations indicated by the
oxygen-isotope curves, refinements in the astronomical data having been

made (Vernekar 1972; see Berger 1980). For Palaeolithic archaeology the outstanding question, as mentioned earlier, is the extent to which the continental climate patterns match the global one.

Orbital parameters
The relevant ones are as follows:

1. The eccentricity of the earth's orbit around the sun. The orbit is an ellipse of quite small eccentricity, the difference between furthest earth–sun distance and the nearest being about 3% at present. Over the past 200,000 years the difference has varied between near 2% and 10%; the most important term in the variation has a period of 413,000 years, but more relevant to the present discussion is the group of terms that comprise what is usually referred to as the 100,000-year cycle.
2. The obliquity, or tilt, of the ecliptic. This is the angle between the equatorial plane of the earth and the plane of the orbit around the sun. The present value is 23.4 °. In the past it has varied between 21.8 ° and 24.4 °, with an average period of 41,000 years.
3. The precession of the equinoxes. This occurs because the earth's axis of rotation wobbles in a similar manner to the axis of a spinning top (this wobble should not be confused with the variation in obliquity). At present in the Northern Hemisphere midsummer (i.e. the North Pole tilted towards the sun at an angle of 23.4 °) occurs when the earth is almost at that point in its elliptical orbit which is furthest away from the sun; approximately 11,000 years ago the northern midsummer was occurring when the earth was at its nearest point to the sun. There is a major precessional cycle of 23,000 years, and a minor one of 19,000 years, the mean period being close to 22,000 years.

The variations in these parameters are due to gravitational perturbations resulting from the changing configuration of the planets. They are illustrated in Fig. 2.6.

Climatic response
The overall annual insolation falling on the earth is not altered by changes in parameters (1) and (3), and only very slightly by eccentricity variations – by not more than about 0.1% over the past half-million years. Hence in seeking a causal connection between orbital variations and climate more subtle mechanisms have had to be considered.[5] A number of possible mechanisms suggest that the degree of contrast between seasons is likely to be an important factor in the build-up or decay of glaciation. On this basis Milankovitch (1941) considered that when the summer radiation flux in high northern latitudes, particularly 65 °N, fell below a certain value a major glaciation was likely to be triggered, there being a lag in response of some thousands of years. This viewpoint has been followed by most

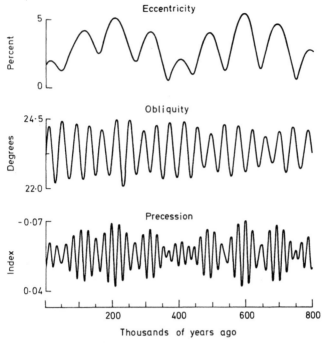

Fig. 2.6 Variation of orbital parameters (according to Berger 1977; redrawn from Imbrie and Imbrie 1980).

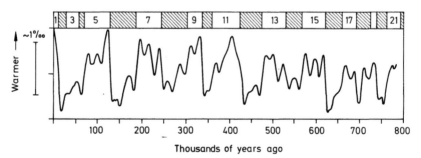

Fig. 2.7 Oxygen–isotope variations for the past 800,000 years with time-scale based on orbital tuning (redrawn from Imbrie *et al.* 1984). The curve is the smoothed record obtained from planktonic foraminifera of five deep-sea cores distributed around the oceans of the world. The numbers along the top indicate warm stages; dates for stage boundaries are included in Table 2.4. The vertical scale is in normalized units such that the standard deviation of the cūrve is equal to 1 unit.

subsequent investigators, though some have considered 45 °N as being more important and others winter flux rather than summer flux.

As might be expected, the insolation curves of Fig. 2.5 show direct response to precessional changes and variations in obliquity (mean periodicities 22,000 years and 41,000 years respectively) with modulation by the 100,000-year eccentricity cycle. It was the finding of these periodicities in the oxygen-isotope record, particularly the two former, that established the validity of the concept of climate control by 'orbital forcing' rather than through a detailed model of exactly how the control occurs. Many investigators participated in the process; see for instance Broecker and van Donk (1970), Hays *et al.* (1976), Emiliani (1978) and Imbrie *et al* . (1984). Not only were the periodicities conclusively identified but also the lags of the climate response – about 8,000 years in the case of the obliquity component – were consistent with the estimated time required for glacial build-up.

Once it was established that the major part of global climatic variation could be ascribed to orbital forcing, climatologists then had the opportunity to devise climatic models that would explain the causal connection (see Imbrie and Imbrie 1980); obviously one particular interest in this aspect is the prediction of future climate. However, it is the past that is the concern of this book and for this the important development is the utilization of the orbital forcing concept to provide an astronomically based time-scale for the variations in global climate revealed in deep-sea cores.

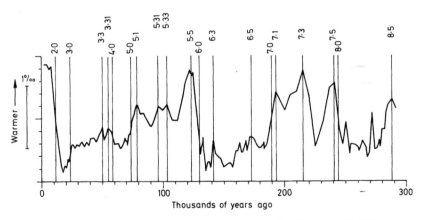

Fig. 2.8 High-resolution oxygen–isotope variation for the past 300,000 years with time-scale based on orbital tuning (redrawn from Martinson *et al.* 1987). The curve is the averaged record from five deep-sea cores from various oceans of the world, but using benthic (bottom-dwelling) foraminifera instead of the planktonic (surface-dwelling) foraminifera that were used for Fig. 2.7; the core locations were different, too. Dates for stage boundaries (2.0, 3.0, 4,0, etc.) are included in Table 2.4.

2.3.5 ORBITAL TUNING AND CHRONOSTRATIGRAPHY

The dating of the oxygen–isotope variations shown in Fig. 2.3 was based on the magnetic reversal at 730,000 years ago and the assumption of a constant sedimentation rate. Comparison with the isotope variations found in other cores has indicated that assumption to be a reasonable approximation as also the uranium–series dating of Termination II (the

Table 2.4 Oxygen-isotopic stage boundaries

Boundary [a]	Termination [b]	Ages (thousands of years)		
		Shackleton[c] and Opdyke (1973, 1976)	Imbrie[d] et al. (1984)	Martinson[d] et al. (1987)
1–2	I	13	12	12
2–3		32	24	24
3–4		64	59	60
4–5		75	71	74
5–6	II	128	128	130
6–7		195	186	190
7–8	III	251	245	244
8–9		297	303	
9–10	IV	347	339	
10–11		367	362	
11–12	V	440	423	
12–13		472	478	
13–14		502	524	
14–15		542	565	
15–16	VI	592	620	
16–17		627	659	
17–18		647	689	
18–19		688	726	
19–20			736	
20–21			763	
21-22			790	

[a] In the terminology of Pisias *et al.* (1984) successive boundaries, reading from the top, are denoted by 2.0, 3.0, 4.0, etc.

[b] The terminations are those defined by Broecker and van Donk (1970) on the basis of their interpretation of the saw-toothed character of their record.

[c] The ages in this core are based on 700,000 years for the Brunhes–Matuyama boundary and the assumption of a constant sedimentation rate. The revised age for that boundary is 730,000 ± 11,000 years (Mankinen and Dalrymple 1979).

[d] The ages are astronomically based with an estimated overall accuracy of 5000 years.

boundary between stages 5 and 6) as 127,000 years ago, and radiocarbon dating in stage 2. The basic idea of orbital tuning is that having used the existing time-scale to establish the reality of orbital forcing, that time-scale is then adjusted (in a long reiteration process) so that there is a constant lag, for each dominant periodicity in the frequency spectrum, of climatic record behind orbital variation (the latter sometimes being referred to as the 'metronome'); there are other more complex procedures too, as well as checks on overall validity. By stacking the isotope variations (and also the faunal variations) found in a number of cores, the effect of irregularities in individual records is minimized. For further exposition of the procedures the reader should consult Imbrie *et al.* (1984).

Figure 2.7 shows a climatic time-scale derived in this way for the last 800,000 years, and Fig. 2.8 a higher resolution time-scale for the past 300,000 years. The ages of stage boundaries for these time-scales are given in Table 2.4 together with those for the core of Fig. 2.3. It should be appreciated that in the iterative process of orbital tuning the constraints of radiometric and magnetic dating are gradually relaxed. Hence it is valid to note the agreement between the latter two methods and astronomically based dates as evidence of reliability. For the boundary between stages 5 and 6 (Event 6.0; Termination II) the time-scales of Figs 2.7 and 2.8 indicate 128,000 years and 130,000 years respectively; this is in excellent agreement with the radiometric dating of 127,000 ± 6,000 years. For the Brunhes–Matuyama boundary the time-scale of Fig. 2.7 indicates 734,000 years, also in excellent agreement with radiometric dating, which gives 730,000 ± 11,000 years. The error limits estimated for the astronomically based time-scales are ± 5,000 years.

2.3.6 ICE-CORE VARIATIONS

Continuous records of oxygen-isotope variation are also available in long cores drilled in polar ice-caps. There are a number of possible factors which may influence the isotope ratio and so interpretation in terms of palaeotemperature is not straightforward. However, not only is there a long-term pattern of variation similar to the deep-sea pattern but also because the annual layers are rather thick (e.g. around 20 cm in the upper part of the core; lower down 'thinning' occurs) seasonal variation in isotope ratio can be measured and the annual layers can be counted. This has been done in a 2 km long core from Greenland (Dye 3; Hammer *et al.* 1986) back to 3870 BC, with an estimated standard deviation of ±10 years. There is also seasonal variation of dust content and acidity; the latter enables the year-by-year counting to be carried back to 8770 BC, with a total estimated error limit of ±150 years.

Further back in time the layers become too thin for counting and age estimates can only be made on the basis of models of glacier flow and ice movement. In this way the Vostok core from Antarctica has been estimated to reach 160,000 years; the profile of temperature inferred from it correlates well with the deep-sea record, deuterium[6] being used as indicator in this case (Jouzel *et al.* 1987).

Relevance to radiocarbon calibration

Beyond the layer in the Dye core corresponding to 8770 BC there were drastic changes in layer thickness and other parameters and that date was interpreted as corresponding to the Younger Dryas/Pre-Boreal boundary (see Table 2.3). This is in good agreement with the date for that boundary of 8750 ±50 BC obtained by varve counting. The boundary is clearly marked in the pollen record and associated dating gives an age in radiocarbon years of *c.* 10,000 ± 75; this suggests the radiocarbon age is about seven centuries more recent than the calendar age – an underestimate of comparable magnitude to that indicated by measurements on dendrochronologically dated wood from a few millennia later.

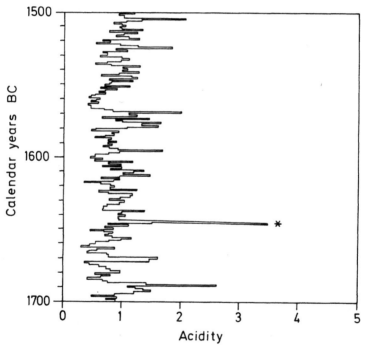

Fig. 2.9 Part of the acidity record from the Dye–3 core, Greenland (redrawn from Hammer *et al.* 1987). Of the two prominent peaks in these two centuries only the one marked with a star is considered to be due to a volcanic eruption. This is because the acidity in the ice layer concerned was predominantly due to sulphuric acid (see Fig. 2.10), whereas the other peak was dominated by nitric acid (indicative of intense melting during summer months). The acidity is measured by means of a special electric conductometric method having a resolution of a few millimetres; it is expressed in terms of equivalent hydrogen-ion concentration.

Evidence of the Bronze Age eruption of Thera

An eruption injects huge amounts of dust and sulphur compounds into the atmosphere. The latter component, mainly in the form of sulphuric acid aerosols reaches the stratosphere and may linger for months, or more – particularly for a major eruption. As a result there is enhanced acidity in the snow deposited soon after an eruption and a distinct acidity signal may be seen in the appropriate layer of an ice-core; many such signals have been correlated with eruptions of known date (Hammer *et al.* 1986). Through shielding of solar radiation there is also a deleterious effect on the climate and this may be detectable in the tree-ring record; in California, frost-damaged annual growth rings in fossil bristlecone pines have been correlated with

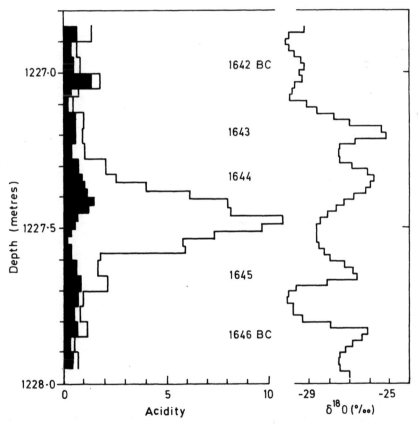

Fig. 2.10 More detail (redrawn from Hammer *et al.* 1987) relevant to the starred peak of Fig. 2.9. The filled histogram on the left of the figure represents nitric acid concentration and the unfilled histogram sulphuric acid plus nitric acid; these concentrations were determined by chemical analysis (ion chromatography). Oxygen–isotope values are shown on the right with calendar dates being given in the middle. The rightward peaks (less negative $\delta^{18}O$) correspond to summer.

eruptions (La Marche and Hirschboeck 1984) and, in Northern Ireland, short periods of severely attenuated growth fossil bog oaks correspond to ice-core indications of eruptions (Baillie and Munro 1988).

Of particular archaeological interest is a strong acidity peak (see Figs 2.9 and 2.10) in the Greenland ice-core mentioned above; this is dated to 1644 ± 20 BC (Hammer *et al.* 1987) and attributed to the eruption, during Minoan times, of the volcano of Thera on the Aegean island of Santorini. Also, in the tree-ring records mentioned above, there is indication of a temporary deterioration of climate around 1628 BC, which is within the error limits of the ice-core dating. On the other hand, the traditional archaeological chronology for the region, based on artefact links to the Egyptian calendar, requires the eruption to be about a century later. The majority of the radiocarbon determinations made on archaeological material associated with the destruction caused by the eruption indicate that a date consistent with the ice-core and tree-ring records had a higher probability than one consistent with traditional archaeological chronology (see Fig. 4.10); independently, there has been reassessment of the archaeological links with Egypt and the revised chronology is concordant with the ice-core and tree-ring records (Betancourt 1987; see also Aitken *et al.* 1988). However, it has been pointed out that because of the frequency of major eruptions the probability that the ice-core/tree-ring signal relates to the eruption is quite low (Warren 1984; Pyle 1989).

2.4 THE POLLEN RECORD (PALYNOLOGY)

2.4.1 ASPECTS OF POLLEN ANALYSIS

The most obvious manifestation of the climate of a terrestrial region, assuming man's activities have not had significant influence, is through the type of tree and plant that flourish there; predominance by tree pollen is indicative of warmth and the relative abundance of different species gives finer detail. Pollen and spores are preserved, particularly in acid soils and peat bogs, and can be identified. Hence from a stratigraphic sequence we can read a record of climatic change by analysing the pollen content; increasingly, other indicators of palaeoclimate, both biological and lithological, are being used, but pollen is singled out for discussion on account of its early use as a dating tool. This dating role arose from the use of pollen in charting the way in which northerly latitudes emerged from the last glaciation. This emergence was described in terms of successive pollen zones, and on the assumption of synchroneity between regions these zones formed a chronological framework. The advent of radiocarbon allowed checking of this framework's validity and at the same time reduced reliance on it so that as far as archaeology is concerned, the main emphasis now is on reconstruction of past climate and of man's ecological interference.

However, as indicated in section 2.4.3, use of the pollen zone framework continues, and also, beyond the range of radiocarbon, the chronological aspect remains important. Of course pollen analysis is also an integral part of botanical research for its own sake; the ubiquitous nature of pollen coupled with its regional diversity also makes it a forensic tool – the pollen types found on clothing give a guide as to regions that have been visited; likewise the pollen types found on the Shroud of Turin are consistent with it having spent some time in the region of Palestine.

For visualization of pollen, readers are recommended to the illustrated introductory guide by Moore and Webb (1978); more comprehensive treatises include Faegri and Iversen (1975), Godwin (1975) and Birks and Birks (1981).

2.4.2 POLLEN

Most pollens (from flowering trees and plants) and spores (principally from ferns and mosses) are extremely small, few exceeding 100 μm (0.1 mm) in diameter, with the majority being around 30 μm. It is the outer portion of the cell, the *exine*, which is preserved, by means of a waxy coat of material called *sporopollenin*. The size and shape of this outer wall, along with the number and distribution of the apertures in it, enable identification to be made using a *pollen key* (photographs and reference slides made up from modern pollen). Table 2.5 lists some of the important *taxa*.

Table 2.5 Latin names for some important plant taxa (after Bradley, 1985)

Latin	English	Latin	English
Abies	Fir	Juglans	Walnut
Acer	Maple	Juniperus	Juniper
Alnus	Alder	Larix	Larch
Ambrosia	Ragweed	Liquidambar	Sweet gum
Artemisia	Wormwood/sage	Lycopodium	Clubmoss
Betula	Birch	Nyssa	Tupelo
Carpinus	Ironwood	Ostrya	Hornbeam
Carya	Hickory	Picea	Spruce
Chenopodiaceae	Goosefoot	Pinus	Pine
Corylus	Hazel	Populus	Poplar
Cyperacaea	Sedges	Pseudotsuga	Douglas fir
Ephedra	Horsetail	Quercus	Oak
Eucalyptus	Eucalyptus	Salix	Willow
Fagus	Beech	Taxodium	Bald cypress
Fraxinus	Ash	Tilia	Basswood/lime
Gramineae	Grasses	Tsuga	Hemlock
		Ulmus	Elm

Laboratory procedures; pollen diagrams

Following sieving or differential flotation the samples undergo appropriate chemical treatments in order to remove as much of the sediment matrix as possible. The residues are stained with an organic dye to bring out the surface characteristics of the grains and then mounted on glass slides in a suitable medium such as glycerine jelly or silicone oil. It is usual to identify several hundred grains per sample, using a microscope at ×400 magnification.

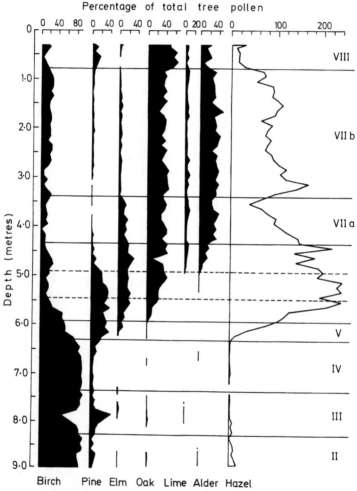

Fig. 2.11 Pollen diagram from Hockham Mere, East Anglia (after Godwin 1975). The Roman numerals indicate the pollen zones defined by Godwin. Zone II corresponds to the Allerød interstadial, III to the Younger Dryas, IV to the Pre-Boreal, VI to the Boreal, VIIa to the Atlantic, VIIb to the Sub-Boreal and VIII to the Sub-Atlantic. Subsequent work at the site has led to some reassessment.

The simplest way of expressing results is in a diagram indicating each species as a percentage of the total – see Fig. 2.11; depending on the application, 'total' may be restricted to a particular range of pollen, e.g. arboreal pollen (AP) or non-arboreal pollen (NAP). The drawback of the percentage method is that the influx of a prolific taxa will cause all other percentages to be depressed. Expression as *absolute pollen frequency* (APF – grains per gram, or per unit volume) avoids this interdependence. A further step is to eliminate distortion due to variation in sedimentation rate. This is possible only when dating is sufficiently detailed for the rate to be known; occurrence is then expressed as *pollen influx* – grains per year per unit area of land surface.

Quantity; preservation

The higher the probability of success in fertilization the lower the quantity of pollen produced by a plant. Thus self-fertilizing plants produce least of all, while those that rely on wind for dispersal produce more than those that utilize insects; oak relies on wind and a single tree may disperse about 100 million grains per year, and in a northern hardwood forest the 'pollen rain' may reach the order of a 1 kg/m^2 per century. Dispersal distance does not usually exceed the order of 1 km for trees and a few tens of metres for plants; hence sampling in one particular spot is likely to be strongly influenced by what is growing in the immediate vicinity. On the other hand, there are reports of pollen which has travelled hundreds of kilometres and such far-travelled pollen is liable to cause confusion in environments where local pollen production was low, e.g. tundra.

Obviously, in order to get a true picture of the past vegetation, adjustment has to be made for pollen productivity; thus pine, oak, birch and alder are almost an order of magnitude more prolific than lime, ash and maple. Such adjustment is beset with interferences, but it is mostly for ecological reconstruction that it needs to be done. However, even for dating purposes there are pitfalls – e.g. dependence on type of repository (bog, lake bottom, forest, etc.) both because of differential sorting at the input stage and because of differences in vulnerability to physical, chemical and biological attack.

2.4.3 POLLEN ZONES AND DATING

Late-glacial and Postglacial dating in north-west Europe

Following the last glacial period's most intense cold phase there were rapid climatic changes, represented in northern Europe (see Table 2.3) by the Bølling and Allerød interstadials in Late-glacial times and followed in the Postglacial period by steady improvement to the climatic optimum of about 5000 radiocarbon years ago (about 4000 calendar years BC). The Postglacial subdivisions were made on the basis of plant remains in Scandinavian bogs and they were reflected in the pollen content too.

The distinctive pattern of tree species which were successively dominant (birch, pine, mixed-oak, etc.) was found elsewhere in northern Europe and led to the definition of pollen zones corresponding to the subdivisions of Table 2.3. Figure 2.11 illustrates the zonation developed for Britain.

As recalled by Godwin et al. (1957:353): 'Because the zone-systems had been constructed on the basis that a zone in one region was equivalent to, rather than identical with, that in another, pollen-analysts . . . assumed the zones to be broadly synchronous across Europe'. The zones were established long before the advent of radiocarbon, absolute dating being obtained by reference to the Scandinavian glacial varve chronology; hence the assumption of synchroneity allowed transference of this chronology to sites elsewhere and this enhanced the role of pollen analysis beyond the importance it would have had anyway as a relative dating tool. Of course the zones are rather broad and served to distinguish between archaeological periods rather than to provide detail within a period.

When radiocarbon became available the critical question of synchroneity could be tested and the essential validity of the assumption was confirmed (see, e.g. Godwin et al. 1957; Godwin and Willis 1959; Godwin 1960). Again quoting Godwin (1981:187) '. . . one was finally assured of the broad effectiveness of the pollen zone system and of the chronological frameworks that had been evolved to sub-divide the Flandrian period . . .' and '. . . research workers from this time forward . . . were now naturally able to move about the Flandrian period, and for that matter the preceding Weichselian (Glacial), with altogether fresh assurance'.

Although the conclusion of broad synchroneity remains valid today, further, more detailed research has found not uncommon examples of *time-transgression*. Thus in the Postglacial of the British Isles, between upland and lowland there are marked differences, of the order of 2000 years, in the radiocarbon dates for some pollen changes (Smith and Pilcher 1973), although there are some indicators, e.g. the elm decline, which appear to have been approximately synchronous. However, there is a general tendency for retardation of upland regions with respect to lowland, and of westerly regions in north-west Europe with respect to deeply continental regions (see Hibbert et al. 1971); this is as might be expected since the vegetational response to climate amelioration, particularly by slow-growing species such as trees, can hardly have been instantaneous; there would have had to be time for a species to travel from refugia where it had continued to flourish during the colder period. On the other hand, declines and extinctions, whether due to man or to climate, have tended to be more synchronous.

Pollen assemblage zones (PAZ); chronozones
Although radiocarbon reduced the dating significance of pollen zones they continue to be an important framework for archaeology, also providing a

check against rogue dates. However, the rigid system of numbered zones has given way to more descriptive *pollen assemblage zones* defined on the basis of the dominant types.[7] As proposed by West (1970) the pollen assemblage zones at a type site are used as a basis for *chronozones* defined in terms of radiocarbon years, i.e. at the type site the boundaries of the major assemblage zones are dated by radiocarbon and these dates then define the chronozone boundaries. The latter are transferred to other regions by means of radiocarbon dating and the assemblage zones observed there are related to the chronozones established at the type site, hence avoiding any reliance on synchroneity of pollen change. Table 2.6 shows the system as applied to the type site for England and Wales, Red Moss.

In archaeological application the assemblage zone established for a given site can be roughly dated by reference to a site in the same, or geographically similar region at which the relationship of the assemblage zone sequence to the chronozone system has been established.

Correlation with oxygen-isotope time-scale; La Grande Pile; Les Echets
Pollen sequences have an important role in establishing the extent to which continental climate correlates with the isotope time-scale; also, if correlation is established they become the means by which the time-scale is transferred to land. At the time of writing it is well established that the

Table 2.6 Pollen assemblage zones for Red Moss[a]

Climatic unit	Assemblage zone	Characteristics	Chronozone [b]	Radiocarbon years before present
Sub-Boreal (warm, dry)	f	Oak-alder	F III	
				5,010±80
Atlantic (warm, wet)	e	Oak-elm-alder	F II	
				7,110±120
	d	Pine-hazel-elm	F I d	
				8,200±150
Boreal (warmer than before, dry)	c	Hazel-pine	F I c	
				8,880±170
	b	Birch-pine-hazel	F I b	
				9,800±200
Pre-Boreal (sub-Arctic)	a	Birch-pine-juniper	F I a	
				(10,250)

[a] Red Moss is the type site for the Flandrian stage in England and Wales. This table is derived from Tooley (1981) and Hibbert *et al.* (1971).

[b] Chronozone boundaries defined for the same time period in Scandinavia are given in Table 2.3.

Eemian, usually considered as the last interglacial of northern Europe, correlates with substage 5e, centred on 124,000 years ago. One of the sequences indicating this is from coastal marine sediments in western Norway (Mangerud *et al.* 1979, 1981). The pollen record in these could be directly related to marine fauna, and thence to the biostratigraphy of cores from the Norwegian Sea. The oxygen–isotope stratigraphy of the latter showed the same major features as Fig. 2.8 and in particular the 5e peak of the last interglacial. At the corresponding depth in the coastal sediment the pollen record showed characteristic features of the Eemian interglacial.

Figure 2.12 shows one aspect of the pollen sequence from a site more remote from the oceans – the peat bog of *La Grand Pile* in north-eastern France, some 1000 km from the Atlantic. The aspect shown is the amount of tree pollen relative to total land pollen; hence high values correspond to warm climate and the diagram can be regarded as the pollen equivalent of the deep-sea isotope curves of section 2.3. From detailed pollen analysis the oldest of the three major maxima was identified as the Eemian interglacial, and hence presumed to correspond to isotope substage 5e. Radiocarbon

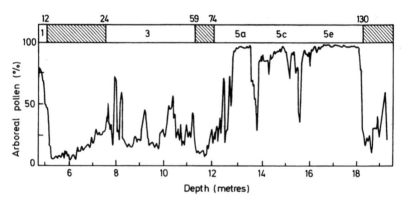

Fig. 2.12   Extract from the pollen analysis of a peat bog, La Grande Pile, in north-eastern France (redrawn from Woillard and Mook 1982). The curve indicates the tree (and shrub) pollen expressed as a percentage of total tree, shrub and herb pollen; also shown are the deep-sea isotope stages to which correspondence of warm periods was made; this was tentative for the early stages and on the basis of radiocarbon dating for the later ones. The ages shown (in kiloyears) for stage boundaries are from Martinson *et al.* (1987). The earliest warm period (high percentage) was interpreted by Woillard (1978) as the Eemian interglacial and the succeeding ones also as interglacials – Saint-Germain Ia, Ic and II – though by others these were regarded as corresponding to the first three interstadials of the Weichselian glacial period (see Table 2.2). The depth scale is not uniform with age, there having been rapid sedimentation (loess deposition) during cold periods and compaction during warmer ones according to G. Seret (pers. comm.); the latter also notes that organic carbon content parallels arboreal pollen, sometimes giving more detail.

dating (using the isotope enrichment technique) indicated the most recent of the three maxima to be beyond 70,000 years (Woillard and Mook 1982) – consistent with its correspondence to substage 5a; dating of more recent parts correlated well with later stages.

Figure 2.13 shows the tree pollen sequence obtained from another peat bog in France, at *Les Echets* some 200 km further south. Major maxima are evident here too and for the oldest the same attribution to the Eemian interglacial and isotope substage 5e was made (de Beaulieu and Reille 1984a, b); however, the maxima between 34 and 30 m were interpreted as interstadials (corresponding to the three earliest interstadials of northern Europe given in Table 2.2), whereas at La Grande Pile the maxima following the Eemian interglacial had been interpreted as interglacials also (Woillard 1978). This interpretation, which displaced the Eemian from being the last interglacial, brings up the question of the criteria used to distinguish an interglacial from an interstadial, and also the characteristics by which different warm stages can be distinguished. According to Woillard (1978: 15) an interglacial '. . . represents an important warming characterized by a vegetational evolution which presents a logical succession from an ecological point of view . . .', whereas an interstadial '. . . represents a shorter and less-marked warming which has not allowed thermophilous species to immigrate again from their refuges in successive well-ordered waves. On the contrary, a sudden and anarchic extension of thermophilous species can be seen . . . .' However, the absence of certain species led to Beaulieu and Reille (1984a, b) to place the northern limit of extension of deciduous trees as being near both sites during the warm periods in question and hence to regard them as interstadials.

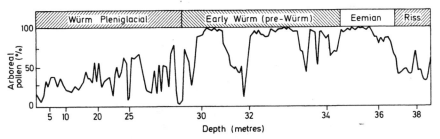

Fig. 2.13 Extract from the pollen analysis of a core from the peat bog at Les Echets, eastern France (redrawn from de Beaulieu and Reille 1984a). The curve indicates the tree and shrub pollen expressed as a percentage of total tree, shrub and herb pollen. On the basis of the relative abundance of the various species the earliest major maximum was interpreted as the Eemian interglacial and the maxima between 34 and 30 m as interstadials of the succeeding Würm glacial period (equivalent to the Weichselian in more northerly terminology). The depth scale is non-uniform so as to allow better presentation of detail.

Phases of an interglacial

The logical succession in an interglacial is from very cold types of vegetation landscape to several phases of forest landscape, corresponding to increasing degrees of warmth, followed by a return to cold forests and eventually tundra again. The ecological phases are sometimes described using the terminology *cryocratic, protocratic, mesocratic* and *telocratic*, for which the characteristics are indicated in Table 2.7. Alternatively, the characterization is in terms of pollen zone assemblages such as indicated in Table 2.8. Minor differences between these assemblages allow different interglacials to be distinguished. Thus in Britain the present interglacial is characterized by having had prolific hazel during the Boreal (Zone I), whereas for the Ipswichian it was strong in Zone II, and in Zone

Table 2.7 Ecological zones of an interglacial

Zone	Climate	Vegetation	Flora
Cryocratic	Cold	Open herb and low shrub	Arctic and Alpine
Protocratic	Warm	Park–tundra to light wood	Residual Arctic-Alpine
Mesocratic	Thermal maximum	Closed deciduous forest	Woodland plants and thermophiles
Telocratic	Cooling	Coniferous woodland and acidic heath	Recession of thermophiles

Table 2.8 Pollen zones of an interglacial (after West, 1970)

Zone I (pre-temperate)	Boreal trees such as birch and pine; significant amounts of light-demanding shrubs and herbs
Zone II (early temperate)	Mixed oak forest comprising oak, elm, ash and hazel
Zone III (late temperate)	Expansion of forest trees such as ironwood, fir and spruce at the expense of mixed oak forest
Zone IV (post-temperate)	Reappearance and dominance of boreal trees such as birch, pine and spruce; thinning of the forest and appearance of dwarf shrubs

III ironwood abounds. Similarly there can be differentiation between interstadials.[8] This characterization of warm periods, and cold periods also, gives pollen analysis, often in combination with other biological and lithological studies, a dating role that is particularly important on sites beyond the range of radiocarbon (e.g. Girard and Renault-Miskovsky 1983; Renault-Miskovsky 1986) and within it (e.g. Leroyer and Leroi-Gourhan 1983). This role is integral with the picture given of ancient man's environment (e.g. Leroi-Gourhan 1980).

2.5 VARVE CHRONOLOGY

The summer melting of glaciers produces streams carrying a fine suspension of sand, silt and clay. In lakes fed by this meltwater the coarse particles settle first followed by finer material as the year goes on. The resulting annual laminations (*varves*) are distinguishable to the eye in sections cut into the beds of dried-out lakes because of the change of colour as the sediment goes from coarse to fine. The thickness of a layer, typically between a few millimetres and a few centimetres, reflects the amount of melting, an abnormally hot summer giving rise to an abnormally thick layer (which may reach several tens of centimetres) and a cold summer giving a layer which may only be the fraction of a millimetre. Hence, since the sequence of thin and thick layers is determined by climate, glacially deposited clay in different localities of the same climatic region can be cross-dated. Using the same overlapping techniques as will be described for dendrochronology, reference plots spanning thousands of years can be established by linking together successive sections from different lakes; however, it is not usually possible to reach the present day, and anchoring by means of some dated event is necessary. Although such cross-dating can be successful within a given region, notably Scandinavia, attempts to establish linkages between continents (*teleconnections*) have not been successful.

Rhythmites is the general geological term applied to laminated sediments, the term 'varves' being used when the laminations are annual.

The Scandinavian varve chronology

The climate amelioration at the end of the last glacial period caused the glaciers to retreat northward across Sweden and Finland, leaving behind a series of glacial lakes which gradually dried up once their source of supply had disappeared. The varve sequences observed in these, first by Baron de Geer around 1912, form a unique and remarkable system extending back to around 13,000 years ago for varves in the southern tip of Sweden (Strömberg 1985).

This system has more than regional significance for two reasons. First, it gives an absolute chronology for part of the Scandinavian pollen zone system – because both systems are manifestations of climate.

Secondly, and more importantly in the context of this book, it provides an additional basis for absolute calibration of the radiocarbon time-scale (Tauber 1970). Linkage to this scale is obtained from radiocarbon dating of peat-bog samples at pollen zone boundaries; direct radiocarbon dating of the varves themselves is not reliable because most of the organic content is of secondary origin. The calibration obtained by Tauber was substantially at variance with that obtained from varves in the Lake of Clouds (see below) but subsequently re-evaluation of the Scandinavian sequences has gone some way towards resolving the discrepancy (see Strömberg 1985; Stuiver *et al.* 1986).

The long Scandinavian varve chronology is possible because the ice-sheet there retreated in a simple and almost unidirectional manner. This is in contrast to the complicated situation that was prevalent in North America.

The Lake of Clouds, Minnesota
Glacial melting is not the only cause of varves; in non-glacial lakes seasonal variation in accumulation of organic detritus may also give rise to annual laminations, as well as seasonal variation in sedimentation and chemical precipitation. Some 10,000 laminations were found in a 5 m core extracted from the Lake of Clouds and radiocarbon dating of organic matter in the core itself confirmed that the laminations were annual ones (Stuiver 1970); this was in respect of that part of the core where there was overlap with the tree-ring-derived calibration then available. On the assumption that the laminations were annual in the earlier part too, this core made it possible to extend the calibration back to 10,000 years ago; the calibration so obtained has subsequently been used to anchor the Scandinavian varve chronology (treated as a 'floating' chronology on account of uncertainties in the recent part) and hence to extend the calibration to some 13,000 years ago (Stuiver *et al.* 1986).

2.6 DENDROCHRONOLOGY (TREE-RING DATING)

Although varves have been important in extending calibration of the radiocarbon time-scale back to Late-glacial times, it was wood dated by dendrochronology that provided the conclusive evidence that the time-scale was indeed distorted, as well as the detailed calibration that has been critical in giving a better understanding of the relationship between Europe and the Near East during the Neolithic and Bronze Ages. This reassessment has been termed the 'second radiocarbon revolution' (the first being the inception of the radiocarbon technique itself) and the dated wood samples were its munitions. Perhaps stimulated by this role on the world scene, direct dating of archaeological sites by dendrochronology, to an accuracy far surpassing radiocarbon, has been one of the major developments of the last quarter of the twentieth century, particularly in Europe and other lowland regions where its potential has only lately been realized. Likewise a third aspect – dendroclimatology – is of increasing importance, though outside the scope of this book; for a conference compendium on this topic see Hughes *et al.* (1982).

There are several useful texts available for further reading about the direct aspect – such as those by Baillie (1982) and by Eckstein *et al.* (1984); there is a conference compendium edited by Fletcher (1978a). The radiocarbon calibration role is discussed also in Chapter 4; a valuable set of relevant research papers is contained in volume 28 of *Radiocarbon*.

2.6.1 TREE-RINGS

As might be expected there is seasonal variation in growth and in many species this leads to visually recognizable annual rings. The structure of the wood depends on the species and there are three main groups: (i) *ring-porous* hardwoods (e.g. oak), (ii) *diffuse-porous* hardwoods (e.g. beech) and (iii) conifers (e.g. spruce, pine). In the ring-porous type the *earlywood* formed during the spring consists of a band of large pores ('vessels' for water conduction) whereas the *latewood* pores are smaller, with a high content of fibre: the large pores of the earlywood make the annual growth layers easily recognizable. In the other two types the colour of the latewood gives rise to a distinct line at its boundary with the earlywood; this line is also present in the ring-porous type but is less noticeable. The counting of the annual rings in the cross-section of a newly felled tree allow its age to be found.

The width of rings is influenced by climate and for trees grown in stressed conditions, e.g. there is a distinctive pattern of wide and narrow rings. This allows *cross-dating* between trees felled in different years (see Fig. 2.14) and by continuing the process through successively older trees the felling date of archaeological timbers and fossil trees can be determined. On the other hand some species are *complacent*, i.e. there is

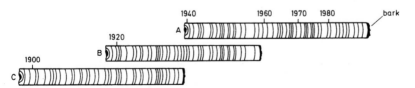

Fig. 2.14 Chronology building (after Bannister 1969). Here A is a radial sample from a living tree cut after the 1989 growing season; B and C are samples from trees felled at earlier dates. Fortunately the life spans of the trees used for sequences reaching into prehistoric times are hundreds (oak) and thousands (bristlecone pine) of years; even so many now-dead trees are needed.

little variation in width, and also there are situations in which an otherwise sensitive species may behave in a complacent manner.

Dendrochronology was pioneered early in the twentieth century by A. E. Douglass, an astronomer seeking a natural record of sunspot activity, in the south-western United States. There the emphasis, initially, was on trees growing in stressed conditions high up in the mountains near the treeline. This is in contrast to the forests of temperate regions such as lowland Europe where the successful development of dendrochronology has been somewhat against expectations, somewhat more subtle techniques being required to extract the pattern of variation.

Although it is evident that trees carry a climatic signal the relative importance of different factors is not easy to assess and interpretation in terms of past climate is far from straightforward. Also, such interpretation – as well as dating – is subject to interference by local environment, e.g. whether the tree was in a dense forest or isolated.

Missing rings; false rings

In conifers a particularly adverse year may result in no growth at all, in which case there is a *missing ring*. Conversely an irregular summer, or insect attack, in which growth is retarded and then starts again may produce a *double ring*, the second component of this being called a *false ring*. The primary guard against being misled is experience in examination and knowledge of the species concerned. It is in highly sensitive trees – the ones that give the most extreme response to climate (and hence the most easily recognizable patterns) – that there is highest risk of these abnormalities; oak, which constitutes the backbone of European dendrochronology, is relatively insensitive and hence has the strong compensatory advantage that there is negligible risk of a missing ring and the likelihood of a false one is low; even so there are uncertainties, such as illustrated in Fig. 2.15.

Examination along at least three radii, preferably the whole circumference, is the next line of defence – a ring missing in one part may be microscopically visible in another. The ultimate defence is by comparison between contemporary young and old trees, because of the former being substantially less sensitive.

Abnormal growth may also be caused by man's interference, disease, insect attack or merely by proximity of another tree. The abnormality is then much less likely to be general and hence it will be shown up by comparison. If there is an undetected abnormality in a beam from an archaeological site that is being dated against a master chronology, then there will be no match with the master chronology no matter what relative dating positions are tried and the beam will be declared undatable – or should be, dendro dating being an all-or-nothing procedure.

Sapwood and heartwood

The nearest that dendrochronology can get to the date of archaeological

(a)   (b)

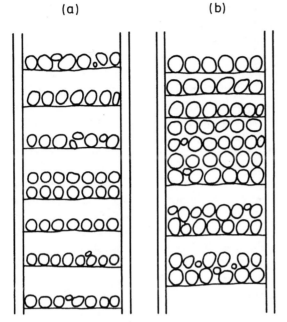

Fig. 2.15 Some examples of counting uncertainties in oak (redrawn from Baillie 1982). The tree in (a) has been regularly producing a single row of large vessels each year, so in the middle of the sequence shown it is not clear whether the double row represents 2 years or an abnormal single year. The tree in (b) has suffered a severe set-back causing it to change from double rows each year to very closely spaced single rows, which gradually separate (at the top of the diagram). Because of such irregularities experience and understanding on the part of the operator are essential, backed up with inter-tree checks for consistent behaviour (see text).

usage is the date of felling. For this to be possible the sapwood must be intact; if not, then an estimate of the number of rings of missing sapwood has to be made. Often the sapwood will have been removed during woodworking processes in antiquity, but even if intact initially the likelihood of its preservation in wet burial conditions is less than for heartwood. The latter remains robust and fibrous even after thousands of years in wet conditions, whereas the sapwood, since it contains food reserves, is prone to deterioration. Even if preserved it is difficult to sample, for in the wet state it will usually have the consistency and strength of wet cardboard; if allowed to dry out it is likely to collapse.

2.6.2 SAMPLING, MEASUREMENT AND DATA HANDLING
For detection of abnormalities it is advantageous to have a complete cross-section and this is possible when dealing with fossil trees found

in bogs and river gravels – such as used in developing the prehistoric European master chronologies; the sampling tool is then a chain saw. Obviously a different technique is required for sampling the timbers of a cathedral or living trees and the tool used then is the increment corer which yields cores of 5–10 mm in diameter and length up to 1 m depending on the hardness of the wood; for oak 30–40 cm is more realistic. Some corers act by cutting, some by milling – in which case they are mechanically driven. Most dry-wood types have the disadvantage that any sapwood present is destroyed. Because of the importance of sapwood in obtaining a precise date, cores should then be supplemented by cutting wedges deep enough to reach the heartwood whenever possible.

Wood panels carrying paintings, as well as oak chests and carvings, provide another type of dendrochronological record. For such objects the ring pattern is read *in situ* from an exposed edge with the aid of a calibrated eyepiece and ruler; an alternative is to use photography and this has the advantage that the pattern can then be read by a microscope.

Ring widths vary between a few tenths of a millimetre to several millimetres and a measurement accuracy of 0.05 – 0.02 mm is desirable. The core, or slice if available, is mounted on a travelling stage and viewed through a binocular microscope. The widths can either be recorded manually or fed automatically into a microprocessor; however, an experienced operator remains an important component of the process so that abnormalities can be noted and checked straightaway. Another possibility is to measure wood density by means of X-rays.

Prior to measurement the sample should be prepared by sanding, planing or paring (with a razor or scalpel), whichever produces the clearest record. Dry samples can be brought to a high polish and then chalk can be used to highlight the earlywood growth. However, most archaeological samples are wet and if sapwood is present it is important to avoid its collapse, as already noted. Therefore it should be kept wet, by freezing or otherwise, until measurement.

Presentation of data

In early work with the highly sensitive trees of the American South-west and other semi-arid regions the skeleton plot (see Fig. 2.16) was adequate as a basis for matching between trees. As dendrochronology developed fuller information was included in the presentation and indeed for less sensitive deciduous trees, such as oak, this was necessary from the start. A straightforward plot of width (versus year) has the disadvantage that for a fast-growing young tree the variation is more striking than for a slower-growing old tree; however, by plotting on semi-logarithmic paper a given ratio between two widths is given the same emphasis irrespective of growth rate. This representation also gives emphasis to narrow rings;

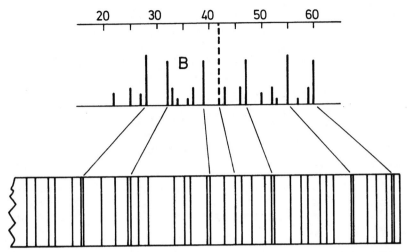

Fig. 2.16 Skeleton plot for a tree of the American South-west (redrawn from Ferguson 1970). The height of the vertical line in the skeleton plot represents the *narrowness* of the ring, i.e. it is inversely proportional to the width of the ring; the dashed line indicates that a missing ring is suspected. The letter 'B' indicates an exceptionally broad ring.

these are usually more diagnostic than wide ones, which are somewhat suppressed in this presentation.

Another method is the '%5 average' in which the width of each ring is expressed as a percentage of the average width of the five rings of which that ring is the central one. More sophisticated computational filtering techniques are also used, a trend line being fitted and each ring width expressed as a ratio to the appropriate width indicated by the trend line – see Fig. 2.17.

An alternative system (see Hollstein 1979) is to express each ring as a function of the width of the previous ring; this has the disadvantage that the indices so produced show, for a single tree, the long-term trend of slowing growth.

Cross-correlation
Having obtained one or other form of plot for two trees, the next step is to judge at what relative position in time the plots give a match. This can be done visually, by time-shifting the two patterns with respect to each other. However, it is desirable to have also some quantitative assessment of the goodness of the match and there are several procedures for obtaining this.

In the *percentage parallel variation method* the number of years in which the two plots both show an increase in width or both show a decrease in

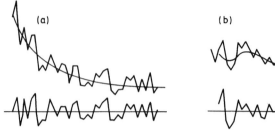

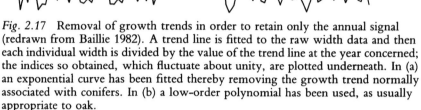

Fig. 2.17   Removal of growth trends in order to retain only the annual signal (redrawn from Baillie 1982). A trend line is fitted to the raw width data and then each individual width is divided by the value of the trend line at the year concerned; the indices so obtained, which fluctuate about unity, are plotted underneath. In (a) an exponential curve has been fitted thereby removing the growth trend normally associated with conifers. In (b) a low-order polynomial has been used, as usually appropriate to oak.

width is expressed as a percentage of the number of years of overlap. If there is no match the number of years of agreement should be about the same as the number of years of disagreement and value obtained will be close to 50%. The critical question is what value must the percentage reach in order to say with confidence that there is a match. This depends upon the number of years of overlap and is shown in Fig. 2.18 for a confidence level of 99.9%, i.e. the probability that the indicated value or greater occurs for the random situation, i.e. no match, is only 1 in 1000 ($P = 0.001$). Thus we see that for an overlap of 100 years the percentage agreement should be 65% or greater in order to have confidence in the match.

An alternative is the *t-test system* (Baillie and Pilcher 1973). The *t-value* is a measure of the correlation between the ring-width values of the two series between which a match is being sought; although not a rigorous statistical test it is highly effective in routine use, giving a greater contrast between 'match' and 'no match'. It should be seen as complementing the visual cross-dating; in practice for an overlap of 100 years, the minimum value acceptable for a match is $t = 3.5$; statistical probability levels for significant matches have been calculated (Munro 1984).

Replication and averaging
In the same way as with deep-sea cores it is advantageous to accumulate a stacked record based on a number of sequences. This dilutes individual irregularities and enhances the common signal to which the trees are responding, i.e. the signal-to-noise ratio is improved. However, this is only the case if the individual sequences are correctly matched to each other and so the first step in producing a master sequence, whether for a site or for a region, is to test by cross-correlation the *replication* of the

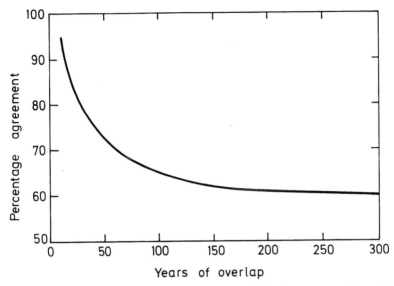

Fig. 2.18 The percentage parallel variation method of cross-correlation (Eckstein and Bauch 1969). The goodness of match between two patterns for a given relative position in time is assessed as the percentage of years in which both patterns have moved in the same direction. The curve above indicates, for a given length of overlap, the minimum percentage that must be attained in order for probability of chance agreement to be less than 1 in 1000 ($P < 0.001$), i.e. the confidence level that the match is significant is greater than 99.9%.

individual components; this will also exclude those that are invalid because of missing or false rings.

If the master sequence is produced by averaging the actual ring widths of the components it will be weighted in favour of fast-growing trees; also there will be a spurious trend if the proportion of fast-growing trees changes at some point in the master sequence. Hence the component sequences are converted to indices, discussed above, before averaging.

Signatures and signature years
In the terminology of the American South-west a *signature* is a distinctive pattern of narrow and broad rings, such as illustrated in Fig. 2.11. With the less sensitive trees of Europe such signatures are uncommon, but it has been found useful to note *signature years*, these being years in which 75% of all relevant trees either show an increase or show a decrease. Such years are sometimes indicated in the master sequence by a heavy bar connecting the two widths concerned.

2.6.3 CALIBRATION OF THE RADIOCARBON TIME-SCALE

Dendrochronology provides precisely dated samples of wood, a material highly suitable for radiocarbon dating. Hence it has been of paramount importance in calibrating the radiocarbon time-scale. A number of tree-ring chronologies have been used for special purposes (e.g. in establishing that the calibration applicable to the Southern Hemisphere is the same, to within a few decades, as that applicable to the Northern Hemisphere), but there are two major chronologies of exceptional length, one based on high-altitude trees from western USA and the other on lowland trees from western Europe.

Except for special purposes when samples spanning only 1 or 2 years have been provided, the samples used have spanned 10 or 20 years.

The bristlecone pine chronology

High up in the White Mountains of California, at altitudes somewhat over 3 km, there are dead bristlecone pines of remarkable antiquity, as well as some living trees which started growing more than 4000 years ago. Conditions for preservation are good because of the high altitude and because of the resinous nature of the species. Also because of the high altitude each year's growth period is restricted to no more than a couple of months, with the result that the rings are narrow (as little as 0.25 mm) and the pattern is highly sensitive to climate. Initially the tree was known as *Pinus aristata*, but this name has now been superseded by *Pinus longaeva* except for one particular form. Besides California the tree grows in mountainous regions of Arizona, Colorado, Nevada, New Mexico and Utah.

By leap-frogging from living trees to successive older fossil trees (as illustrated in Fig. 2.11) a continuous master chronology has been built up which currently extends back to 6700 calendar years BC. This remarkable achievement has been the work of the late Wesley Ferguson and his colleagues at the Tree-Ring Research Laboratory at the University of Arizona at Tucson (Ferguson 1968, 1979; Ferguson and Graybill 1983). Because of occurrence of missing rings in trees of the highest sensitivity (typically 5% being absent along a given radius, 2–3% absent over the whole cross-section) less highly stressed specimens were used initially with the difficult ones being brought in at a later stage. The accuracy of the master sequence so produced was later confirmed by comparison with a bristlecone pine chronology developed independently (La Marche and Harlan 1973), though from the same region. The ultimate validation has been through the mutual agreement between the radiocarbon calibration based on the bristlecone pine chronology and that based on the lowland oak chronology of Europe, a truly remarkable triumph for all techniques concerned.

There is good prospect of further extension of the chronology as older trees are recovered; 'floating' sequences have been established that, according to radiocarbon measurement of the wood, are beyond the range of the continuous sequence. It is a matter of waiting until trees are found that bridge the gap.

The European oak chronology

Being the prime building material in most of north-west Europe, oak was the obvious first choice in attempting to build a European sequence, having as objective the dating of buildings, archaeological sites and art-historical objects. By the middle 1960s sequences for Germany spanning the last 1000 years, and beyond, had been developed, notably by Huber at Hamburg and by Hollstein at Trier, and together with further extension these formed one major building block of the consolidated European chronology. The other was the Irish bog-oak chronology developed at the Belfast Palaeoecology Centre; when a consensus was reached between the German and Irish workers a European chronology spanning 7300 years became available (Pilcher *et al.* 1984). At the time of this bridging, the German sequences reached back only to 4000 years ago, though subsequently this has been substantially extended.

Because of their much shorter life span many more trees are required in developing an oak chronology than for a bristlecone pine chronology. On the other hand, being less sensitive they are much less prone to abnormalities, as noted earlier. Also, because the average ring widths are greater, larger samples are available for radiocarbon measurements, thereby allowing higher precision. It was somewhat unexpected that the bog-oaks of Ireland, on the Atlantic seaboard, would cross-date with oaks of Germany grown in different climatic and ecological conditions; the validity of this cross-dating, established by steps from Ireland to England to Germany, is another implication of the agreement of the European time-scale calibration with that based on bristlecone pines.

As with the bristlecone pine there are European 'floating' sequences, in pine as well as oak, beyond the present range of the master chronology that is dendrochronologically anchored with respect to the present day. By matching the radiocarbon 'wiggles' (see section 4.4.4) in the late part of one of these floating sequences with the wiggles in the very early part of the bristlecone pine chronology (which currently extends some 1500 years beyond the European master chronology) it has been possible to reach back to 11,000 calendar years ago, allowing further extension of the time-scale calibration (Becker and Kromer 1986). For further extension by dendrochronology trees in river gravels from more southerly regions, such as Greece, are being sought; in northerly parts the tree cover was sparse or non-existent due to adverse conditions.

2.6.4 DATING OF ARCHAEOLOGICAL SITES AND STRUCTURES

Dendrochronological dating is potentially applicable wherever trees were growing, except in tropical regions. Its use is now so widespread and in so many diverse situations that it is not feasible to give any representative picture of its application. Instead a few generalized comments will be made, most of them implicit in the foregoing sections. Examples of application will be found in Baillie (1982) and Eckstein *et al.* (1984); indication of currently available dendrochronological data will be found in Hughes *et al.* (1982) and in Eckstein and Wrobel (1985). An extensive project is in progress in the eastern Mediterranean region using oak, pine, cedar, juniper and fir; unfortunately neither olive nor plane trees are suitable (Kuniholm and Striker 1987).

First and foremost it is a technique of quite remarkable accuracy, far surpassing the 'hard science' techniques of the subsequent chapters. When the sapwood is intact the felling date can sometimes be determined to better than a year – by noting whether growth concluded with earlywood or latewood. On the other hand a master chronology for the region concerned is a necessary prerequisite, and even when this is available it is not necessarily the case that a match for the unknown timber will be found – because its pattern has been distorted by non-climatic interferences. So even a rough estimate of date may not be available. Of course in the absence of a relevant master chronology, it may be possible to determine duration of occupation by interrelating the timbers of the site to form a floating site chronology. The master chronology may also be a floating one, perhaps with some indication of calendar age provided by a non-dendrochronological technique having been applied on a relevant site.

The linking of the Irish and German oak chronologies gives an indication of the size of region over which cross-dating may be possible. However, rather than use a common master chronology for such a large region it is more effective to establish individual ones for smaller regions; the correlation obtained for an unknown timber then tends to be at a higher level of confidence on account of local climatic signals. In the case of Europe, sub-regional chronologies are given absolute dating by region-to-region bridging to either the Irish or German chronologies. Hence, potentially, dendro dating in Europe can reach just as far back as the Irish/German chronology; at present this means to 7300 years ago with full confidence and accuracy, and with poorer accuracy, back to 11,000 years.

A major limitation is the need to find timbers containing enough rings. It is rarely possible to find a reliable match with less than 80, and the general rule is that upwards of 100 are required; it depends upon the distinctiveness of the pattern. It is advantageous to use contemporary timbers to make a 'site master'; as in constructing the master chronology for a region, this averages out individual irregularities and enhances the wanted signal.

Besides oak and pine, species such as beech, spruce, fir and juniper have been used. In general the reference chronology needs to be based on the same species as the item being dated, though not always.

Sapwood estimates
Often the sapwood is not complete (i.e. it does not reach to the bark) and in the worst possible case the sapwood/heartwood boundary is missing too; there is then an unknown member of years between the date of the last ring and the date of felling. If the sapwood/heartwood boundary is present then a sapwood allowance may be added; unfortunately, however, the amount depends not only on species and region but also – at any rate in oak the most studied species – on age of tree and distance up the trunk. According to Eckstein *et al.* (1984) the oak estimates of various workers lie between 14 and 50, with a mean figure of 30 being suggested for western England, with a 95% probability that any individual value lies between 19 and 50. Thus for an oak sample in which the heartwood/sapwood boundary is present, but not the bark, the accuracy of dating is to 'within a decade or two'. More data on sapwood are given in Fig. 2.19.

2.6.5 ART-HISTORICAL DATING
A remarkable dendrochronological source is the edges of oak panels used for medieval paintings such as portraits by Rembrandt, Rubens and others. The panels were evidently cut as radial boards along the length of the tree; hence two opposite edges show the rings. When the heartwood/sapwood boundary is present the likely date of the portrait is obtained by adding an appropriate sapwood allowance (but see Fig. 2.19) plus a further allowance for seasoning; in the more frequent case when the boundary is absent then only an estimate of the earliest date can be made. A check on the validity of the dendrochronological estimates is provided in cases when the artist has added a date after his signature or when there are historical records concerning the person depicted in the portrait. In other cases the dendrochronological estimate provides useful information to the art historian, sometimes to the extent of revealing a forgery.

Wooden chests, cupboards and carvings are another dendrochronological source and extensive study of these, together with panel portraits, has been made for material found in The Netherlands, Germany and southern England (see Eckstein *et al.* 1975; Fletcher 1977, 1978b; Bauch 1978).

Cross-dating
A puzzling feature of the so-called art-historical sequences derived from the above materials was that in the period AD 1200–1650 there was difficulty in matching them to the master chronologies derived from historic and archaeological building timbers. Because of this it was postulated (e.g. Fletcher 1978c) that for the English material at any rate the

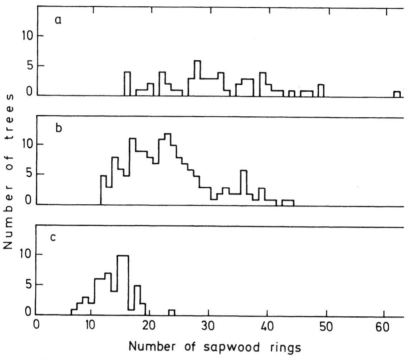

Fig. 2.19 Histograms of observed numbers of sapwood rings for oaks from: (a) England, (b) West Germany and (c) Finland (redrawn from Baillie *et al.* 1985).

provenance was lowland regions around the southern basin of the North Sea, where rainfall was substantially lower than the regions from which the historic and archaeological timbers had been obtained. Subsequently, however, it was suggested (Baillie 1984) that a more exotic origin in the eastern Baltic was likely and this was later confirmed (Baillie *et al.* 1985; Eckstein *et al.* 1986). Cross-dating to a continuous sequence developed in that region for the last 1000 years resulted in a forward shift of the art-historical sequences by half a decade; however, this shift is more or less compensated by a smaller sapwood allowance being appropriate for that region of origin (see Fig. 2.19) with the consequence that the art-historical results derived using the earlier placement of the sequences remain valid to within their error limits (Eckstein *et al.* 1986).

The removal of the notion that there was a lowland region in which growth pattern did not fit that of adjacent regions greatly enhances the potentiality of the technique. The development of the notion in the first place demonstrates the dangers inherent in ignoring warning signs.

Subsequent to AD 1650 there is no dichotomy between the art-historical and the other sequences, and it was difficult to see why the whole of the hypothesized lowland region should have ceased production. However, with a Baltic origin for the oak there is a more acceptable explanation – trade routes across the Baltic sea were cut by the Thirty Years War and never resumed (see Eckstein *et al.* 1986).

NOTES

1. This means 0.1% of value of the ratio, e.g. a change from 0.2000 to 0.2002%

2. It is usual to express the isotopic composition by reference to a particular standard, thus

$$\delta \, ^{18}O = \frac{(^{18}O/^{16}O)_{sample} - (^{18}O/^{16}O)_{standard}}{(^{18}O/^{16}O)_{standard}} \times 1000 \qquad (2.1)$$

Hence a sample that has a ratio that is 0.1% higher than the standard, has a $\delta^{18}O$ value of $+ 1$ per mil (‰). For isotopic measurements on shells the standard used is a belemnite from the Peedee formation of North Carolina (PDB-1). There is also a water standard, known as SMOW (Standard Mean Ocean Water).

3. Subsequently, indications have been obtained (Chappell and Shackleton 1986) that during the last interglacial deep-ocean temperatures were about 2 °C lower than at present or during the last interglacial. It is concluded that though the major influence on isotope variation was from global ice-volume the effect of water temperature was appreciable (see also Labeyrie *et al.* 1987; Shackleton 1987).

4. Detailed examination suggests slight non-synchroneity, e.g. whereas the Brunhes–Matuyama boundary is 'warm' in the deep-sea record, it is 'cold' in the Chinese loess – as also in other continents and in sediments other than loess. However, it is possible that the apparent non-synchroneity arises because of variable delay between deposition of sediment, whether on land or on the ocean floor, and acquisition of its magnetic remanence.

5. Another question is why, prior to the present succession of glaciations lasting about 2 million years, there had been no glacial age for the previous 300 million years. One possible explanation (see Imbrie and Imbrie 1986, part III) is in terms of the very slowly changing configuration of the continents, resulting from slight drift. It is only certain particular patterns that make the earth vulnerable to being triggered into an ice age (by the occurrence of a dip in solar radiation in northerly latitudes). Diversion of the Gulf Stream is one example of a mechanism through which continental configuration may act.

6. Deuterium is one heavy isotope of hydrogen; its nucleus consists of a proton and a neutron, whereas that of hydrogen consists of a proton only; in nature the atomic abundance of the heavy isotope is 0.016%. Temperature-dependent fractionation occurs as for oxygen. In water there are various possible combinations of light and heavy isotopes, the most relevant to the palaeoclimatic record being $^1H^2H^{16}O$, generally written as HDO, and $^1H_2{}^{18}O$.

7. Inevitably there is some ambiguity in defining the boundaries of zones and there are two possible criteria, the second being the one commonly used (see Smith and Pilcher 1973). (1) *Empirical limit:* the point at which pollen of the species first becomes consistently present, i.e. for a number of consecutive samples. (2) *Rational limit:* the point at which the pollen curve begins to rise to sustained high values.

8. Some warm phases have pollen characteristics which are not sufficiently dissimilar to be distinguishable; thus in Britain the three substages 5a, 5c and 5e were initially regarded by palynologists as a single warm phase.

REFERENCES

Aitken, M. J., Michael, H. N., Betancourt, P. P., and Warren, P. M. (1988) The Thera eruption: continuing discussion of the dating, *Archaeometry* 30, 165–82.

Baillie, M. G. L. (1982) *Tree-ring Dating and Archaeology*, Croom Helm, London, 274 pp.

Baillie, M. G. L. (1984) Art-historical dendrochronology, *Journ. Archaeol. Sci.* 11, 371–93.

Baillie, M. G. L. and Pilcher, J. R. (1973) A simple crossdating program for tree-ring research, *Tree-Ring Bulletin* 33, 7–14.

Baillie, M. G. L., Hillam, J., Briffa, K. R. and Brown, D. M. (1985) Re-dating the English art-historical tree-ring chronologies, *Nature* 315, 317–19.

Baillie, M. G. L. and Munro, M. A. R. (1988) Irish tree rings, Santorini and volcanic dust veils, *Nature* 332, 344–6.

Bannister, B. (1969) Dendrochronology, in *Science in Archaeology* (eds. E. R. Higgs and D. Brothwell), Thames & Hudson, Bristol, UK.

Bauch, J. (1978) Dating of panel paintings, *BAR* (International Series) 51, 307–14.

de Beaulieu, J.-L. and Reille, M. (1984a) The pollen sequence of Les Echets (France): a new element for the chronology of the Upper Pleistocene, *Géographie physique et Quaternaire* 37, 3–9.

de Beaulieu, J.-L. and Reille, M. (1984b) A long Upper Pleistocene pollen record from Les Echets, near Lyon, France, *Boreas* 13, 111–32.

Becker, B. and Kromer, B. (1986) Extension of the Holocene dendrochronology by the preboreal pine series, 8800 to 10,100 BP, *Radiocarbon,* 28, 961–7.

Begét, J. E. and Hawkins, D. B. (1989) Influence of orbital parameters on Pleistocene loess deposition in central Alaska, *Nature* 337, 151–3.

Berger, A. (1977) Long-term variations of the Earth's orbital elements, *Celestial Mech.* 15, 53–74.

Berger, A. (1980) The Milankovitch astronomical theory of paleoclimates. A modern review, *Vistas Astron.* 24, 103–122.

Betancourt, P. P. (1987) Dating of the Aegean Late Bronze Age with radiocarbon, *Archaeometry* 29, 45–9.

Birks, H. J. B. and Birks, H. H. (1981) *Quaternary Palaeoecology*, Edward Arnold, London.

Bradley, R. S. (1985) *Quaternary Palaeoclimatology*, Allen & Unwin, Boston.

Broecker, W. S., Thurber, D. L., Goddard, J., Ku, T.-L., Matthews, R. K, and Mesolella, K. J. (1968) Milankovitch hypothesis supported by precise dating of coral reefs and deep-sea sediments, *Science* 159, 297–300.

Broecker, W. S. and van Donk, J. (1970) Insolation changes, ice volumes and the ^{18}O record in deep-sea cores, *Rev. Geophys. Space Phys.* 8, 169–98.

Cato, I. (1985) The definitive connection of the Swedish geochronological time scale with the present, and the new date of the zero year in Döviken, northern Sweden, *Boreas* 14, 117–22.

Chappell, J. and Shackleton, N. J. (1986) Oxygen isotopes and sea level, *Nature* 324, 137–40.

Dansgaard, W. and Tauber, H. (1969) Glacier oxygen-18 content and Pleistocene ocean temperatures, *Science* 166, 499–502.

Derbyshire, E. (1987) A history of glacial stratigraphy in China, *Quaternary Science Reviews* 6, 301–14.

Eckstein, D. and Bauch, J. (1969) Beitrag zur Rationalisierung eines dendrochronologischen Verfahrens und zur Analyse seiner Aussagesicherheit, *Forsturissenschaftliches centralblatt* 88, 230–50.

Eckstein, D., Brongers, J. H. and Bauch, J. (1975) Tree-ring research in the Netherlands, *Tree-ring Bulletin* 35, 1–13.

Eckstein, D., Baillie, M. G. L. and Egger, H. (1984) *Handbook for Archaeologists No. 2 – Dendrochronological Dating*, European Science Foundation, Strasbourg, 55 pp.

Eckstein, D. and Wrobel, S. (1985) Dendrochronologie in Europa, *Dendrochronologia* 1, 9–20.

Eckstein, D., Wazny, T., Bauch, J. and Klein, P. (1986) New evidence for the dendrochronological dating of Netherlandish paintings, *Nature* 320, 465–6.

Edwards, R. L., Chen, J. H., Ku, T.-L and Wasserburg, G. J. (1987) Precise timing of the last interglacial period from mass spectrometric determination of thorium-230 in corals, *Science* 236, 1547–53.

Emiliani, C. (1955) Pleistocene temperatures, *J. Geol.* 63, 538–78.

Emiliani, C. (1978) The cause of the Ice Ages, *Earth Planet, Sci. Lett.* 37, 349–52.

Faegri, K. and Iversen, J. (1975) *Textbook of Pollen Analysis* (3rd edn), Hafner Press, New York; Munksgaard, Copenhagen.

Ferguson, C. W. (1968) Bristlecone pine: science and esthetics, *Science* 159, 839–46.

Ferguson, C. W. (1970) Concepts and techniques of dendrochronology, in *Scientific Methods in Medieval Archaeology* (ed. R. Berger), University of California Press, pp. 183–200.

Ferguson, C. W. (1979) Dendrochronology of bristlecone pine, *Pinus longaeva, Environment International* 2, 209–14.

Ferguson, C. W. and Graybill, D. A. (1983) Dendrochronology of bristlecone pine: a progress report, *Radiocarbon* 25, 287–8.

Fink, J. and Kukla, G. J. (1977) Pleistocene climates in central Europe: at least 17 interglacials after the Olduvai event, *Quat. Res.* 7, 363–71.

Flenley, J. R. (1984) Andean guide to Pliocene-Quaternary climate, *Nature* 311, 702–3.

Fletcher, J. M. (1977) Tree-ring chronologies for the 6th to 16th centuries for oaks of southern and eastern England, *Journ. Archaeol. Sci.* 4, 335–52.

Fletcher, J. M. (ed.) (1978a) Dendrochronology in Europe, *BAR* (International Series), **51**, 356 pp.

Fletcher, J. M. (1978b) Tree-ring analysis of panel paintings, *BAR* (International Series), **51**, 303–6.

Fletcher, J. M. (1978c) Oak chronologies for eastern and southern England, *BAR* (International Series), **51**, 139–56.

Fletcher, J. M. (1986) Dating of art-historical artefacts, *Nature* **320**, 466.

Girard, M. and Renault-Miskovsky, J. (1983) Datation et paléoenvironment de la mandibule de Montmarin (Haute-Garonne): analyses polliniques dans la Niche, *C.R. Acad. Sci. Paris* **296**, 669–71.

Godwin, H. (1960) Radiocarbon dating and Quaternary history in Britain, *Proc. Roy. Soc.* **B153**, 287–320.

Godwin, H. (1975) *The History of the British Flora* (2nd edn), Cambridge University Press, Cambridge.

Godwin, H. (1981) *The Archives of the Peat Bogs*, Cambridge University Press, Cambridge.

Godwin, H., Walker, D. and Willis, E. H. (1957) Radiocarbon dating and post-glacial vegetational history: Scaleby Moss, *Proc. Roy. Soc.* **B147**, 352–66.

Godwin, H. and Willis, E. H. (1959) Radiocarbon dating of the Late-glacial period in Britain, *Proc. Roy. Soc.* **B150**, 199–215.

Hammer, C. V., Clausen, H. B. and Tauber, H. (1986) Ice-core dating of the Pleistocene/Holocene boundary applied to a calibration of the C-14 timescale, *Radiocarbon* **28**, 284–91.

Hammer, C. V., Clausen, H. B., Friedrich, W. L. and Tauber, H. (1987) The Minoan eruption of Santorini in Greece dated to 1645 B.C.? *Nature* **328**, 517–19.

Hays, J. D., Imbrie, J. and Shackleton, N. J. (1976) Variations in the earth's orbit: pacemaker of the ice ages, *Science* **194**, 1121–32 (see also *Science* **198**, 528–30).

Heller, F. and Liu, T. S. (1982) Magnetostratigraphical dating of loess deposits in China, *Nature* **300**, 431–3.

Heller, F. and Liu, T. S. (1984) Magnetism of Chinese loess deposits (astr.), *Geophysical Journal of Research* **77**, 125–41.

Heller, F. and Liu, T. S. (1986) Paleoclimatic and sedimentary history from magnetic susceptibility of loess in China, *Geophysical Research Letters* **13**, 1169–72.

Hibbert, F. A., Switzur, V. T. and West, R. G. (1971) Radiocarbon dating of Flandrian pollen zones at Red Moss, Lancs., *Proc. Roy. Soc. Lond.* **B177**, 161–76.

Hillam, J. (1979) Tree-rings and archaeology, *Journ. Archaeol. Science* **6**, 271–8.

Hollstein, E. (1979) *Mitteleuropaische Eichenchronologie*, Mainz am Rhein.

Hughes, M. K., Kelly, P. M., Pilcher, J. R. and La Marche, V. C. (eds) (1982) *Climate from Tree Rings*, Cambridge University Press, Cambridge, 223 pp.

Imbrie, J. and Imbrie, J. Z. (1980) Modeling the climatic response to orbital variations, *Science* **207**, 943–53.

Imbrie, J. and Imbrie, K. P. (1986) *Ice Ages*, Harvard University Press, Cambridge, Mass. 224 pp.

Imbrie, J., Hays, J. D., Martinson, D. G., Mcintyre, A., Mix, A. C., Morley, J. J., Pisias, N. G., Prell, W. L. and Shackleton, N. J. (1984) The orbital theory of Pleistocene climate: support from a revised chronology of the marine $\delta^{18}O$ record, in *Milankovitch and Climate, Part I* (eds A. Berger, J. Imbrie, J. Hays, G. Kukla and B. Saltzman). Reidel, Dordrecht, The Netherlands, pp. 269–305.

Jouzel, J., Lorius, C., Petit, J. R., Genthon, C., Barkov, N. I., Kotlyakov, V.

M. and Petrov, V. M. (1987) Vostok ice core: a continuous isotope temperature record over the last climatic cycle (160,000 years), *Nature* **329**, 403–8.

Kukla, G. (1987) Loess stratigraphy in central China, *Quaternary Science Reviews* **6**, 191–219.

Kukla, G., Heller, F., Liu, X. M., Xu, T. C., Liu, T. S. and An, Z. S. (1988) Pleistocene climates in China dated by magnetic susceptibility, *Geology* **16**, 811–814.

Kuniholm, P. I. and Striker, C. I. (1987) Dendrochronological investigations in the Aegean and neighbouring regions, *Journal Field Archaeology* **14**, 385–98.

Labeyrie, L. D., Duplessy, J. C. and Blanc, P. L. (1987) Variations in mode of formation and temperature of oceanic deep waters over the past 125,000 years, *Nature* **327**, 477–82.

La Marche, V. C. and Harlan, T. P. (1973) Accuracy of tree ring dating of bristlecone pine for calibration of radiocarbon time scale, *Journ. Geophys. Res.* **78**, 8849–58.

La Marche, V. C. and Hirschboeck, K. K. (1984) Frost rings in trees as records of major volcanic eruptions, *Nature* **307**, 121–6.

Leroi-Gourhan, A. (1980) Les analyses polliniques au moyen-orient, *Paleorient* **6**, 79–91.

Leroyer, C. and Leroi-Gourhan, A. (1983) Problèmes de chronologie: le castelperronien et l'aurignacien, *Bull. de l'Association française pour l'étude du Quaternaire* **80**, 41–4.

Liu, X. M., Liu, T. S., Cheng, M. Y., Liu, C. and Xu, T. C. (1985) The primary study on magnetostratigraphy of a loess profile in Xifeng area, Gansu Province, *Proceedings of International Symposium of Loess Research*, 5–16 Oct., Xian, p. 100.

Lowe, J. J. and Gray, J. M. (1980) The stratigraphic subdivision of the Lateglacial of North-west Europe, in *Studies in the Lateglacial of North-west Europe* (eds J. J. Lowe, J. M. Gray and J. E. Robinson), Pergamon, Oxford and New York, pp. 157–75.

Lowe, J. J. and Walker, M. J. C. (1984) *Reconstructing Quaternary Environments*, Longman Scientific and Technical, London 389 pp.

Mangerud, J., Anderson, S. Th., Berglund, B. E. and Donner, J. J. (1974) Quaternary stratigraphy of Norden, a proposal for terminology and classification, *Boreas* **3**, 109–26.

Mangerud, J., Sonstegaard, E. and Sejrup, H.-P. (1979) Correlation of the Eemian (interglacial) stage and the deep-sea oxygen–isotope stratigraphy, *Nature* **277**, 189–92.

Mangerud, J., Sonstegaard, E., Sejrup, H.-P. and Haldorsen, S. (1981) A continuous Eemian–Early Weichselian sequence containing pollen and marine fossils at Fjosanger, western Norway, *Boreas* **10**, 137–208.

Mankinen, E. A. and Dalrymple, G. B. (1979) Revised polarity time scale for the interval 0–5 m.y. BP, *Journ. Geophys. Res.* **84**, 615–26.

Martinson, D. G., Pisias, N. G., Hays, J. D., Imbrie, T. C. and Shackleton, N. J. (1987) Age dating and the orbital theory of the ice ages: Development of a high-resolution 0 to 300,000-year chronostratigraphy, *Quat. Res.* **27**, 1–29.

Mesolella, K. J., Matthews, R. K., Broecker, W. S. and Thurber, D. L. (1969) The astronomical theory of climatic change: Barbados data, *J. Geol.* **77**, 250–74.

Milankovitch, M. M. (1941) *Canon of Insolation and the Ice-age Problem*, Königlich Serbische Akademie, Beograd. (English translation by the Israel Program for Scientific Translations, published for the US Department of Commerce, and the National Science Foundation, Washington, DC, 1969.)

Mix, A. C. and Pisias, N. G. (1988) Oxygen isotope analyses and deep-sea temperature changes: implications for rates of oceanic mixing, *Nature* 331, 249–51.

Moore, P. D. and Webb, J. A. (1978) *An Illustrated Guide to Pollen Analysis,* Hodder & Stoughton, London.

Morley, J. J. and Hays, J. D. (1981) Towards a high-resolution, global, deep-sea chronology for the last 750,000 years, *Earth Planet, Sci. Letters* 53, 279–95.

Munro, M. A. R. (1984) An improved algorithm for cross-dating tree-ring series, *Tree Ring Bulletin* 44, 17–27.

Nilsson, T. (1982) *The Pleistocene,* Reidel, Dordrecht, The Netherlands.

Olausson, E. (1965) Evidence of climatic changes in deep sea cores with remarks on isotopic palaeotemperature analysis, *Progr. Oceanogr.* 3, 221–52.

Pilcher, J. R., Baillie, M. G. L., Schmidt, B. and Becker, B. (1984) A 7,272-year tree-ring chronology for western Europe, *Nature* 312, 150–2.

Pisias, N. G., Martinson, D. G., Moore, T. C., Shackleton, N. J., Prell, W., Hays, J. and Boden, G. (1984) High resolution stratigraphic correlation of benthic oxygen isotope records spanning the last 300,000 years, *Marine Geology* 56, 119–36.

Pyle, D. M. (1989) Ice core acidity peaks, retarded tree growth and putative eruptions, *Archaeometry* 31, 88–91.

Renault-Miskovsky, J. (1986) Relations entres les spectres archéo-polliniques du sud-est de la France et les oscillations climatiques entre 125,000 ans et le maximum glaciare, *Bull. de l'Association française pour l'étude du Quaternaire* 83, 56–62.

Robinson, S. G. (1986) The late Pleistocene palaeomagnetic record of North Atlantic deep-sea sediments revealed by mineral magnetic measurements, *Phys. Earth Planet. Int.* 42, 22–47.

Shackleton, N. J. (1967) Oxygen isotope analyses and Pleistocene temperatures re-assessed, *Nature* 215, 15–17.

Shackleton, N. J. (1987) Oxygen isotopes, ice volume and sea level, *Quaternary Science Reviews* 6, 183–90.

Shackleton, N. J. and Opdyke, N. D. (1973) Oxygen isotope and paleomagnetic stratigraphy of equatorial Pacific core V28–238: oxygen isotope temperatures and ice volumes on a 10^5 year and 10^6 year scale, *Quat. Res.* 3, 39–55.

Shackleton, N. J. and Opdyke, N. D. (1976) Oxygen-isotope and paleomagnetic stratigraphy of Pacific core V28–239. Late Pliocene to latest Pleistocene, in *Investigation of Late Quaternary Paleooceanography and Paleoclimatology* (eds R. M. Cline and J. D. Hays), Geological Society of America Memoir 145, Geological Society of America, Boulder, Colo., pp. 449–64.

Sibrava, V., Bowen, D. Q. and Richmond, G. M. (eds) (1986) Quaternary glaciations in the Northern Hemisphere, *Quaternary Science Reviews* 5, 514 pp.

Smith, A. G. and Pilcher, J. R. (1973) Radiocarbon dates and vegetational history of the British Isles, *New Phytol.* 72, 903–14.

Stringer, C. B., Currant, A. P., Schwarcz, H. P. and Colcutt, S. N. (1986) Age of Pleistocene faunas from Bacon Hole, Wales, *Nature* 320, 59–62.

Strömberg, B. (1985) Revision of the lateglacial Swedish varve chronology, *Boreas* 14, 101–5.

Stuiver, M. (1970) Long-term C-14 variations, in *Radiocarbon Variations and Absolute Chronology,* (ed. I. U. Olsson), Wiley, New York, pp. 197–213.

Stuiver, M., Kromer, B., Becker, B. and Ferguson, C. W. (1986) Radiocarbon age calibration back to 13,300 years BP, *Radiocarbon* 28, 969–79.

Tauber, H. (1970) The Scandinavian varve chronology and C-14 dating, in

Radiocarbon Variation and Absolute Chronology (ed. I. U. Olsson), Wiley, New York, pp. 173–96.

Tooley, M. J. (1981) Methods of reconstruction, in *The Environment in British Prehistory* (eds I. Simmons and M. J. Tooley), Duckworth, London, pp. 1–48.

Turner, C. and Hannon, G. E. (1988) Vegetational evidence for late Quaternary climatic changes in southwest Europe in relation to the influence of the North Atlantic ocean, *Phil. Trans. R. Soc. Lond. B 318*, 451–485.

Turon, J.-L. (1984) Direct land/sea correlations in the last interglacial complex, *Nature 309*, 673–6.

Urey, H. C. (1948) Oxygen isotopes in nature and in the laboratory, *Science* 108, 489–96.

Vernekar, A. D. (1972) Long-period global variations of incoming solar radiation, *Met. Monog.* 12 (34) Amer. Meteorol. Soc., Boston.

Warren, P. M. (1984) Absolute dating of the Bronze Age eruption of Thera (Santorini), *Nature 308*, 492–3.

West, R. G. (1970) Pollen zones in the Pleistocene of Great Britain and their correlation, *New Phytol.* 69, 1179–83.

Winograd, I. J., Szabo, B. J., Coplen, T. B. and Riggs, A. C. (1988). A 250,000-year climatic record from Great Basin vein calcite: implications for Milankovitch theory, *Science* 242, 1275–1280.

Woillard, G. M. (1978) Grand Pile Peat Bog: a continuous pollen record for the past 140,000 years, *Quat. Res.* 9, 110–33.

Woillard, G. M. and Mook, W. G. (1982) Carbon-14 dates at Grande Pile: correlation of land and sea chronologies, *Science* 215, 159–61.

Zeuner, F. (1946) *Dating the Past* (1st edn), Methuen, London.

3 RADIOCARBON – I

In this chapter we discuss the physical basis of radiocarbon dating and the causes of its complications, concluding with brief mention of other cosmogenic nuclides which have been suggested for dating such as calcium-41. In the succeeding chapter attention is focused on practicalities relevant to archaeological application, including conversion of radiocarbon years to calendar years.

An account of the early development of the technique has been given by its originator W. F. Libby (1955, 1965) who later received a Nobel Prize for this work. A great deal has subsequently been written in research journals and conference proceedings; various monographs are available, such as that by Taylor (1987) which also includes a historical perspective. Lists of dates were published in *Radiocarbon* until the late 1980s, and then accumulated in a database organized by that journal. Around the world there are upwards of 100 radiocarbon laboratories; there is an international specialist conference every three years, as well as one restricted to accelerator dating. Additional special meetings are held from time to time; there is a regular series orientated towards archaeologists, this being based on the radiocarbon laboratory at Groningen, The Netherlands.

Besides archaeology the technique has extensive applications in Quaternary geology and the environmental sciences.

3.1 THE ESSENTIAL BASIS

3.1.1 RADIOACTIVITY AND OCCURRENCE; PRINCIPLE OF DATING

Carbon-14 is chemically identical with non-radioactive carbon (carbon-12 and carbon-13); it differs only in having extra neutrons in its nucleus and this causes slight instability. When it decays it transmutes to nitrogen-14, which is not radioactive. In the process of decay nuclear radiation is emitted in the form of beta particles, one from each atom of carbon-14 that decays. Decay is spontaneous and proceeds at an immutable rate,[1] being totally unaffected by climate or environment. In the case of carbon-14 the number of atoms in an isolated sample decreases by 1% every 83 years; this means that in 5730 years (the *half-life*) there is decrease to one-half of the number initially present – and after a further 5730 years the number remaining will be halved again, and so on.

Formation of carbon-14 atoms occurs in the upper atmosphere due to the interaction of cosmic-ray neutrons with nitrogen-14, the principal isotope of nitrogen (to which it eventually decays back, as mentioned above). After formation carbon-14 atoms quickly combine with oxygen to form 'heavy' carbon dioxide molecules, the chemical behaviour of which is almost identical with ordinary carbon dioxide. There is rapid mixing in the atmosphere and through photosynthesis there is entry into plant life (see Fig. 3.1); animals eat plants and consequently all the living animal and vegetable world (the *biosphere*) contains carbon-14. Atmospheric carbon dioxide also enters the oceans as dissolved carbonate, so that this too contains carbon-14; so too do any shells and deposits formed from it. The totality of atmosphere, biosphere and oceans is known as the *carbon exchange reservoir*. The concentration ratio between carbon-14 atoms and

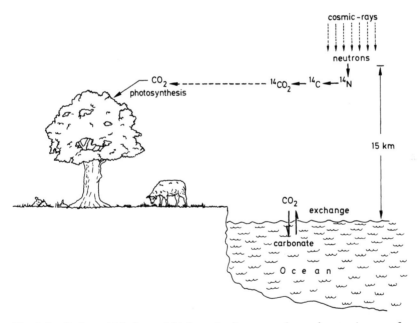

Fig. 3.1 Carbon–14 is formed high up in the atmosphere, the maximum of production being at about 15 km (50,000 ft). After oxidation to carbon dioxide it mixes in with the non-radioactive carbon dioxide of the atmosphere. Entry into the biosphere is by photosynthesis into plants and thence by ingestion into animals. Ocean carbonate has roughly the same concentration ratio of ($^{14}C/^{12}C$) as atmospheric carbon dioxide because of the exchange that occurs at the surface of the ocean. More detail of the 'carbon exchange reservoir' is given in Fig. 3.4.

non–radioactive carbon atoms is approximately the same (about one in a million million) throughout the reservoir; also it stays approximately constant with time. This concentration ratio represents the *equilibrium level* that is established, on a global scale, between loss by radioactive decay and production by cosmic rays.

In organic matter that is no longer exchanging its carbon with the reservoir there is loss of carbon-14 by radioactive decay but no replenishment; this is the case when cellulose molecules of wood are formed, for instance. Hence from the time of formation the concentration ratio in wood decreases at a rate determined by the immutable 5730-year half-life. The procedure for dating is then straightforward, as illustrated in Fig. 3.2. Instead of concentration ratio it is convenient in discussion to use specific carbon-14 activity, i.e. the rate of emission of beta particles per unit mass of total carbon; this rate is exactly proportional to the concentration ratio.

Time zero for timber
Note that the radioactive clock starts at the time of the sample's formation; hence time zero for the inner rings of a tree is earlier than for the outer part and it is only for the latter that time zero corresponds to the felling date.

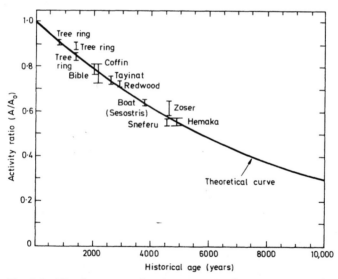

Fig. 3.2 The first comprehensive test using known-age samples (from Arnold and Libby, 1949). The theoretical curve is based on the Libby half-life of 5568 years; this was the preferred value at the time. The older samples are from Egyptian pyramids, the king's name being given. The vertical scale shows the ratio between the carbon–14 activity in the ancient sample to that in a modern one.

Exponential decay; lifetime

The probability of radioactive decay is such that in a large number of carbon-14 atoms 1% will decay in 83 years. This determines the form of the curve shown in Fig. 3.2, viz.:

$$A = A_0 \exp(-t/8267) \tag{3.1}$$

where A is the carbon-14 activity for a sample of age t years, A_0 is the value of A for $t = 0$, i.e. the starting activity and 8267 years is the *lifetime* (or *mean life*) of carbon-14. The mathematical function 'exp' is available on many hand calculators and it may be verified[2] that an increase of 83 years in the value of t gives a decrease of 1% in the value of A, irrespective of the value of t.

The lifetime, τ, is the average life expectancy of a carbon-14 atom and it is related to the half-life, $t_{1/2}$, according to

$$t_{1/2} = 0.693\,\tau \tag{3.2}$$

Thus $t_{1/2} = 5730$ years and it may be checked that for this value of t, $A = 0.5A_0$. At the time when radiocarbon was being developed the best available measurements on the decay rate of carbon-14 indicated a half-life of 5568 years (and a lifetime of 8033 years). These are known as the conventional, or 'Libby' values, whereas it is the revised or 'Cambridge' values that have been given above, Cambridge (UK) being the venue of the 1955 Radiocarbon Conference at which the revised values were announced. As discussed in section 4.4.1 conventional radiocarbon ages are calculated on the basis of the Libby half-life.

In order to determine the age corresponding to a given value of (A/A_0), equation (3.1) is converted to its logarithmic form, viz.:

$$\begin{aligned}
t &= -8267 \ln(A/A_0) \\
&= -19{,}035 \log(A/A_0)
\end{aligned} \tag{3.3}$$

The mathematical functions 'ln' and 'log' are also available on hand calculators. Figure 3.3 shows a plot of (A/A_0) versus t in which the former is on a log scale. It may be seen that a given percentage change in (A/A_0) corresponds to a fixed change in years irrespective of the value of t. Thus if the measured value of A is erroneously high by 1% the age obtained will be too small by about 80 years; similarly if the value used for A_0 is erroneously low by 1% the age obtained will be too great by about 80 years. This is a useful rule of thumb to keep in mind during discussion.

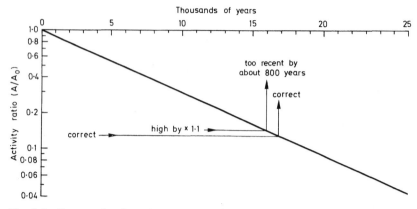

Fig. 3.3 Decay of carbon–14 activity with its half-life of 5730 years using logarithmic scale for (A/A_0). With this scale a change in (A/A_0) by a given factor, say × 1.1, corresponds to the same linear vertical distance irrespective of value; hence if the evaluated ratio is erroneously high by that factor the apparent age is too recent by about 800 years irrespective of age.

3.1.2 HISTORICAL

Carbon-14 can be produced artificially and it was consideration of relevant laboratory data, together with the results of cosmic ray measurements made by means of high-altitude balloons, that led Libby to predict, in the mid-1940s, that carbon-14 should be present throughout the biosphere. This of course includes human excreta, and first confirmation of Libby's prediction was obtained by measurements on samples of methane gas given off by city of Baltimore sewage (Anderson *et al.* 1947). Subsequently, measurements were made on living wood and the same level of carbon-14 was found; on extending the investigation to different continents the level was found to be uniform on a worldwide basis, and so too for samples of recently formed sea shell (Libby *et al.*, 1949).

All this was very satisfying confirmation of prediction; in addition Libby and his collaborators saw the possibility of age determination and they included in their measurements samples of wood from the tombs of the Egyptian kings Zoser and Sneferu, who died around 2700–2600 BC. Arguing that, once formed, the cellulose molecules of wood should no longer be part of the exchange reservoir, i.e. there would be no replenishment by new carbon-14 to balance the amount lost by decay, they expected to find a substantially lower level. This was indeed the case, a concentration of carbon-14 of roughly half that in living wood being found.

Then followed more comprehensive measurements of known age samples (Arnold and Libby 1949). The satisfactory results obtained (see Fig. 3.2) confirmed the validity of reversing the process and using carbon-14 concentration in deducing the age of an undated specimen from measurement of its carbon-14 concentration. This was the birth of the radiocarbon revolution in archaeology with its dramatic impact on prehistoric chronology. One of the first fruits was the finding that the neolothic town of Jericho had begun several thousand years earlier than had been conjectured.

3.1.3 MEASUREMENT

Until the late 1970s the sole technique for evaluation of the carbon-14 concentration ratio in a sample was by the measurement of its radioactivity: the emission rate of beta particles per gram of total carbon. Libby and his collaborators used a modified Geiger counter to do this. Subsequently *gas proportional counters* were used and for these the carbon of the sample is converted into carbon dioxide, methane or acetylene. Later, *liquid scintillation counters* were introduced and these use benzene made from the sample's carbon, conversion to carbon dioxide being the first step in the chemical process. *Accelerator mass spectrometry* (AMS) is now increasingly used. In this the carbon-14 concentration is measured directly – as the ratio between carbon-14 and carbon-12 (or carbon-13). A nuclear accelerator is needed and so the measurement facility is expensive. But the throughput of samples is much higher than in the other techniques and the sample size required is less by several orders of magnitude, allowing dating of a single seed for example. Further discussion of measurement techniques is given in section 4.1.

3.2 THE CARBON EXCHANGE RESERVOIR

3.2.1 THE EQUILIBRIUM CONCENTRATION RATIO

Figure 3.4 is a simplified 'box' model of the reservoir into which the carbon-14 mixes. There are 42 million million tonnes of ordinary carbon in the reservoir of which 93% are in the deep ocean, 2% in the surface (mixed) ocean, 1.6% in the atmosphere, 0.8% in the terrestrial biosphere and 2.6% in humus. The meaning of 'exchange' reservoir is that the carbon atoms circulate comparatively rapidly and the residence time in any component (except some parts of the deep ocean) is very much shorter than the carbon-14 lifetime. Hence although carbon-14 is produced predominantly in polar regions of the stratosphere (the maximum of the production being at a height of 15 km) the concentration in the reservoir is approximately uniform. The total amount of cosmogenic carbon-14 in the reservoir (i.e. the component produced by cosmic rays, there is also a component from nuclear explosions – see section 3.4.2) is about 62 tonnes; this is the equilibrium value resulting from the balance between the global production rate of 7.5 kg per year and radioactive decay. Hence on a weight-for-weight basis the overall equilibrium concentration ratio

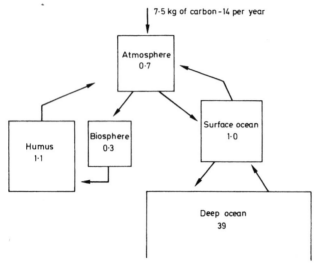

Fig. 3.4 A simplified box model of the carbon exchange reservoir. The arrow at the top represents the production of carbon–14 in the upper atmosphere by cosmic-ray-induced neutrons. The figure in each compartment is the carbon–12 content in units of a million million tonnes (10^{12}). The surface ocean is the mixed layer which is separated from the deep ocean by the thermocline at about 100 m. The average residence time of a carbon atom in the atmosphere is about 5 years, and the same for the surface ocean; the residence times in the biosphere and humus are some tens of years. Unlike the other compartments the deep ocean is not well mixed and there are gradients within it; the average residence time in some parts is several thousand years.

is 1.5 parts of carbon-14 to a million million parts of carbon-12; this corresponds to a carbon-14 activity of 14 beta particles per minute per gram of total carbon.

The essential basis of dating is by comparison of the activity found in a sample today with the activity it was presumed to have had at the time its carbon ceased to exchange with the reservoir. Obviously the latter will have been different from the present-day value if the production rate was different in the past, or if the total amount of ordinary carbon in the reservoir was different; these two time-dependent effects, both of which can give rise to the need for calibration by known-age samples, are the subject of section 3.3. We now discuss the small differences in activity existing today between different compartments of the reservoir and between different samples.

3.2.2 ISOTOPIC FRACTIONATION
Although plants obtain their carbon from the atmosphere, the actual carbon-14 activity in them is lower by 3 or 4% (equivalent to an

apparent excess age of 240–320 years). This is because in the process of photosynthesis carbon-14 is not taken up as readily as carbon-12. There are small variations from species to species in the degree of this isotopic fractionation, and it is now common practice to evaluate the effect for each sample that is dated. This is done by measurement of the carbon-13

Table 3.1 Isotopic fractionation[a] occurring in various materials[b]

Sample material	δ^{13} C
Wood, charcoal, peat	−25 ± 3
Beet sugar	−25 ± 2
Bone collagen, amino acids	−20 ± 2
NBS[c] Oxalic acid	−19 ± 1
Succulent plants	−17 ± 2
Freshwater plants	−16 ± 2
Arid zone grasses, sedges	−13 ± 2
Marine plants	−12 ± 2
Cane sugar	−11 ± 2
Maize, millet	−10 ± 2
Bone apatite	−10 ± 2
Atmospheric carbon dioxide	−9 ± 2
Non-marine carbonates	−5 ± 5
Marine carbonate	0 ± 3

[a] δ^{13} C represents the difference, in parts per thousand, between the ratio of carbon-13 to carbon-12 in the sample to the ratio for the chosen standard (PDB carbonate).

[b] The values quoted are the averages given by Gillespie (1984) who cautions that there are many cases where values outside these ranges are found, giving as examples the dependence for bone collagen on the source of carbon in the diet. A summary of values reported in the literature for archaeological samples has been given by Burleigh *et al.* (1984).

[c] National Bureau of Standards, USA.

concentration in the sample; this stable isotope is present to about 1% and so it can be measured with an ordinary mass spectrometer (equally well as in the much more expensive accelerator system used for AMS dating). The percentage depletion for an isotope is proportional to the difference in atomic mass; hence the depletion for carbon-14 is calculated simply by doubling the depletion found in the sample for carbon-13. A less satisfactory procedure is to use the average value for the type of material concerned (see Table 3.1).

Isotope fractionation also occurs in the exchange reaction between carbon dioxide and ocean carbonate, there being an enrichment of 1.5% when carbon goes from atmosphere to ocean. Hence, relative to plant life there is an isotopic enrichment of ocean carbonate by about 5%. It so happens that this just compensates for the deficiency of carbon-14 in ocean carbonate that arises from the long residence time there (discussed next) and the directly measured carbon-14 activities are the same. But when correction for isotopic fractionation is made, the carbonates from the surface ocean show an apparent age relative to plant life of around 400 years.

Isotopic fractionation complicates the experimental determination of a date but, unlike mixing rates, it is not a fundamental source of uncertainty.

3.2.3 MIXING RATES AND RESIDENCE TIMES

Carbon atoms spend only a few tens of years in the atmosphere and surface ocean before reaching the deep ocean. The residence time there is of the order of 1000 years; this refers to the average time spent there by a carbon atom before return to the atmosphere by the exchange reaction at the surface between carbonate and carbon dioxide. Consequently there is a measurable deficiency of carbon-14 in carbonate of the deep ocean because loss by radioactive decay is occurring without full replenishment by freshly produced atoms; some deep-water samples from the Pacific Ocean show apparent ages of several thousand years. The surface ocean is intermediate since the carbon in it is a mixture of 'reinvigorated' carbon from the atmosphere and 'old' carbon from the deep ocean; the apparent age is about 400 years as mentioned above.[3]

More complex models than the one shown in Fig. 3.4 are necessary in order to get a proper understanding of the actual situation. For instance, the atmospheric circulation systems of the Northern and Southern Hemispheres are sufficiently separate for there to be a slight difference in carbon-14 activity between the two: the activity in the southern mid-latitudes is lower by about 0.45% – corresponding to an apparent excess age of 35 years. The presumed reason for this is that the area of ocean in the Southern Hemisphere is 40% greater than that in the Northern, and this means that there is a higher rate of return of old carbon to the Southern atmosphere.

Another irregularity is the upwelling of deep water. Where this happens the carbonate in the surface layer will have an apparent age substantially greater than the usual 400 years. Because there may have been changes in oceanic circulation patterns the regions of upwelling may have changed, i.e. although modern marine samples from a region may indicate absence of upwelling this does not rule out the possibility that it may have been the regime at the time when the sample being dated was formed.

While this possibility is not often relevant to archaeology, there is a more general effect that could have influenced the atmospheric carbon-14 concentration in the past and be responsible for some of the short-term distortions in the time-scale. The upwelling of deep water means there is a direct interchange between atmosphere and deep ocean and the extent of it is one of the factors determining the atmospheric carbon-14 activity; an increase in upwelling would cause the latter to decrease and vice versa. Increased coverage by ice, during a glacial period, is one way in which the interchange might have been reduced.

The hard water effect

In a limestone region a substantial part of the dissolved carbon in ground or river water is derived from the carbonate of the rocks over which the water has flowed. This carbonate was removed from the exchange reservoir a very long time ago and hence the carbon-14 that was in it once has decayed. As a result the carbon in ground or river water may have an apparent age in excess of several thousand years or more.

Although deposited carbonate can be removed from a sample by acid washing, there is no pre-treatment that can deal with old carbon that has been incorporated by photosynthesis, such as may occur with aquatic plants, or by other processes of formation such as in the case of shells.

Volcanic emanation

The carbon dioxide emitted by volcanoes is deficient in carbon-14 and hence plants growing in close proximity are liable to have an apparent age which is in excess. This has been observed,[4] as also for shells grown in water into which volcanic carbon dioxide has been injected directly from gas springs or fumaroles, though of course this is difficult to distinguish from the hard water effect.

In the case of carbon dioxide emitted into the air it is to be expected that the effect would have been so rapidly diluted as to be unimportant; nevertheless there is always the chance that the sample being dated did grow in close proximity to the source of emanation, or downwind of it.

However, the comprehensive data necessary for a definitive assessment of the relevance of the effect to archaeology are not yet available.

3.3 RADIOCARBON ACTIVITY VARIATIONS DURING PAST MILLENNIA

By way of revision let us recall that the essential basis of radiocarbon dating is comparison between the carbon-14 activity measured in the sample and the activity presumed to have been present in the sample when it was formed. If in reality the starting activity was higher than presumed then the date obtained will be too recent, and vice versa. An underestimation of 1% in starting activity leads to an age deficit of about 80 years irrespective of date (see Fig. 3.3).

3.3.1 KNOWN-AGE SAMPLES

The starting activity that laboratories use in calculating dates is based upon wood grown in the late nineteenth century; this is to avoid the effects of the man-made perturbations that are discussed in section 3.4. After allowance for the amount of decay that corresponds to the age of this wood the value obtained for the starting activity is a beta emission rate of 13.6 particles per minute per gram of total carbon. These values are known as the values for 'modern' wood despite being based on mid-nineteenth-century wood; they are the values that would have been present in modern wood if the man-made perturbations had not occurred. For other types of sample the modern values are obtained after allowance for any difference in isotopic fractionation compared to wood, and in the case of sea shells and other marine samples for the presumed finite age of the carbon from which they were formed.

In retrospect it seems to have been unduly optimistic to assume that the modern values were the true starting values for all time past. There was of course no alternative but to make this assumption, and its validity was indeed discussed by Libby (1955); however, with the pressures and excitements of dating application its validity was not too seriously questioned until mounting evidence to the contrary had built up (see Suess 1986). This initially came from two sources. Discordant ages were found both for dated tree-rings and for wood from the Egyptian pyramids (de Vries 1958; de Vries *et al.* 1958; de Vries and Waterbolk 1958; Ralph and Stukenrath 1960). Extensive measurements on dated tree-rings were then made in a number of laboratories; of predominant importance was the 8000-year dendrochronological sequence established at the University of Arizona for the bristlecone pines which grow at an altitude of 3 km in the White Mountains of California. Radiocarbon measurements on these were made at the Universities of Arizona, California (La Jolla) and Pennsylvania (Philadelphia), the first results being available from La Jolla laboratory in the form of the now classic 'Suess curve' (Suess 1970). This indicated a long-term trend which prior to the third millennium BC amounted to the radiocarbon dates being too recent by about 800 years, corresponding to the starting activity being nearly 10% higher than the presumed value. Superimposed on this trend were short-term fluctuations ('wiggles') with periodicities of the order of 200 years; these and other rapid variations are sometimes referred to as *de Vries effects* (de Vries 1958). Data from other laboratories were in broad agreement and some of the various calibration curves that have been in use are mentioned in section 4.4.4, together with the high-precision calibrations that are now available; Fig. 3.5 indicates the activity variation implied by these latter.

One important question was whether a calibration derived from trees that grow at high altitude on the west coast of America is applicable to lowland Europe and elsewhere. Geophysical expectation was that, except for the slight difference between Northern and Southern Hemispheres already mentioned, atmospheric mixing would give effective uniformity. This has been confirmed by radiocarbon measurements on wood from the dendrochronological sequences that were gradually established for Europe; these show agreement with American-based data to within a few years (Stuiver and Pearson 1986; Pearson and Stuiver 1986).

Another source of known-age samples is through the annual layers of

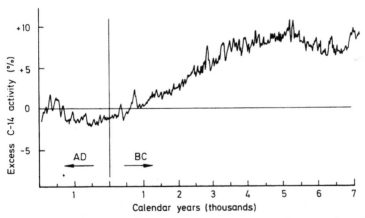

Fig. 3.5 Carbon–14 radioactivity in the atmosphere relative to the value for the late nineteenth century (redrawn from Stuiver *et al.* 1986). The data have been derived from measurements on dendrochronologically dated wood. The long-term trend is probably due either to a change in the earth's magnetic field (which affects the cosmic-ray flux incident on the upper atmosphere) or to climatic changes following the end of the last glacial period, or to a combination of both. The short-term 'wiggles' are probably associated with sunspot activity; interplanetary magnetic fields are intensified during periods of high activity and these too deflect cosmic rays.

glacial varve sequences (see section 2.5). These reach back to the start of glacier retreat at the end of the last glacial period and provide an extension beyond the current limit of the dendrochronological calibration, though it seems likely that the limit will continue to be extended through the finding of older and older fossil trees. Initial results obtained from Swedish varves were in disagreement with North American varves for millennia prior to 5000 BC, but subsequently there has been a revision in the dating of the former.

Beyond the range of both varves and trees it is a matter of comparison with other laboratory-based techniques, such as uranium series and thermoluminescence. Although the precision of the latter is rather poor by comparison with radiocarbon, new developments in uranium–series dating give prospect of error limits of the order of ±100 years (for 20,000-year-old samples). We return to the details of calibration in Chapter 4. In the meantime we consider some of the causes for the concentration variations that have been suggested.

3.3.2 INFLUENCE OF GEOMAGNETIC FIELD

Because the cosmic-ray particles which produce the neutrons which produce the carbon-14 are electrically charged they are deflected by the earth's magnetic field. Particles approaching polar regions of the stratosphere are not much affected, but increasingly for lower latitudes and equatorial regions there is deflection away from the earth. Hence if in the past the magnetic field was weaker the production of carbon-14 would have been greater,[5] and vice versa; although there would be latitude dependence in production variation, atmospheric concentration variation would be uniform because of rapid mixing. However, although the mixing (in the atmosphere and surface ocean) is rapid there is only gradual change in the concentration because the reservoir as a whole takes a rather long time to adjust to a new level of production. This means that for a short-term change in production the resulting change in concentration is very much less than for a long-term change; calculation[6] is complex, particularly for rapid variation, on account of 'hold-up' in the atmosphere and surface ocean due to delay in mixing into the deep ocean.

It is also to be noted that when we talk of the earth's magnetic field in this context we are referring to the world-wide field; this is the *dipole field* that arises from the overall magnetic moment of the earth (see section 9.2). Superimposed on this field are *non-dipole* components which affect only a localized region of several thousand kilometres in extent; these components fall off sharply with height and in any case, being localized, they tend to average out as far as overall production rate is concerned.

Thus in considering the influence of the geomagnetic field we are primarily concerned with the long-term variations, of a few thousand years or more, that may have occurred in the earth's overall magnetic moment. It has been calculated that a ±50% variation in magnetic moment with a periodicity of 8000 years would be needed to account for the carbon-14 activity variations indicated by the bristlecone pine measurements. The rather sparse archaeomagnetic data available at the time of the calculation (Suess 1970) gave support to this explanation, but it is questionable whether the data used really represent world-wide rather than localized variation (Aitken *et al.* 1989); it is very difficult to obtain archaeomagnetic results for early millennia on a world-wide basis.[7]

Geomagnetic reversals

Much more dramatic than any slow periodic variations in the geomagnetic moment are the reversals in direction that have occurred intermittently in the past at widely spaced intervals – the basis of magnetic reversal stratigraphy (see section 9.5). During the act of reversal the strength of the dipole field falls to a rather low value so that there is a strong enhancement of carbon-14 production; the duration is of the order of several thousand years and hence a substantial effect on atmospheric carbon-14 activity is to be expected.[8] During the millennia of radiocarbon applicability there is some evidence for one or two brief *polarity excursions*[9] (a quick flip to and fro) but it is not established that these were world-wide rather than localized; only if world-wide would there have been an appreciable effect on radiocarbon activity.

3.3.3 SUNSPOT ACTIVITY: HELIOMAGNETIC MODULATION

When sunspot activity is high there is an intensification of the weak interplanetary magnetic field carried by the solar wind, and this deflects cosmic rays away from the earth's vicinity, particularly the low-energy component responsible for carbon-14 production. Records of sunspot activity have been kept in Zurich since AD 1700 and estimates based on such phenomena as aurora borealis and solar flares have been made for earlier centuries. These data suggest a 200-year periodicity in sunspot activity on which the well-known 11-year cycle is superimposed.

Because the latter are so rapid the corresponding age shift is unlikely to be more than 10 years.[10] On the other hand, the attenuation for periodicities of several hundred years is less severe and variations in atmospheric carbon-14 concentrations of the order of 1% are to be expected. This is about the amplitude of the short-term 'wiggles' in Fig. 3.5 and hence it is reasonable to presume that heliomagnetic modulation is the cause of these. A secondary effect to be expected is for the wiggles to be less pronounced during periods when the geomagnetic moment is strong; the heliomagnetic modulation affects the lower energy cosmic rays and when the geomagnetic moment is high these are deflected away from the earth anyway.

During high solar activity there is also the occurrence of solar flares;

the associated particles will produce carbon-14 and it has been estimated that the increase in atmospheric carbon-14 activity due to a single event could be of the order of 1%, thus tending to compensate the effect of heliomagnetic shielding. Increases in carbon-14 production may also arise from supernovae explosions.

3.3.4 RESERVOIR SIZE AND MIXING RATES

The average carbon-14 activity in the reservoir depends not only on the global equilibrium amount of carbon-14 but also on the size of the reservoir. The most obvious way in which this may have changed is through the increase in the volume of the oceans due to the gradual melting of glaciers at the end of the last Ice Age; an increase of 2.5% has been estimated. Carbon that is locked up in the carbonate of glaciers is not part of the exchange reservoir and so it is 'old' carbon deficient in carbon-14; hence its release would have caused a decrease in the average carbon-14 reservoir concentration.

However, there is no indication of this in the calibration record; a rather high concentration seems to have been prevalent in the early millenia long after the glaciers had melted. Probably there is masking either by the effect of geomagnetic moment change or by a more transient climatic effect. One such is the decrease in carbonate solubility with warmer climate causing some conversion to carbon dioxide in the atmosphere; this does not cause a change in reservoir size since the amount lost by the ocean is gained by the atmosphere. But since the carbon in the ocean is slightly 'older' than that in the atmosphere, its release causes a transient decrease in atmospheric activity. There are other more subtle transient effects, e.g. an increase in the release of carbon from the deep ocean by increased upwelling; changes in relative sizes and mixing rates of reservoir compartments. In support of some such effect there is evidence that 15,000–20,000 years ago the age difference between deep ocean and surface ocean was about 500 years less than at present (Shackleton *et al.* 1988).

It should be noted that the influences of geomagnetic moment and of sunspot activity are not necessarily confined to the direct effect resulting from magnetic modulation of cosmic rays. Certainly there is correlation of climate with sunspot activity and there may be an additional sunspot effect on carbon-14 concentration resulting from the associated climatic change.

3.3.5 IN SITU PRODUCTION

This is an effect that might have been strong enough to falsify the bristlecone pine calibration record, but there is now strong evidence that it was not. There is a slight amount of nitrogen-14 in wood and at the altitude of 3 km at which the bristlecone pines grew, the cosmic-ray flux is an order of magnitude greater than at sea-level (though still only 3% of the maximum flux value reached in the stratosphere at 15 km). However, apart from the marginally significant increase in carbon-14 content that is predicted by calculation, incorporation of carbon-14 produced in this way into the molecules forming the cellulose structure of a tree is unlikely, and unless this happens it will be removed in the course of chemical pre-treatment before measurement.

The agreement of the low-altitude European calibration with the high-altitude bristlecone pines is conclusive evidence that *in situ* production is not a significant effect.[11]

3.4 RECENT, MAN-MADE DISTURBANCES

3.4.1 THE FOSSIL-FUEL EFFECT (SUESS EFFECT)

The combustion of coal and oil releases into the atmosphere large quantities of carbon dioxide in which the carbon-14 has long since decayed – because coal and oil were removed from the exchange reservoir millions of years ago. This 'old' carbon significantly dilutes the carbon-14 concentration in the atmosphere and the radiocarbon activity found in wood grown in AD 1950 (prior to nuclear weapons testing) is lower than samples grown in AD 1850 (prior to the Industrial Revolution) despite the decay that has occurred in the latter; this was first reported by Suess (1955). Another manifestation of fossil-fuel combustion is the depression of atmospheric carbon-14 concentration in the neighbourhood of large cities.

After allowance for decay the activity in wood grown around 1950 is 3% lower than would be expected from measurements on wood grown before 1850. Estimation of the amount of fossil fuel burnt between 1850 and 1950 indicates that if the resulting carbon dioxide was uniformly mixed throughout the reservoir, there should be a lowering in carbon-14 activity by only 0.2%. The observed effect is more than ten times as strong because of a hold-up in the atmosphere arising from the finite mixing time into the deep ocean as already mentioned.

3.4.2 NUCLEAR WEAPONS TESTING

Around 1960 there was much atmospheric testing of nuclear weapons and it is estimated that the neutrons released in the fission and fusion explosions would have caused the formation of several tonnes of carbon-14. Distributed uniformly throughout the reservoir this would increase the carbon-14 activity by a few per cent but, as with the fossil-fuel effect, there is a hold-up in the atmosphere and the actual rise is much stronger; in the mid-1970s the atmospheric activity was approximately double the level in the pre-nuclear era. As the extra carbon-14 continues to spread into the deep ocean the level will gradually fall to the few per cent representing uniform distribution – assuming hopefully that there are no further atmospheric nuclear explosions (underground tests do not contribute) and no nuclear reactor disasters on a larger scale than at Chernobyl in 1986.

There are three useful side-effects from nuclear weapons testing. First, the delay between the peak of the atmospheric excess and the arrival of 'bomb carbon' in the various compartments of the reservoir gives valuable information about mixing rates – being produced at high altitude the bomb carbon-14 mimics the carbon-14 produced by cosmic rays and so reveals the route taken by the latter.

Secondly, in the years during which atmospheric testing continued there was a sharp increase in the activity of short-lived plants with each successive growing season, followed by an annual decrease after the peak of the atmospheric testing had been passed. Malt whisky has provided useful samples for documenting this annual change just as vintage wines have been used in respect of the fossil-fuel effect. The reference data so obtained can then be used in reverse to give precise dating (to the year) of undated samples – hardly relevant to archaeology but useful on occasions in forensic investigations.

Thirdly, the excess level of atmospheric carbon-14 activity gives a valuable way of testing the integrity of sample materials. For instance in tree-rings that grew prior to the onset of the atmospheric excess the cellulose shows no influence from it, whereas for the resin extract the level of carbon-14 may be affected for rings up to a dozen years earlier than the onset of the atmospheric change.

It is sometimes suggested that the carbon-14 produced by these nuclear events invalidates radiocarbon dating. But of course, reiterating what has been said in the last paragraph, the only samples affected are those that were unreliable anyway.

3.5 OTHER COSMOGENIC RADIOISOTOPES

Given the complexities now associated with the derivation of a calendar date from carbon-14 data it is not surprising that some archaeologists ask if there is not a better radioisotope to use. There are about a dozen or so radioisotopes produced by cosmic rays which have an archaeologically relevant half-life (see Table 3.2), but it turns out that carbon-14 is unique in the combination of properties that make it suitable for archaeological dating: a half-life of the right order for much of prehistory, chemical properties that ensure distribution throughout the biosphere, production at an approximately constant rate, feasibility of measurement and a dating clock for which $t = 0$ corresponds to an archaeologically significant event.

Calcium-41
Although there is some possibility of using beryllium-10 and aluminium-26 for dating sediment cores it is only calcium-41 that is being seriously

Table 3.2 Some other cosmogenic radioisotopes
(With half-lives given in thousands of years)

Aluminium-26:	730	Chlorine-36:	300
Beryllium-10:	1600	Silicon-32:	*c.*0.1
Calcium-41:	*c.*100		

considered for archaeological application (suggested by Raisbeck and Yiou 1979; see also Henning *et al.* 1987; Taylor *et al.* 1989; Middleton *et al.* 1989); this is on account of its occurrence in bone and the appropriateness of its half-life for dating hominid evolution. Formation of calcium-41 is through the action of cosmic-ray neutrons on calcium-40 (non-radioactive) and this occurs in the soil rather than in the atmosphere. Because the neutrons are attenuated in soil, formation occurs only in the top 1 m or so. Calcium is taken up into plant tissue through absorption in the root system and hence into bone through ingestion of plants by animals. Decay of calcium-40 activity does not commence until the sample is underneath soil or rock overburden in excess of about 3 m; hence bones found within an appropriately deep rock shelter would have a well-defined time zero.

However, the problems are severe, the immediate one encountered being the difficulty of detection, even using accelerator mass spectrometric techniques. A more fundamental one is uncertainty about the initial activity at time zero, i.e. the equivalent of the radiocarbon activity in the exchange reservoir, A_0. In the case of calcium-41 there is no world-wide exchange reservoir and local variations influenced by soil history are to be expected. Results so far reported for measurement of calcium-41 activity in modern bones from various regions are not encouraging (Middleton *et al.* 1989).

We have used the term 'activity' in order to retain the analogy with radiocarbon. However, because of the very much lower decay rate it is more realistic to talk of the ($^{41}Ca/^{40}Ca$) concentration ratio; it is estimated that for the top 1 m of soil this will be about 1 in 100 million million (10^{14}), i.e. 100 times lower than the ($^{14}C/^{12}C$) concentration ratio in the reservoir.

NOTES

1. Although on average the rate is constant there are short-term random fluctuations – see section 4.1.3. Also, in this context 'rate' means the percentage decrease in unit time; for an isolated sample of radioactive atoms the actual number that decay in unit time is proportional to the number that remain. Put otherwise – for any remaining atom the probability of decay per unit is constant.

2. Note, however, that above 5% the rule becomes increasingly approximate; also, the error limits in age corresponding, for example, to $\pm 20\%$ in A/A_0, are substantially unequal being -1500 and $+1800$ years.

3. It has been suggested (Olsson 1979) that this could give rise to an 'island effect' on account of the atmospheric carbon dioxide in an oceanic region being partly composed of exhaled gas from the sea.

4. Relevant measurements have been reported by various authors including Chatters *et al.* (1969) on Hawaii, Bruns *et al.* (1980) in West Germany and on the Aegean island of Santorini, Saupé *et al.* (1980) in Italy, and Olsson (1983, 1987) in Iceland. Note that emanation continues during inactive periods.

5. A given percentage increase in the geomagnetic field strength causes decrease in carbon-14 production by about half that percentage, i.e. a 20% increase in field causes a 10% decrease in production and vice versa.

6. Compared to the change in concentration due to a permanent change in production, the change resulting from a periodic variation in the latter is about $\times 0.07$ for a periodicity of 1000 years, $\times 0.05$ for a periodicity of 100 years, and $\times 0.006$ for a periodicity of 10 years.

7. Another approach is to compare the available archaeomagnetic data with the magnetic moment variation calculated as necessary to have caused the observed variation in radiocarbon activity (but ignoring the attenuation due to short periodicity). This is referred to as the *radiocarbon geomagnetic moment*.

8. Relevant to other effects associated with magnetic reversals, e.g. extinction of species, it should be noted that although the low-energy component of cosmic rays responsible for carbon-14 production is strongly affected, this is not the case for the high-energy component. It is this latter that penetrates the atmosphere and reaches the earth's surface. The correlation of extinction of species with magnetic reversals probably arises because the latter cause climatic changes.

9. Within the period 30,000–40,000 years ago there is the *Lake Mungo* excursion, recorded in aboriginal fireplaces in Australia, and the *Laschamp* excursion, recorded in lava flows in France (but see section 9.3.1). Dating is not yet accurate enough to establish whether or not they were contemporary; even if they were contemporary they did not necessarily represent a reversal in the overall geomagnetic moment – they could have been strong but separate localized disturbances. Although suggestions have been made there is so far no well-established dramatic distortion in the radiocarbon time-scale for the period in question.

    The *Lake Mono* event, *c.* 25,000 years ago, was almost certainly a localized disturbance.

10. Observations made on recent 11-year cycles indicate that the overall variation in carbon-14 production would have been between 10 and

20%. If the atmospheric carbon-14 activity had varied by the same percentage then radiocarbon dating would hardly be a practical proposition – the percentages quoted correspond to age shifts of 800 and 1600 years respectively. However, as discussed in note 6 above, because of the slow response time of the reservoir a production-rate variation having a periodicity of around 10 years would be severely attenuated and the resultant activity variations would be only about 0.1% – corresponding to an age shift of 8 years – see Stuiver and Quay (1981).

11. Besides cosmic rays there is the possibility that lightning bolts could give rise to *in situ* production (because lightning produces neutrons). Lightning-generated neutrons could also contribute to atmospheric carbon-14 production (Libby and Lukens 1973).

It has also been suggested (Cowan *et al.* 1965) that the Tunguska meteor that fell in 1908 in Siberia could have been accompanied by neutron generation, through annihilation of anti-matter. However, there is no experimental evidence to support this.

REFERENCES

N.B. References to Chapters 3 and 4 are located at the end of Chapter 4.

4 Radiocarbon – II

In the previous chapter we have discussed basic principles and various relevant geophysical/geochemical effects. We now come to the practical procedures involved in obtaining a date – sampling and measurement – and face up to those *bêtes noires*: statistics, calibration and error limits.

4.1 MEASUREMENT

4.1.1 THE TWO APPROACHES: BETA ACTIVITY AND ATOM COUNTING

In the previous chapter discussion has been in terms of the carbon-14 activity of the sample, i.e. the rate of emission of beta particles per gram of total carbon. This is in line with the conventional approach, which is based on measurement of the sample's beta activity. This activity is directly proportional to the concentration ratio, i.e. the ratio between the number of carbon-14 atoms and the number of carbon-12 atoms; the discussion in the previous chapter could have been equally well in terms of concentration ratio and indeed this is the more fundamental quantity. It is this that is measured in the atom-counting approach, i.e. the technique of accelerator mass spectrometry (AMS); ordinary techniques of mass spectrometry are inadequate because the smallness of the ratio to be measured makes it necessary to couple-in a nuclear accelerator. About half a dozen such installations came into use during the 1980s despite the high cost of construction, approaching a million dollars. This is about an order of magnitude higher than that of a conventional beta-counting installation, but the advantages of AMS are substantial.

These advantages stem from the very much greater count-rate that can be obtained with AMS from a given weight of sample. In beta counting, because only 1% of the carbon-14 atoms in a sample emit a beta particle in about 80 years, the number of particles emitted in a feasible laboratory counting time is very many orders of magnitude below the number of atoms present; for an installation which handles several grams of total carbon the counting time necessary to record sufficient counts (40,000) for a statistical precision of ±0.5% is a day or more, depending on the age of the sample. With AMS nearly the same precision can be obtained in a few hours, using only a few milligrams. Not only does the lower weight requirement give access to a new range of samples, e.g. single seeds, but it also allows determinations to be made on separate chemical components of a sample, some of which may be more reliable than others – particularly important in the case of bone.

On the other hand, if plenty of sample is available then, for the present at any rate, the highest precision of all (±0.25% or better, corresponding to less than ±20 years in age) is obtainable by beta counting – in one of a few special high-precision laboratories. These laboratories are able also to extend beyond the 40,000-year limit of most other installations.

4.1.2 CONVENTIONAL BETA COUNTING

In the first measurement by Libby and his co-workers the *solid-carbon* technique was used – the sample being converted into carbon black and painted on to the inner wall of a modified Geiger counter. The sample needs to be inside the counter because besides the emission rate being low, the beta particles are weak in terms of penetrating power, the measured rate being halved by a 0.01 mm thickness of aluminium.

The solid-carbon technique was soon superseded by the *proportional gas counter* because of its great efficiency and lower vulnerability to external contamination. The carbon is converted into carbon dioxide, methane or acetylene and then used as the counting gas of a proportional counter. Each beta particle creates a burst of ionization and this produces an electrical pulse at the counter's electrodes. The size of the pulse is proportional to the energy deposited in the gas by the beta particle and this allows discrimination against any contaminating alpha-particle activity (which produces much bigger pulses) and to some extent against cosmic rays. Heavy steel and/or lead shielding, several tons of it, is the primary protection against the beta counts being swamped by cosmic-ray background. In addition anticoincidence detectors are necessary; a ring of these surrounds the central counter that contains the sample gas and if there is simultaneous recording of a pulse both in a detector of the ring and in the central counter the electronics ignore it. In a typical installation the sample counter has a volume of several litres and it is filled to a pressure of 1 or 2 atm, so that the amount of carbon is a few grams; the count rate for modern carbon is of the order of 20 per minute, and with good shielding the background can be as low as 1 count per minute.

Whichever gas is used in the sample counter the first step in chemical preparation is to burn the sample in a stream of oxygen, thereby forming carbon dioxide. If this is to be the counter gas it is then very carefully purified. Alternatively, it may be converted into methane or acetylene, but either way the chemical preparation represents a substantial proportion of the man-hours involved in processing a sample. For *liquid scintillation counting*, after forming acetylene from carbon dioxide there is a conversion into benzene. This is then used as solvent for a liquid scintillator; in this case the emission of a beta particle is detected by means of the flash of light produced in the scintillator; the vial containing benzene plus scintillator is viewed by two photomultipliers and these convert each flash into an electrical pulse which is then processed and recorded electronically as in the beta-counting technique. Because it is in liquid form a given amount of carbon can be contained in a much smaller volume, typically in a 20 ml vial. Not only does this present a smaller target for cosmic rays but the size of the shielding is much less too. Another important advantage is the ease with which sample, standard and background measurements can be alternated by automatic changing of vials. The technique deals with large samples more easily than does gas counting; it is straightforward to use a sample containing about 10 g of carbon and this gives a count rate for modern material somewhat over 100 per minute with a background typically around 5 per minute. On the other hand the chemical preparation is more complex and it is not such a convenient system for handling small samples (of less than 1 g of carbon). Hence the choice of method is dependent on the main type of application for which the installation is intended.

Mini- and microcounters. These are small gas counters designed for measurement of samples having only 5–100 mg of carbon. Consequently the count rate is very low and several months of counting are necessary to accumulate enough counts for adequate statistical accuracy. A dozen or so such counters are operated simultaneously within the same shielding so that the output of dates is not dramatically less than for a single large counter – but the waiting time for the customer is longer.

High-precision laboratories. Through development of technique and meticulous care certain laboratories have developed systems capable of a measurement precision equivalent to ±20 years, both for gas counting (e.g. at Groningen, at Seattle and at Heidelberg) and for liquid scintillation counting (e.g. at Belfast). Besides being able to handle large samples (10–100 g of carbon) such laboratories incorporate special measures which ensure ultra-constant efficiency over long periods, and which allow very precise correction for background variation, etc. It is from this type of laboratory that the high-precision calibration curves discussed in section 4.4.4 were obtained.

4.1.3. STATISTICAL PRECISION

Because radioactive decay is a random process the rate of emission of beta particles as determined by counting for a finite interval of time is liable to be different to the average rate that would be determined if the counting time was infinitely long. It is a similar effect to the deviation, from the average, of the number of raindrops falling on a small area in rain of constant intensity; the percentage deviation becomes smaller as the observation time is made longer. There is a similar improvement in precision with beta particles for longer counting time (or a bigger counter). If N is the number of particles counted then there is a 68% probability that the true value (corresponding to the average rate multiplied by the counting time) lies within the limits $N \pm \sigma$, where σ, the standard error, is equal to $N^{1/2}$. Thus if

$$N = 100 \qquad \sigma = 10, \text{ i.e. } 10\% \text{ of } N$$
$$N = 1000 \qquad \sigma = 33, \text{ i.e. } 3.3\% \text{ of } N$$
$$N = 10,000 \qquad \sigma = 100, \text{ i.e. } 1\% \text{ of } N$$
$$N = 100,000 \text{ etc. } \quad \sigma = 330, \text{ i.e. } 0.33\% \text{ of } N$$

If the error limits are widened to $\pm 2\sigma$, then there is a 95% probability that the true value is contained within them, and for $\pm 3\sigma$ the probability is 99.7%. This statistical uncertainty reflects through as uncertainty about the true value of the radiocarbon age – see Fig. 4.1.

This statistical uncertainty due to the randomness of radioactive decay is a fundamental limitation in the precision to which beta activity may be measured; there are other experimental uncertainties too (and also the uncertainty introduced in conversion of radiocarbon years to calendar date – see section 4.4), but however much laboratory effort is devoted to making these negligible the statistical uncertainty remains.[1] Figure 4.2 illustrates the advantage of using large samples.

The error multiplier
As just indicated, statistical fluctuations are by no means the full story as far as experimental error is concerned. Lack of constancy of counter background and counter efficiency are two obvious additional sources, as well as introduction of contamination during sample preparation. There are a host of more subtle interferences that a laboratory must guard against (e.g. isotopic fractionation – see below) and reliable age determination requires all the many component procedures to be carried out at a high level of competence.

An increasing number of laboratories make an assessment of the additional experimental uncertainty and the error limits quoted include an appropriate contribution; particularly in the past, however, the quoted error limits have tended to include only the statistical uncertainty and to obtain a more realistic estimate of precision it is necessary to increase the limits by an estimated *error multiplier*. Around 1980 some twenty well-established laboratories around the world participated in a first programme of comparative measurements on replicate 5000-year-old wood samples. The results indicated, as expected, that the scatter of repeated measurements within the same laboratory was appreciably greater than predicted by counting statistics alone, appropriate error multipliers

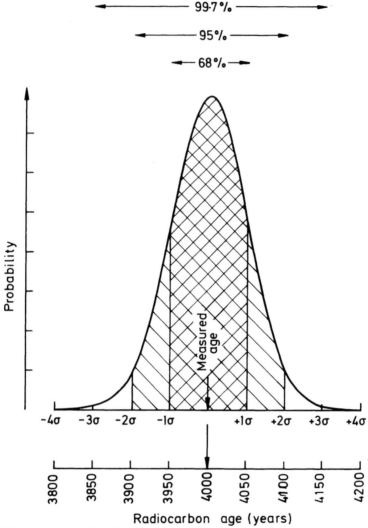

Fig. 4.1 Probability that true age differs from measured age by a given amount –
expressed in terms of the standard error (or deviation), σ. The probability that the
true age lies within a certain interval is given by the area under the curve for that
interval; the probabilities of the true age lying within ±1σ, ±2σ and ±3σ of the
measured age are indicated at the top. The scale at the bottom refers to a sample
for which the measured age is quoted as 4000 ± 50 years. The probability curve
shown is known as the *normal* or *Gaussian* distribution.

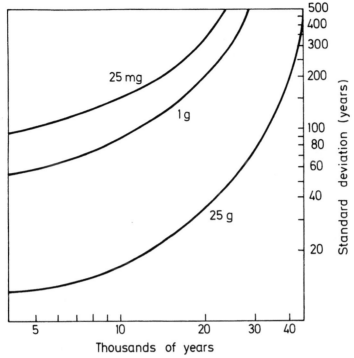

Fig. 4.2 Error limits (at 1 standard deviation) arising from statistical uncertainty versus age for several weights of carbon. Counting times: 1 month for 25 mg, 2 days for 1 g and also for 25 g. The data are from Mook and Waterbolk (1985) and based on routine procedure at the Groningen laboratory.

lying in the range 1.3–2; the comparisons also revealed strong systematic biases in several laboratories (see under International Study Group 1982). These biases were of course investigated and corrected, and indeed the whole programme focused the attention of all radiocarbon laboratories on measures to reduce both systematic and experimental uncertainties, and to make continuing realistic assessment of their error limits. Another more comprehensive comparison programme is currently in progress (see Scott *et al.* 1989).

In an attempt to guard against being misled by a laboratory's systematic bias some archaeologists make a practice of splitting their samples between two laboratories. While this has the advantage that both are unlikely to have the same systematic bias, differences noted should not be regarded as permanent – laboratories are continually improving their standardization procedures.

4.1.4 ISOTOPIC ENRICHMENT; ISOTOPIC FRACTIONATION

However good the experimental quality of a laboratory the ultimate limitation in reaching further back in time with beta-counting installations is, as indicated above, the statistical uncertainty in the net sample count rate.[2] For very old samples, because the sample-plus-background count rate is barely distinguishable from the background count rate, impossibly long counting times are needed to get a meaningful age and the only solution is to enhance the ratio of carbon-14 to carbon-12 using controlled *isotope fractionation* before measurement; this is by means of a laboratory version of the fractionation effect that occurs during various carbon conversion processes in nature (see section 3.2.2). The process so far employed, in *extended range laboratories* (e.g. at Seattle and at Groningen), utilizes a thermal diffusion column,[3] and a five fold enrichment of carbon-14 relative to carbon-12 can be achieved in about 2 months; this pushes back the limiting age to around 70,000 years for material such as peat, a substantial quantity of sample being required. In the installation at Seattle the counting room is located 11 m underground (and heavily shielded in addition).

Interference by isotopic fractionation. Fractionation may also occur in the chemical reaction involved in sample preparation and here it is deleterious because, unless monitored, it can distort the age obtained. Because slight changes in conditions can alter the degree to which fractionation occurs, as far as possible the effect is monitored for each sample measured; this is by means of the (carbon-13/carbon-12) ratio (see section 3.2.2). An alternative approach is to achieve 100% conversion of the sample's carbon into the gas or liquid used for counting, thereby giving immunity to the effect.

4.1.5 ACCELERATOR MASS SPECTROMETRY (AMS)

When an electrically charged particle moves in a magnetic field there is a force on it which causes its path to be curved; the heavier the particle the less the curvature. This is the basic phenomenon by which a stream of carbon ions (i.e. atoms having an excess or a deficit in number of electrons) can be bent into separate streams of carbon-12, carbon-13 and carbon-14. In order to employ various sophisticated nuclear physics techniques for detection of the carbon-14 ions they must be travelling at high speed, hence the need for a nuclear accelerator (see Fig. 4.3). The special detection techniques are needed in order to discriminate against residual contamination by nitrogen-14 and by molecular ions such as ^{13}CH which have the same weight.

Injection into the accelerator of carbon ions is achieved by means of an *ion source* in which carbon from the sample forms the target.[4] In the tandem accelerator usually employed the negative ions so produced are accelerated by electrostatic attraction to a terminal at around 2 million V positive. Within this terminal the ions pass through a gas 'stripper'; this

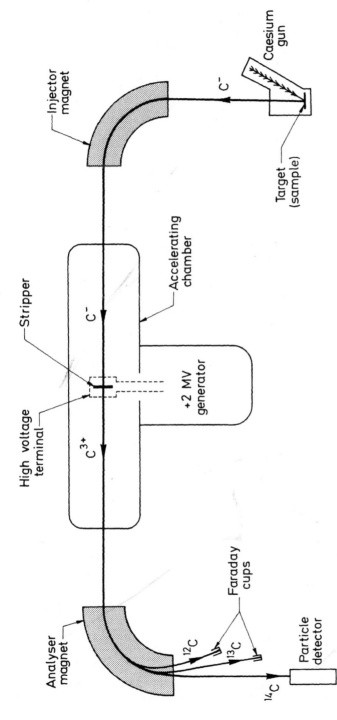

Fig. 4.3 Schematic representation of an accelerator mass spectrometer (AMS). The sample is presented as a target (e.g. as graphite on a tantalum wire) and, by sputtering this with caesium ions, negative carbon ions are produced. By means of various electrostatic focusing devices (not shown) these are guided towards the injector magnet which bends their paths into the accelerator chamber in which there is a terminal at 2 million V positive. Within the terminal there is a gas 'stripper' which converts the negative ions into triply charged positive ions. After further focusing devices the ions reach the analyser magnet which separates them as indicated. Before the particle detector there are velocity filters, etc. in order to discriminate against ions which are not carbon–14; also there is stringent particle identification by means of the pulses produced in the detector. The diagram is not to scale; the distance between injector magnet and analyser magnet is typically about 10 m, and the diameter of the high-voltage generator about 1.5 m. The latter is pressurized, whereas all tubes in which the ions travel are evacuated.

causes an ion to lose several electrons and hence it emerges positively charged; it is now repelled by the positive voltage on the terminal and in returning to a region of zero volts (i.e. 'earth') it gains further energy. Ions that now have a triple charge (C^{3+}) reach a speed corresponding to the acceleration of a single-charged ion through 8 million V (2 MV on arrival at the terminal plus 3×2 MV on departure).

Each carbon-14 ion entering the particle detector produces an electrical pulse just as a beta particle produces a pulse in a conventional counter. Being relatively more numerous the carbon-12 and carbon-13 ions are detected by collection on a type of electrode known as a Faraday cup and measured as electrical current. During measurement of a sample the overall relative efficiency of the system for the carbon–12, carbon–13 and carbon–14 is intermittently monitored by switching to a target made from a reference standard; the background due to residual carbon-14 within the accelerator is similarly checked by means of a target made from 'dead' carbon. At the time of writing the contamination acquired during sample preparation sets a limit of about 50,000 years to the maximum age that can be reliably measured; once this contamination can be reduced it is hoped to reach 70,000 years, thereby including a particularly interesting stage of man's development. 'Accelerator contamination' due to residual carbon-14 in the accelerator, already mentioned, needs to be kept low also, but this is not usually a problem. Both types of contamination can exhibit *memory effects*, i.e. be higher after the processing of a sample rich in carbon-14.

With the accelerator technique chemical preparation represents the major part of the time and effort involved and so it is economic to have several preparation lines running in parallel feeding on accelerator. These may be based in the customer institution so that the input into the accelerator laboratory consists of prepared targets ready for immediate measurement.

Error limits; sample size

In 1 mg of 5000-year-old carbon there are about 20 million atoms of carbon-14. To obtain 10,000 counts from these by beta decay, so as to obtain ±1% precision, would require a counting time of about 4 years, but using AMS 10,000 carbon-14 ions would reach the detector in less than an hour.[5] However, except for very old samples the precision attainable is limited not so much by counting time as by experimental uncertainties such as those arising from change in machine efficiency between measurement of sample and measurement of standard, and other more complex effects. Routinely, an accuracy of better than ±1%, i.e. ±80 years in radiocarbon age, can be achieved, at any rate for samples of the last 10,000 years, with ±0.5% (40 years) for special samples – although not as good as the

±20 years of a high-precision installation there are strong compensatory advantages.

Impact on archaeology

As mentioned at the beginning of the chapter the reduction in the amount of carbon required – of the order of 1 mg instead of 1 g or more (except for mini- and microcounters) gives access to a new range of samples, allowing the archaeologist to select the more significant finds on a site without regard to size, but with full regard to suitability for the technique. It also allows the chemist in the laboratory to select the organic components from a sample that, from experience, are most reliable. The initial impact of this greater selectivity, and other aspects, have been reviewed by Harris (1987), among others, and there are various collated accounts of applications such as that edited by Gowlett and Hedges (1986). Another advantage is the ease with which a measurement can be repeated. For technical discussion the reader may refer to publications such as those by Litherland (1987) and by Hedges (1987).

4.1.6. LIMITS OF MEANINGFUL AGE: TERMINOLOGY

Whatever type of installation is employed for measurement there is a limit at which the sample-plus-background count rate is not distinguishable from background. The recommended practice (Stuiver and Polach 1977) is that a sample for which the *net* count rate is within 1σ of zero should be reported as *sample activity not distinguishable from background*; on the other hand, some laboratories report an age such as $(45,000^{+00}_{-3000})$ if the net count rate is positive, or as *infinite* if negative.

If the net count rate is between 1σ and 2σ of zero the recommended practice is to report a *minimum age* corresponding to net count rate *plus* 2σ, though some laboratories report such a sample in the usual way.

At the other end of the time-scale the recommendation is that samples for which the radiocarbon age (after reservoir correction – see section 4.4.2) is less than 200 years should be reported as *modern* and that samples having an apparent age in the future (e.g. due to contamination with bomb carbon) should be reported as > *modern*.

4.2 EFFECT OF CONTAMINATION

Because the concentration ratio of carbon-14 to carbon-12 is lower in old samples, contamination with a small amount of modern carbon causes a disproportionately large shift in apparent age, the effect becoming more serious with increasing age of sample. Thus in a sample which is 17,000 years old the addition of 1% of new carbon will cause the age to be too recent by 600 years, for a 34,000-year-old sample the same percentage causes an error of 4000 years and for a 50,000-year-old sample the apparent age will be 36,000 years. For an infinitely old sample, the addition of 1% of modern carbon will give an apparent age of 38,000 years.

Contamination by 'dead' carbon, i.e. carbon in which the carbon-14 has long since decayed as in carboniferous material beyond the age of 100,000 years (e.g. coal and oil), does not have such a dramatic effect though it can still be serious. An addition of 1% increases the age by about 80 years, irrespective of age.

Besides the extrinsic contamination acquired, for instance in the laboratory (within the measurement system or during sample preparation), there is the question of contamination which is intrinsic to the sample itself, as now discussed.

4.3 SAMPLES AND SAMPLING

4.3.1 SAMPLE INTEGRITY; CONTAMINATION

An essential characteristic of a sample is that over the centuries of burial it has not acquired any fresh carbon from the atmosphere (e.g. by fungal growth) or other components of the exchange reservoir (e.g. in the case of shell, by later incorporation of ocean carbonate). The requirement must be fulfilled stringently, since as we have seen above, only a minute amount of modern carbon can cause a significant error in the age. As noted in section 3.4.2 there was a sharp increase in atmospheric carbon-14 activity due to nuclear weapons testing; hence one indication of high integrity for a type of sample material is that there should be no excess carbon-14 in samples of this material that were grown before commencement of testing. The various components of wood (cellulose, lignin, etc.) have been investigated in this way.

In respect of dead carbon it is not a matter of later incorporation but of the possibility of incorporation at formation, e.g. aquatic plants growing in a limestone region where the carbonate in the ground water may be 'old' because derived from the limestone.

Although the sample material itself may have high integrity there may be intrusive contamination acquired during burial. The humic acids carried in percolating ground water are an example, likewise carbonates; both of these are likely to have an age different to that of the sample.

4.3.2 SAMPLE TYPES AND LABORATORY PRE-TREATMENT

It follows that the extent to which a sample is reliable is bound up with the stringency of the laboratory pre-treatment that can be applied. At minimum there must be removal of humic acids by washing in alkali, and removal of carbonates by washing in acid. The severity that the laboratory can afford to use is dependent both on the size of the initial sample and on the amount of carbon required by the measurement facility; the severity needed depends also on the age. Obviously the use of AMS with the requirement of only a few milligrams of carbon is highly advantageous in this context. The following notes, intended only as indicative of the sort of samples being dated and of the procedures being applied, are based mainly on the useful and concise handbook by Gillespie (1984); the reader is also referred to the European Science Foundation handbook (Mook and Waterbolk 1985), and to the comprehensive text by Taylor (1987).

Wood. The most reliable component of wood is cellulose and extraction of this component avoids lignin, which is less reliable, and humic acids from the soil; however, this is a drastic procedure and the amount of cellulose obtained may be as low as one-fifth of the initial sample. As far as humic acids are concerned these can be extracted and discarded. The more serious problem with wood and charcoal is estimation of the extent to which its formation pre-dated the archaeological event of interest, and in the case of charcoal certainty of archaeological association is often questionable.

Bone. For reliable dates from bone it is necessary to extract the protein fraction (collagen, gelatin); the carbonate fraction is not usually reliable because of the difficulty of removing secondary carbonates that have washed in from the soil. The difficulty over protein is that the amount remaining decreases with age, to a degree depending on burial environment, and there may not be much left; there is then greater risk that what is measured is dominated by contamination acquired during burial. A check on this can be made by amino acid analysis thereby determining the extent to which the amino acid 'signature' corresponds to that for collagen. With AMS dating a refinement in special cases (but too time-consuming routinely) is to obtain dates for individual amino acids (see Fig. 4.4); one of these – hydroxyproline – is particularly advantageous since it is almost unique to bone (though it has also been detected in natural water).

Shell. This material – composed almost entirely of calcium carbonate – is difficult because of continued exchange of carbon with the environment, particularly in the case of land shells; a powdery appearance indicates that substantial exchange has taken place. One approach is to subject the sample to increasing severity of acid and to date a portion after each treatment. Layers in which exchange has occurred are on the outside and more vulnerable; when these have been removed there is a levelling off of the dates obtained – this may require removal of up to 50% of the starting weight.

This does not deal with the problem of carbon exchange through recrystallization; in respect of this, shells for which the calcium carbonate is in the form of argonite are safer than those for which it is in the form of calcite. This is because on recrystallization argonite forms calcite; thus if the shell is free from calcite there is built-in evidence that no exchange has occurred. The presence of calcite can be detected by X-ray diffraction or thin section microscopy. Another possibility with shell is to use the

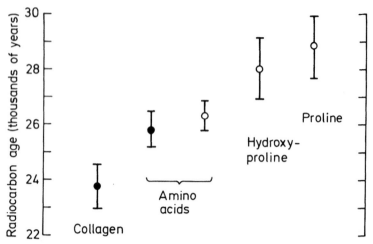

Fig. 4.4   Radiocarbon ages for different fractions extracted from a rhinoceros bone. Open symbols indicate AMS dating (at Oxford) and closed symbols conventional beta–decay counting (at the British Museum). The older ages given by the proline and hydroxyproline, which are amino acids generally specific to bone, suggest contamination by intrusive amino acids in the other fractions.

organic protein constituent, conchiolin; however, even in modern shell this is present only to 1 or 2%.

With marine shells a dominant uncertainty is the extent of the reservoir correction (see section 3.2.3) – the present-day value does not necessarily have validity in the past.

Sediments and soils. The usual approach is to date the bulk organic carbon but success is variable, the dates often being too young due to the presence of modern humic acids. Conversely, small particles of shale or coal may lead to dates which are too ancient. Although in arid regions the dating of soil carbonates may be meaningful, remains of plants and lower organisms, separable by sieving, are a preferable component and particularly applicable if the minicounter or AMS technique is being used. These techniques also give the possibility of dating specific chemical compounds, e.g. fatty acids and other lipids.

Peat. The remains of the original vegetation from which the peat was formed are represented by *humins*, which are insoluble in alkali; hence this fraction is more reliable than the alkali-soluble humic and fulvic acids, which may or may not be intrusive.

Mortar. As mortar sets, carbon dioxide is absorbed from the atmosphere to form calcium carbonate; hence in principle mortar should be datable, likewise lime burials (e.g. Stuiver and Waldren 1975). In practice the dates obtained for mortar are liable to be too old by several thousand years;

possible causes include admixture of carbonate rock chips (of infinite age) and incomplete heating of the limestone (also of infinite age) used to make the quicklime. Encouraging results have been obtained in some cases by removal of chips and also by monitoring with stable oxygen–isotope measurements (e.g. Dauchot-Dehon *et al.* 1983; Van Strydonck *et al.*1986; Zouridakis *et al.* 1987).

Other materials. There are also procedures for seeds, grain, ivory, paper and textiles; with all of these the small sample aspect of AMS dating is advantageous. The same is true for charred organic matter within pottery, straw within mudbricks and traces of charcoal in iron objects originating in the fabrication process. Dating of stalagmites (e.g. Gascogne and Nelson 1983; Bastin and Gewelt 1986; Geyh and Hennig 1986) and other carbonate deposits (e.g. Muzzolini 1982) is also attempted, but there is uncertainty because some of the carbon incorporated is 'old', originating from limestone.

4.3.3 COLLECTION (ALSO BASED MAINLY ON GILLESPIE 1984)

Of more immediate concern to the archaeologist than the extent to which pre-treatment can remove intrinsic contamination is the possibility of external contamination during collection and storage. Cigarette ash and food scraps are well known in this context, but it is sometimes forgotten that paper, cloth and cotton wool, etc. are rich in carbon too. Polythene (polyethylene) bags (i.e. ordinary plastic bags, though they should be strong ones) are acceptable as containers, but other plastics such as PVC or PVA must be avoided since they may contain plasticizers which can be absorbed by the sample material. Aluminium foil and glass bottles are excellent, as long as the latter are carefully packed for transit. For padding within the container glass wool should be used, not cotton wool or paper tissues. Obviously labelling is of paramount importance but cards should not be put inside the same immediate container as the sample.

Sampling strategy

The expense and effort involved in obtaining a date is substantial, warranting careful thought in advance about objectives and the means to achieve them. There are two types of consideration here. First there is the archaeological one of the directness of association with the occupational phase under consideration. However reliable the laboratory's dating, sending a sample of reused timber is not usually relevant, likewise a ritual or inherited object from a grave. Similarly, there is a need to distinguish between long-lived and short-lived samples. Even if not reused the date obtained for the timber in a building will relate not to its construction nor to the felling of the tree, but to the formation of the wood as the tree grew; of course it is sometimes possible to relate the latter event to the date of felling by counting the annual rings – as long as there is sapwood remaining on the timber.

A second consideration is the laboratory one that different types of samples are subject to different problems. Burial conditions on a particular site may alter the usual hierarchy of reliabilities and if several types of sample are available it is prudent to collect them; if all types give the same date then confidence in the answer is substantial. Another point here is that a laboratory may be interested in having different types of sample from the same horizon in order to test the efficacy of pre-treatment procedures. Obviously this involves collaboration, but in any case, even for routine dating the more liaison between archaeologist and laboratory the better.

Archaeological association
Returning to the question of certainty of association the following categorization is derived from Waterbolk (1971, 1983):

A. Full certainty: the measured sample comes from the archaeological object itself. Examples: human bone from grave, tree-trunk canoe, wagon wheel, post from house, organic backing material in pottery.
B. High probability: there is a direct functional relationship between the organic material which is measured and the diagnostic archaeological finds. Examples: carbonized coffin in a grave with finds, carbonized grain in rubbish pit with sherds, charcoal in an urn, hearth in floor of house.
C. Probability: there is not a demonstrable functional relation between measured sample and archaeological material, but the quantity of organic material and the size of the fragments argue in favour of a relationship. Example: charcoal concentration in a rubbish pit or occupation layer.
D. Reasonable probability: as C, but the fragments are small and scattered. Examples: 'dark earth' in occupation layer, particles of charcoal in a grave.

Waterbolk also notes the lower reliability that should be assigned to samples from test excavations in which the interpretation is tentative compared with those from prolonged systematic excavations. In addition he categorizes samples in respect of the delay that there may have been between sample formation and archaeological association.

A. The difference in date is so small as to be negligible ($<$ 20 years). Examples: twigs, grain, leather, bone, outermost tree-rings.
B. The time difference can amount to several decades (between 20 and 100 years). Examples: charcoal from wood species with a short life span; outermost tree-rings from durable wood species when there is no reason to expect a long period of use.

Table 4.1 Optimum sample weights (in grams)

Material	Beta counting		Accelerator
	Conventional	Minicounter	
Charcoal	5–10	0.1–0.5	0.01–0.1
Wood, dry	10–20	0.5–1	0.05–0.1
Wood, wet	40–80	1–2	0.1–0.2
Bone	100–500	10–50	0.5–5
Shell	50–100	0.5–2	0.05–0.1
Carbonates	100–200	2–10	0.1–0.2
Peat, dry	50–100	1–3	0.1–0.2
Peat, wet	100–200	3–5	0.2–0.5
Sediment, dry	100–200	3–5	0.5–5
Sediment, wet	200–500	10–50	1–10

Note: This table is from Gillespie (1984) who adds that these are approximate weights and for samples free of soil, sand and artefacts, etc.; also that in some cases smaller samples will be acceptable but with possible increase in cost and poorer precision. If the sample is likely to be contaminated and/or more than 20,000 years old then the amounts given above should be doubled.

C. The time difference may amount to centuries (> 100 years). Example: charcoal from wood species with a long life span possibly subject to re-use).
D. The nature of the dated organic material is not precisely known. Examples: samples consisting of 'dark earth', 'ash', 'soil'.

Amount of sample
Table 4.1 shows optimum sample amounts for the three types of measurement facility. This is a guide only, and if a greater amount is available, it should be collected; the laboratory can then intensify its pre-treatment procedures. Another prudent policy in the case of plenty is for the archaeologist to retain a reserve sample against various contingencies, e.g. the need to check an unexpected result, the development of improved pre-treatment procedures or other aspects of technique, or simply the loss of the first sample due to equipment failure or other causes.

The minimum amounts from which an age can be obtained in special circumstances are substantially less than those given in Table 4.1, particularly if the sample is not more than a few thousand years old. As has been mentioned, using AMS a single seed can be dated, or a few threads of linen (as with the Shroud of Turin); pushing the technique to the limit it has been demonstrated that it is feasible to date the order of 0.1 mg of blood residue from a prehistoric stone tool (Nelson *et al.* 1986).

Documentation

To an archaeologist each radiocarbon sample is one of a few, but in the laboratory it is one in an annual throughput of several hundreds or even a thousand. Therefore efficient labelling is essential, together with all the information about archaeological context that the particular laboratory requests and needs for publication; the standardized form proposed by Kra (1986) is a guide to what is required. Indication of expected age is useful because it guides the laboratory in its pre-treatment procedures and the measurement time that will be needed. For an old sample the emphasis is on removal of modern contamination and the measurement time is long. For a young sample it is 'old' contamination that matters most and the measurement time is shorter. In general, inadequate pre-treatment causes an old sample to have an apparent age that is too recent and a young sample to have one that is too ancient. It should be recognized that pre-treatment procedures are continually being improved and that a date obtained a decade or so ago cannot have the same reliability as one recently performed, unless the sample was a straightforward one.

Pre-cleaning

It is worth while for the archaeologist to take a critical look at his material before dispatch, picking out all obvious foreign matter such as stones, artefacts, plant roots and leaves, loose soil or sand. Each material type, e.g. charcoal, bone, wood, marine shells, non-marine shells, etc. should be packaged on its own. Indication of contaminants known to be likely is helpful so that the laboratory can be prepared in its pre-treatment approach.

Before the laboratory starts on the pre-treatment proper there is further removal of foreign matter using a low-power microscope, and flotation techniques where appropriate. It is not only a matter of avoiding a wrong answer but also of avoiding overload in the subsequent processing procedures.

4.4 STEPS TOWARDS A CALENDAR DATE

4.4.1 THE NEED FOR CALIBRATION

Laboratory measurements on a sample yield an age – the *age in conventional radiocarbon years* – based on the premiss that the atmospheric ratio of (carbon-14/carbon-12) has been constant. As discussed in section 3.3.1 this premiss is only approximately true and the age so obtained is not the same as the age in calendar years; the latter is derived by means of calibration curves based on known-age samples, mostly wood dated by dendrochronology – hence the terms *dendrodates* and *dendrochronological calibration* (alternatively *tree-ring calibration, bristlecone pine calibration*.

There are two reasons for needing to convert to calendar years:

first, to permit comparisons with dates obtained by other methods, and second, to make a correct assessment of speed of development – there are periods when only a small difference in radiocarbon years corresponds to a substantial change in calendar date, and vice versa. For example, in the first millennium BC the difference between radiocarbon ages corresponding to samples having calendar dates of 800 BC and 400 BC is only about 250 years. Obviously it is important for an archaeologist to know of this, and other less extreme distortions of the radiocarbon time-scale.

Conversion to calendar date is confusing because of the irregular form of the calibration curve; the difficulty of translating error limits from one time-scale to the other is particularly acute and here we are inevitably in the hands of the statisticians. First, however, we deal with the derivation of an age in radiocarbon years.

4.4.2 CONVENTIONAL RADIOCARBON YEARS

The basic principle has been illustrated in Figs 3.2 and 3.3. For the latter the curve was drawn using the revised half-life of 5730 years which was determined, by laboratory measurement, in the early 1960s. This value is 3% greater than the Libby half-life of 5568 years used for Fig. 3.2, and it is this latter value that is used for calculation of conventional radiocarbon years. The reason for retaining it is to avoid confusion and risk of multiple correction. The consequence is that even if there was no distortion of the time-scale the age in calendar years would be 3% greater than the age in conventional radiocarbon years, e.g. 1000 radiocarbon years correspond to 1030 calendar years; however, in general the half-life correction is dwarfed by the correction for distortion. In practice the correction made by the calibration curve subsumes the half-life correction; it is only beyond the limit of the calibration that separate attention needs to be given to the latter.

Years before present (BP)

Because samples get older as the years go by all radiocarbon ages are referred to AD 1950 as 'present'. Of course it is only for very precise dates that this is more than a trivial consideration, but the situation will gradually change in the future. It is less confusing to regard BP as meaning 'before physics' – AD 1950 being the year in which radiocarbon dates began to be published. In radiocarbon terminology 'BP' means an uncalibrated age, with 'cal BP' indicating calibration.

Reference to modern standard

Rather than to attempt a direct evaluation of a sample's carbon-14 activity it is more convenient and more precise to make comparison with a reference standard measured in the same installation just before or just after the sample. The basic reference material is the oxalic acid specially prepared by the US National Bureau of Standards from a crop of sugar-beet. Standard 'modern' activity, A_m, is defined as 0.95 times the activity of this standard[6] when measured[7] in the same installation as the sample at about the same time. Other standards, which have been related to A_m, are used in addition; it is common practice to use one of the same material as the sample being measured.

Isotopic fractionation

Before the age is calculated it is necessary to make correction for any isotopic fractionation that occurred during uptake of carbon by the sample while forming[8] (see section 3.2.2). The standard modern activity refers to wood having the average carbon-13/carbon-12 concentration ratio for wood. In order to allow for the different degree of fractionation occurring in other types of sample, one approach would be to define a standard modern activity for each type. Instead of this the measured sample activity, A', is adjusted so as to correspond to wood, the fractionation-corrected value being denoted by A.

The adjustment is made on the basis that the fractionation effect for carbon-14 is twice that for carbon-13. As an example consider bone collagen, for which the average carbon-13/carbon-12 ratio is 0.5% higher than that for wood, i.e. during formation collagen takes in the heavier isotopes more readily than does wood. Hence the starting carbon-14 activity for a collagen sample would have been higher than for a wood sample formed at the same time, by 1%. To allow for this the measured activity of a collagen sample is reduced by 1%, i.e. $A = 0.99A'$. Failure to make the adjustment would give an age erroneously too recent by 80 years.

High-precision, and some other laboratories, measure the carbon-13/carbon-12 ratio, for each group of samples being processed, by means of an ordinary mass spectrometer. Otherwise the standard value for the sample type concerned is used (see Table 3.1); there is then a small increase in the uncertainty of the date obtained arising from the spread of values for a given sample type.

The age equation

Having adjusted the measured activity A' to the fractionation-corrected activity A, the age[9] in conventional radiocarbon years before AD 1950 is given by

$$\text{Age} = 8033 \ln\left(\frac{A}{A_m}\right) \qquad (4.1)$$

$$= 18,497 \log\left(\frac{A}{A_m}\right)$$

where, as indicated above, A_m is the standard modern activity.

The numerical factors, 3% lower than those in equation (3.3), correspond to the Libby half-life of 5568 years instead of the revised half-life of 5730 years.

For further discussion of the basis on which conventional radiocarbon ages are derived, and the symbols used,[10] the reader should refer to Stuiver and Polach (1977); these authors also give recommendations in respect of rounding-off of reported ages, e.g. if the error limits are below ±50 the age should be rounded off to the nearest multiple of 5, and if between ±50 and ±100 to the nearest multiple of 10. However, with the advent of high-precision calibration curves there is a tendency to delay the rounding-off of high-precision results until quoting the calendar date.

Reservoir-corrected age
As discussed in section 3.2.3 present-day carbonate in deep ocean water may have an apparent age of several thousand years because of its long residence time there. Because there is some admixture of deep water into the surface ocean shells grown there have some apparent age too – around 400 years for mid-latitudes, rising to the order of 1000 years in regions of upwelling. The reservoir correction is determined by measurements on historically dated samples of the same material and origin as the sample being dated; samples prior to the Industrial Revolution need to be used in order to avoid interference by fossil-fuel effect. It is also necessary to consider the way in which the ocean responds to the atmospheric fluctuations in carbon-14 activity (see Fig. 3.5), and appropriate calibration curves for marine samples have been given by Stuiver *et al.* (1986); these are substantially smoother than for atmospheric samples. The same authors give corrections appropriate to various marine regions, based on reported values.

There are also other types of sample which are affected by abnormalities in the carbon-14 activity of carbon taken in during formation, e.g. shells and aquatic plants in limestone regions; other examples were mentioned in section 3.2.3. Reliable correction is only possible in some cases.

The conventional radiocarbon age of a sample refers to the age *before* correction; if the reservoir-corrected age is reported the former is usually given also. It should also be remembered that there is a slight overall reservoir effect between Northern and Southern Hemispheres; late-nineteenth-century dendrochronologically dated wood from southern mid-latitudes gives an apparent radiocarbon age that is about 35 years less recent than contemporary wood from northern mid-latitudes.

4.4.3 COMBINING DATES
'One date is no date' for several reasons – contamination, intrusive material, mistaken attribution, laboratory error, etc. A second determination for the same archaeological phase is many times more useful than a single one:

if the ±1σ spans (68% level of confidence) overlap then confidence in both is enormously strengthened, but if there is no overlap even at the 95% level of confidence (±2σ spans) then both are in doubt.[11] It may be, in the latter case, that the separation is indicative of the duration of the phase, but it is also possible that one of the dates is a 'rogue' – through an interference such as mentioned above. More determinations will throw light on these and comparable questions though in the end there are no hard-and-fast answers, only assessments of probabilities – as indeed is the case with nearly all the techniques of this book; of course in some circumstances there may be confidence in a given interpretation at, say, the 99.7% level or higher, qualifying as 'hard-and-fast', but unfortunately this is not often so.

Reliable assessment of probabilities can be made through rather daunting statistical procedures (e.g. Long and Rippeteau 1974; Ward and Wilson 1978; Wilson and Ward 1981) and increasingly these are becoming accessible through availability as computer programs. Discussion of these is somewhat outside the scope of this book, but some basic considerations relevant to preliminary assessment of a group of dates will be given. Among the aspects involved are (i) whether it is justified to average the dates, (ii) whether it is justifiable to discard some of the outliers as 'rogues' and (iii) the error limits appropriate to the average. In general, averaging is best done before conversion to calendar dates, i.e. the average age in conventional radiocarbon years should be obtained and then calibrated as indicated in section 4.4.4. An exception is when the samples being combined are not coeval but have a known spacing in calendar years, i.e. they form part of a 'floating' tree-ring sequence. *Wiggle-matching* and special statistical treatment are then possible, as discussed at the end of section 4.4.4. When the spacing in calendar years is not known but the samples all relate to a well-defined archaeological period, a useful way of expressing them *in toto* is by means of quoting the interquartile range (Ottaway 1973); the dates are arranged in order and the limits of this range are set so as to exclude the upper quarter and the lower quarter.

The expected spread
The curve of Fig. 4.1 indicated the probability that the true age differed by a given amount from a single measured age. The same curve can be used to express the expected spread in the measured ages obtained from a number of coeval samples. The average for these will be close to the true age and the scatter of individual ages should be such that for 68% of the samples the average is encompassed by the error limits for the sample concerned; of course the 68% is rather approximate unless the number of samples is large and Fig 4.5 illustrates two cases where small numbers are involved. In case (a) the ±1σ error limits of four of the seven

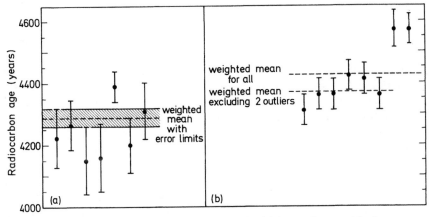

Fig. 4.5 The scatter of individual ages shown in (a) is consistent with the samples being coeval, the weighted mean being 4290 ± 30 years. The samples in (b) cannot be accepted as a group and it is not justifiable to use the weighted mean for all of them; after exclusion of the two outliers the remaining six samples form an acceptable group with a weighted mean of 4370 ± 20 years. The data are discussed further in the text and in notes 12 and 13.

samples encompass the average value, whereas in case (b) only two out of eight do so.

Statistical assessment[12] confirms acceptance of the samples of case (a) as being coeval and without rogues; hence it is justifiable to use the average value as the best estimate of the true radiocarbon age and to quote somewhat tighter error limits than the individual error limits – see below. For case (b) statistical assessment confirms that averaging is not justified for all eight samples but that it is justified for the six that remain after discarding the two outliers; we may note that four out of these six encompass the new average.

In rejecting the two outliers the supposition is either that those two samples were not coeval with the rest, or that they were specially subject to some measurement interference (contamination, etc.). Rejection of outliers is of course a thorny subject liable to stimulate accusations that the data are being manipulated to fit preconceived ideas. Hence it is highly desirable to use soundly based statistics in this context (see above p. 96 for references); the dating of the Bronze Age eruption of the volcano of Thera in the Aegean is a case where different rejection procedures lead to different final dates (Aitken *et al.* 1988; Manning 1988; also Fig. 4.12).

Weighted mean and its error limits

A result with small error limits carries more weight than one with wider limits and this needs to be taken into account in calculating[13] the *weighted mean age* (or *pooled mean*) for a group of coeval samples. Thus for the samples of Fig. 4.5(a) the weighted mean is 4290 years, whereas the unweighted mean (or *arithmetic mean*) is 4240 years; the former is older because of the extra weight given to the sample having an age of 4390 years; the quoted error limits for this one are ±50 years, whereas for the others the limits are ±80 years or greater.

An average is likely to be nearer to the true value than any individual age and this is reflected in the error limits calculated[13] for the mean. In the simple case of individual ages all with the same individual error limits, σ_i, the error limits for the mean age are ($\pm\sigma_i/n^{1/2}$), where n is the number of samples; thus the error limits for the mean in the case of n = 4 and σ = 80 are ±40 years and for n = 16 they are ±20 years.

It is sometimes asked whether there is advantage in measuring, say, four samples compared to counting one sample only for at least four times as long. The answer is emphatically in favour of the former as long as four samples of high suitability (in terms of archaeological association and type of material) are available. There are two reasons: first, the coherence of multiple ages allows assessment of reliability, as indicated above; second, the uncertainty arising from statistical fluctuations in count rate is not the only contribution to the error limits but there is also the rather intangible contribution from minor variations in the sample preparation process. This latter is evaluated by intermittent test runs involving replicate preparations of the same sample, and in the discussion above it is taken for granted that the quoted error limits for an individual age include that contribution (sometimes introduced as the 'error multiplier' – see section 4.1.3).

4.4.4 CALIBRATION

In using calibration curves there are three main aspects. The first is the appreciable divergence between radiocarbon age and calendar age as one goes back in time beyond 500 BC (see Fig. 4.6); prior to that date radiocarbon ages are consistently too recent, the underestimate being steady at around 800 years for the three millennia beyond 4000 BC. From 500 BC to AD 1300 there is a tendency for radiocarbon ages to overestimate the calendar age, but not by more than 150 years. It is in the millennia of underestimation that calibration has its archaeological impact and when it became available for application in prehistory there followed a dramatic reappraisal of the relationship of western Europe and the Balkans to the Near East; this was 'the second radiocarbon revolution', the first having been the impact that radiocarbon ages themselves had had already in indicating a greater than expected antiquity for Neolithic developments.[14]

The second aspect is the increased ambiguity in interpretation that usually results from the 'wiggliness' of the calibration curve. As illustrated in Fig. 4.7 the span in calendar date corresponding to the error limit span of the radiocarbon age may be substantially in excess of the latter; in other

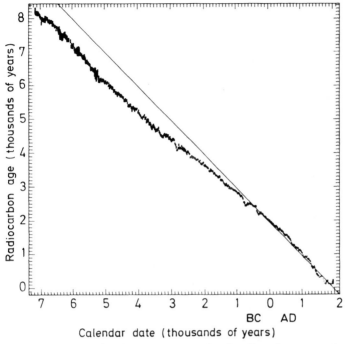

Fig. 4.6 Relationship between conventional radiocarbon age and calendar date, based on dendrochronologically dated wood samples. The solid line shows the 'ideal' relationship that would exist if the half-life used for calculation of conventional radiocarbon ages was exactly correct. (From Pearson 1987.)

cases there may be several possible calendar date spans corresponding to a single radiocarbon age.

The third aspect concerns the error limit band of the calibration curve itself. Even in a wiggle-free part of the curve this inevitably widens the calendar date span – as illustrated in Fig. 4.8.

Faced with these aspects[15] it is not surprising that some archaeologists throw up their hands in despair. The more effective response is a realistic appraisal of the situation. For despite these complications radiocarbon continues to provide the main chronological framework of prehistoric periods back to 40,000 years ago. It should also be appreciated that the calibration curves have involved many years of dedicated and meticulous effort by the laboratories and dendrochronologists concerned and represent a quite remarkable achievement.

Historical

Until the early 1980s an additional difficulty for archaeologists was that the radiocarbon community could not agree on a common calibration curve. The first one produced was that of Suess (1970) drawn freehand

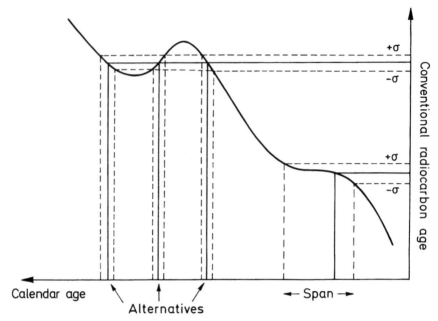

Fig. 4.7   (Left) Because of a wiggle in the calibration curve there are three possible calendar ages corresponding to one radiocarbon age. *(Right)* Because of a 'plateau' in the calibration curve the span in calendar age corresponding to the error limits of the radiocarbon age is substantially increased. On the other hand, in the central steep portion the error limits would be reduced (not shown).

by 'cosmic schwung'. At that time the experimental precision attainable for the calibration samples was about ±50 years, substantially worse than the ±20 years now available from high-precision laboratories. Calibration curves were also produced by Ralph *et al.* (1973) and Damon *et al.* (1972), the former being the basis of the much-used MASCA[16] corrections. Another commonly used calibration curve was that of Clark (1975) based on statistical assessment of all the data then available. These various curves, all based on trees from the western USA, showed the same main features, but there were differences in the smoothing procedures employed. Eventually, using mainly the same data, a *consensus calibration* was proposed (Klein *et al.* 1982); this made a careful assessment of the influence of experimental precision and interlaboratory bias (as indicated by measurement of samples of the same date) and a sound statistical basis for conversion was developed. Inevitably, in order to find common ground it was necessary to accept fairly wide error limits for the accuracy of the conversion. Also instead of keeping to the common practice of quoting the span in calendar date that corresponds to ±1 standard error in radiocarbon age (i.e. the 68% level of confidence) the span that corresponds to ±2 standard errors (i.e.

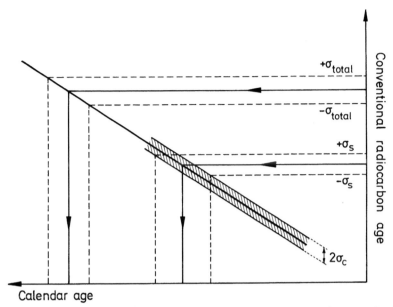

Fig. 4.8 The calibration curve itself has error limits, $\pm\sigma_c$, so that even in the absence of irregularities the calendar age span is wider than the radiocarbon age span to which it corresponds. However, the procedure indicated in the lower part of the figure overestimates the enhancement of the span; the correct procedure (see e.g. Pearson and Stuiver 1986) is to combine the calibration error limits, $\pm\sigma_c$, with those for the sample age, $\pm\sigma_s$ according to $\sigma_{total} = (\sigma_s^2 + \sigma_c^2)^{1/2}$ and use σ_{total} as indicated in top upper part of the figure.

95% level) was used; although the wider spans may be more realistic the different basis for uncertainty assessment does introduce additional confusion. The consensus calibration has now been superseded by the high-precision calibrations which were presented in 1985 at the Twelfth International Radiocarbon Conference at Trondheim, Norway; these opened a new era for archaeologists.

High-precision calibrations
Of particular importance at the conference was the definitive demonstration that there was agreement between calibrations derived from trees growing on the Pacific coast of the USA and trees growing in lowland Europe, derived furthermore in two independent laboratories. These calibrations are the work of the laboratories at Belfast and Seattle and cover the periods 2500–500 BC (Pearson and Stuiver 1986) and 500 BC–AD 1950 (Stuiver and Pearson 1986) with a justified claim to an accuracy of better than ±20 years; because they were replicated in two laboratories they were recognized by the conference as being definitive and were recommended for use by archaeologists. The laboratory at Belfast used the liquid scintillation

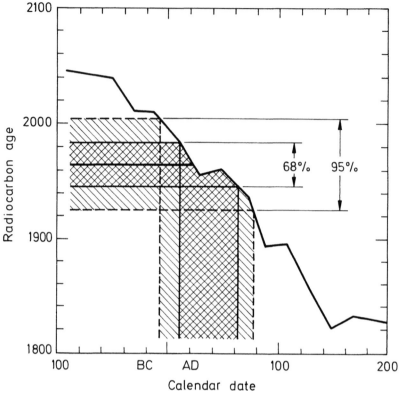

Fig. 4.9 Calibration of the radiocarbon age of 1964 ± 20 years derived from measurements on a control sample by three AMS laboratories involved in dating the Shroud of Turin (see Damon *et al.*, 1989). For the calibration curve (Stuiver and Pearson 1986) σ_c is only about ± 10 years in this period so that, following the procedure given in the caption to Fig. 4.8, $\sigma_{total} = (20^2 + 12^2)^{1/2} = 22$. The calendar date span corresponding to the 68% level of confidence is AD 10–65, and that corresponding to the 95% level of confidence is 10 BC–AD 80.

technique, with samples spanning 20 years of growth (bidecadal), and at Seattle a gas proportional counter was used, with samples spanning 10 years of growth (decadal); any systematic age difference between the two laboratories was shown to be less than a few years. Whereas the former used mainly Irish oak the latter used Douglas fir and sequoia from the US Pacific coast and oak from south Germany; again there was no significant systematic difference between regions.

Full details of all calibrations presented at the conference, together with precise instructions for utilization, are given in a special issue of *Radiocarbon* (vol. 28–2B). Beyond the two recognized calibrations just mentioned the conference recommended use of the Belfast curve – now extended to 6000 BC (Pearson *et al.* 1989). Further back firmly based dendrochronological curves extend to 7200 BC and reliable indications, using varve data also, reach 12000 BC. As elsewhere in the present text 'BC' (or 'AD') means calendar date as obtained after calibration; in the terminology recommended by the conference the correct nomenclature would be 'cal BC' (or 'cal AD').

Most of the calibrations reported utilized either 10- or 20-year growth spans. For some, smoothed curves using a 100-year running mean are presented also; these have an uncertainty in radiocarbon age of only a few years.

Probability spectra

Determination of the calendar date span, or spans, that correspond to the 68% error limits in radiocarbon age (or to the 95% limits) is moderately straightforward, examples being given in Figs. 4.9 and 4.10. However, because of the irregular shape of the calibration curve, the distribution of probability within the span(s) is somewhat more complex than the probability curve appropriate to a radiocarbon age (see Fig. 4.1). Increasingly dates are being expressed in terms of probability spectra, such as shown in Figs. 4.11 and 4.12.

These spectra represent the full information that is available from a determination; given the cost and effort involved in measurement it would seem appropriate that space should be found for spectra in publications, inconvenient though this may be. Although it is possible to derive a central date and confidence level spans from the calendar date probability distribution these gloss over the unevenness of the distribution; thus in Fig. 4.11 the probability is rather low in the centre and the 68% confidence level span excludes dates of substantially higher probability. However, there are other statistical approaches (e.g. Leese 1988) which avoid this feature.

Floating tree-ring sequences; 'wiggle-matching'

Samples which have a known spacing in calendar years, such as those formed by the wood of a large timber beam with well-defined annual rings – or an interrelated sequence of such beams, permit more accurate dating than is otherwise possible. Special statistical treatments have been developed (Clark and Renfrew 1972; Clark and Sowray 1973) which are generally applicable, and in cases where the period in question contains irregularities in the calibration curve, 'wiggle-matching' is possible (e.g. Ferguson *et al.* 1966; Suess and Strahm 1970; Pearson 1986). Essentially this latter consists of finding where the wiggle pattern formed by the sequential sample dates best fits the wiggle pattern of the calibration curve. The time span of the wood used for each sample date (which must be of high precision) needs to be either 10 or 20 years, as appropriate to the calibration curve used; hence the sequence needs to extend over at least 50 years. By this

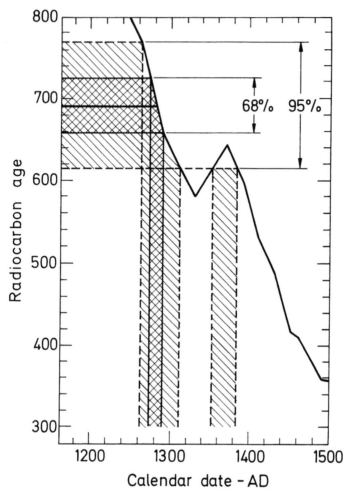

Fig. 4.10 Calibration of the radiocarbon age of 691 ± 31 years as derived from measurements by three AMS laboratories on linen threads from the Shroud of Turin (see Damon *et al.*, 1989). Following a similar procedure to that for Fig. 4.9 the calendar date span corresponding to the 68% level of confidence is AD 1275–1290; corresponding to the 95% level of confidence there are two possible spans: AD 1260–1310 and AD 1355–1385. Note that because of the steepness of the curve the 68% calendar span is appreciably smaller than the radiocarbon age span to which it corresponds. The calibration curve is that of Stuiver and Pearson (1986).

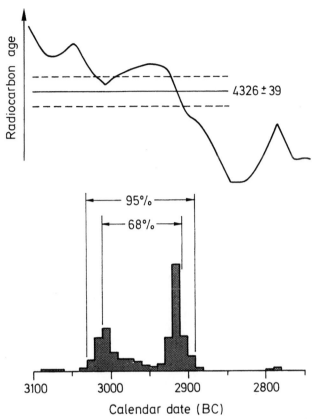

Fig. 4.11 Probability distribution for the calendar age corresponding to a radiocarbon age of 4326 ± 39 years; the upper part shows the calibration curve (Pearson *et al.* 1986) and the histogram below indicates the probability that the calendar date lies in one of the 10 year intervals indicated. The vertical lines indicate the limits of calendar date within which there is a 68% probability of the true date lying; the limits corresponding to 95% probability are also shown. These are not quite the same as the limits of the calendar date span that corresponds to the 68% and 95% levels of confidence limits in the radiocarbon age. The radiocarbon age concerned is the weighted mean for samples from Nubia ('Terminal A-Group') which were contemporaneous with about the beginning of the First Dynasty in Egypt (see Hassan and Robinson 1987, from which this diagram has been obtained[17]).

technique it is possible to obtain quite narrow calendar date spans even in time periods where the calibration curve is flat.

Coherence
Even when the exact separation in calendar years is not known, the coherence of a suite of samples related by stratigraphy, or otherwise, allows better assessment of reliability than can be obtained with unrelated

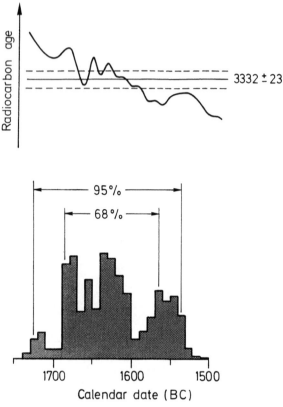

Fig. 4.12 Probability distribution for the calendar date corresponding to a radiocarbon age of 3332 ± 23 years on same basis as for Fig. 4.11 (except that the calibration curve is the decadal one of Stuiver and Becker, 1986). This diagram has been derived by S. W. Robinson (pers. comm.) and the radiocarbon age is based on conventional beta counting determinations made on six fully pre-treated short-lived samples found in a destruction layer associated with the Bronze Age eruption of Thera on the Aegean island of Santorini. Other assessments of the eighteen conventional determinations that are available give lower averages (depending on rejection criteria) but none below 3290 radiocarbon years (see Aitken *et al.*, 1988). Datings of single seeds and grain etc using the AMS technique have now given an average of 3325 ± 30 years (Housley *et al.* 1990) in good agreement with the age illustrated above. The traditional chronology (based on archaeological linkage to the Egyptian calendar) places the eruption *circa* 1500 calendar years BC. As will be seen from the probability spectrum the radiocarbon determinations indicate that an earlier date is much more likely; this is consistent with the revised, 'long', chronology as well as with ice-core and tree-ring evidence – see section 2.3.6. Contrary to the situation in Fig. 4.10 the calibration curve is rather flat here and consequently the 68% range of calendar date probability is substantially wider than the 68% span in radiocarbon age; similarly in respect of 95%.

samples. In most of this chapter we have been concerned with laboratory assessments, but however hard the chef works in his kitchen the ultimate proof of the pudding is in the eating. Figure 4.13 illustrates this.

In judging coherence it is important to pay full regard to the quoted date spans and to remember that at the 68% level of confidence there is a one in three probability that the true date lies outside the quoted span. Thus in checking whether or not two dates are in correct stratigraphic order the spans corresponding to 95% level of confidence should be used; even then there is a one in twenty chance that one of the true dates lies outside the span.

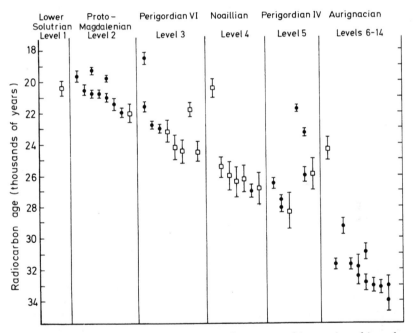

Fig. 4.13 Radiocarbon ages for bone samples, arranged in stratigraphic order, from the Upper Paleolithic site at Abri Pataud, France; closed symbols are for total amino acid extracts dated by AMS (at Oxford); open symbols are for samples dated by beta-decay counting (at Groningen) mostly using collagen. Although the majority are in excellent concordance with stratigraphy there are a few samples for which the date appears to be anomalously too recent; these samples all have a rather small amount of collagen remaining (less than 4% of the original content) suggesting the possibility of contamination by intrusive amino acids from the soil despite precautions taken.

(From Hedges 1987; see also Waterbolk 1971; Mellars and Bricker 1986).

4.5 BEYOND CALIBRATION

Although we may expect gradual extension of the period for which calibration is available through dendrochronology and glacial varve counting, it is unlikely to extend much into the last glaciation. However, other dating techniques are becoming increasingly relevant as far as the long-term trend is concerned. Comparative results using uranium series (Vogel 1987) and thermoluminescence (by H. Valladas, see Aitken 1987) suggest that the period during which radiocarbon gives a substantial underestimate of calender age extends back to at least c. 20,000 years ago. New developments in potassium–argon dating and in uranium-series dating should allow somewhat more precise comparisons to be made, particularly with the latter.

In making such comparisons conventional radiocarbon ages should be multiplied by 1.03 in order to convert to values based on the revised half-life, i.e. 900 years should be added to a radiocarbon age of 30,000 years and 1200 years to one of 40,000.

NOTES

1. As an example consider a proportional counter installation for which the count rate for modern carbon is 16 per minute: for a sample 11,000 years old (two half-lives) the rate will average 4 per minute and so to reach the 10,000 counts necessary for a standard error of ±100 (corresponding to ±1% and hence about ±80 years in age) the counting must be continued for 2500 minutes, i.e. 42 hours. This is one of several factors contributing to the slow and expensive nature of radiocarbon dating.

    The situation worsens for older samples, not only because of the lower count rate but also because the sample count rate becomes comparable with the background count rate observed for a 'dead' sample. Suppose for the same installation the background count rate is 1 per minute and for simplicity assume it to be known precisely and to be constant, which is not necessarily the case. For a sample that is 23,000 years old, i.e. four half-lives, the observed count rate (sample plus background) will average 2 per minute. Hence in the 2 days of counting routinely employed for old samples at many laboratories the total count will be about 6000 with a standard error of ±80. When the background is subtracted the net sample count will be about 3000 but with the same standard error of ±80; the latter corresponds to ±2.7% of the net sample count, i.e. to ±210 years in age.

    The advantage of using a bigger sample may be seen by repeating the above calculation for a scintillation counter for which the modern carbon count rate is 80 per minute and the background 8 per minute.

For a 23,000-year-old sample the sample plus background count rate will average 10 per minute and in 2 days the total count will be about 30,000 ±170; the net sample count is then 15,000 ±170, so the standard error corresponds to ±1.1%, i.e. about ±90 years which is substantially better than the counter which could only accommodate a smaller sample.

2. Using AMS the limitation, at any rate at time of writing, is due to slight contamination introduced during sample preparation. Although this can be subtracted some error is introduced because this is not necessarily the same from run to run.

3. An alternative method of enrichment, demonstrated but not yet utilized, is isotopic enrichment by means of photodissociation using a laser beam. This is faster than using a thermal diffusion column though the amount of sample processed is much less – hence the eventual possibility of using the process in conjunction with AMS measurement. An enrichment factor of 100, corresponding to the same age limit of 70,000 years as achieved with thermal diffusion has been shown to be feasible (Hedges and Moore 1978).

4. There are several types of target in use and more under development. An early procedure used was to produce acetylene, as for gas counting, and from it to deposit carbon (as graphite) on a tantalum wire heated to about 2000 °C. Alternatively, an iron–graphite mixture can be obtained by reduction directly from carbon dioxide, thus cutting out a substantial part of the chemistry, with its attendant risk of isotopic fractionation and contamination. The same advantage applies to the direct use in the accelerator of carbon dioxide as a stream of gas.

5. Assuming that a few per cent of the sample's carbon-14 atoms reach the detector and that the beam current is about 10 μA.

6. The factor 0.95 refers to the first batch that was prepared; for the second batch the factor is 0.7368.

7. If fractionation occurs during preparation of the oxalic acid for measurement the result is normalized to $\delta^{13}C = -19$.

8. There may also be a correction necessary for fractionation during preparation for measurement.

9. The reason why equation (4.1) gives the age relative to AD 1950 is that the activity of the oxalic acid standard, and hence A_m also, decreases with time (by 0.012% per year) due to radioactive decay, and it was only in AD 1950 that it was equal to the *absolute international standard activity*, A_0, the assumed starting activity on which conventional radiocarbon ages are based. The sample activity decreases at the same rate as A_m and hence (A/A_m) measured today gives the value of (A_{1950}/A_0), where A_{1950} refers to the sample activity in 1950. The value chosen for A_0 was based on measurement of known-age nineteenth-century wood grown prior to the Industrial Revolution (and so not affected by fossil-fuel burning); the

measured value was corrected for radioactive decay thereby obtaining the activity of the wood at the time of formation. Of course the assumption that this represents the starting activity of wood of any period is only an approximation and the fluctuations that have occurred (see Fig. 3.5) necessitate conversion of radiocarbon years to calendar years by means of calibration curves.

10. Three quantities frequently used in reporting dates are $d^{14}C$, $\delta^{13}C$, and $D^{14}C$; these are all expressed *per mil* (‰) rather than *per cent* (%). The first quantity refers to the sample's depletion in carbon-14 before correction for the fractionation:

$$d^{14}C = \left(\frac{A' - A_m}{A_m}\right) \times 1000 \tag{4.2}$$

where A' and A_m have the same meaning as in the main text. For a wood sample having an age of 0 BP, $d^{14}C = 0$; for an age of 5568 conventional radiocarbon years, $d^{14}C = -500$; for an age of twice this, $d^{14}C = -750$, etc.; for an infinitely old sample $d^{14}C = -1000$.

Typical values for $\delta^{13}C$ have been given in Table 3.1. These are relative to the PDB standard (a carbonate, *Belemnita americana*, from the Pee Dee formation of South Carolina) and the average value for wood is -25‰. For a sample taking in carbon-13 and carbon-14 more readily than wood, e.g. bone collagen for which $\delta^{13}C = -20$, allowance is made by use of the fractionation-corrected activity defined as

$$A = A'\left(1 - \frac{2(25 + \delta^{13}C)}{1000}\right) \tag{4.3}$$

The fractionation-corrected depletion is then obtained as

$$D^{14}C = \left(\frac{A - A_m}{A_m}\right) \times 1000 \tag{4.4}$$

and in terms of this quantity the conventional radiocarbon age is

$$Age = -8033 \ln\left(1 + \frac{D^{14}C}{1000}\right) \tag{4.5}$$

Since $D^{14}C$ is always negative (except for a sample giving a date in the future, such as occurs for samples grown after the start of nuclear weapons testing), so too is the value of the logarithmic term; hence the negative sign in equation (4.1) is necessary in order to give a positive age for dates in the past.

In geochemical studies and for dendrochronological samples the term *per cent Modern* (pM) is used. It is defined as

$$(pM) = \left(\frac{A}{A_0}\right) \times 100\% \tag{4.6}$$

This is sometimes referred to as the *absolute* per cent Modern, in contrast to former practice when the denominator was A_m rather than A_0.

11. A more quantitative estimate of whether two results are significantly different can be obtained as follows (see Spaulding 1958). Consider two radiocarbon ages, 3810 ±60 and 3500 ±70, the error limits being at the 68% level of confidence. The difference is 310 years with an error limit (68% level) of $\pm(60^2 + 72^2)^{\frac{1}{2}} = \pm 92$; thus the difference is greater (just) than three times the standard error on the difference, and hence the probability of the ages representing different events (or one of them being subject to interference) is greater than 99.7%. (Following from section 4.1.3: a difference of 1σ would correspond to 68% probability, 2σ to 95% probability and 3σ to 99.7%.) Use of the statistic given in note 12 gives comparable answers.

12. For a group of ages Y_1, Y_2, Y_3 ... etc. having a weighted mean Y (see note 13), the relevant test statistic (see Gillespie 1984) is given by

$$T = \left\{\frac{(Y_1 - \bar{Y})^2}{S_1^2} + \frac{(Y_2 - \bar{Y})^2}{S_2^2} + \cdots\right\} \tag{4.7}$$

where S_1, S_2, S_3, etc. are the individual quoted error limits. The individual ages for Fig. 4.5 are given in Table 4.2; for case (a), $T_a = 8.5$ and for case (b), $T_b = 24$. Table 4.3 gives the value of T indicative of 5% probability that the samples represent a coeval group. Since T_a is less than the value appropriate to seven samples, case (a) is acceptable as a group. On the other hand T_b is in excess of the value appropriate to eight samples (confirming intuition) and so those samples cannot be accepted as a group; however, if the two outliers are discarded then we have $T_b = 3.2$ which is well below the value in Table 4.3 appropriate to six samples.

Another way of judging coherence is to evaluate the *observed* standard deviation, σ_{n-1}, available on many hand calculators, and defined as

$$\sigma_{n-1} = \left\{\frac{(Y_1 - \bar{Y})^2 + (Y_2 - \bar{Y})^2 + \cdots}{n-1}\right\}^{1/2} \tag{4.8}$$

Table 4.2 Individual radiocarbon ages used for Fig. 4.5

	(a)	(b)
	4225 ± 95	4570 ± 60
	4265 ± 80	4570 ± 50
	4150 ± 110	4310 ± 50
	4160 ± 110	4360 ± 50
	4390 ± 50	4360 ± 50
	4200 ± 90	4420 ± 50
	4310 ± 90	4410 ± 50
		4360 ± 50
	Weighted mean	4415 ± 18
	excluding two outliers	4370 ± 20
Weighted mean 4290 ± 30		

Table 4.3 Values of test statistics, T, corresponding to 95% probability that a group of samples is coeval

No. of samples	T
2	3.8
3	6.0
4	7.8
5	9.5
6	11.1
7	12.6
8	14.1
9	15.5
10	16.9
11	18.3

Note: The values given for T are often designated such as by $\chi_{6,0.05}$; this refers to $(6 + 1) = 7$ samples and it is the value corresponding to a probability of 5% that they are coeval. It is sometimes wrongly stated that the probability is 95%.

where n is the number of samples. For the eight samples of case (b) the value is 99 years which indicates a scatter much in excess of that predicted by the individual error limits; after discarding the two outliers σ_{n-1} becomes 40 years which is satisfactorily close to the standard deviation of 50 years predicted from the quoted error limits.

It is useful to note that for n samples all having the same quoted error limit S,

$$T = (n - 1)\left(\frac{\sigma_{n-1}}{S}\right)^2 \tag{4.9}$$

13. Using the same nomenclature as in note 12, the weighted mean is given by

$$\bar{Y} = \frac{Y_1/S_1^2 + Y_2/S_2^2 + \dots}{1/S_1^2 + 1/S_2^2 + \dots} \tag{4.10}$$

Hence from Table 4.2 we find $Y_a = 4290$ years, $Y_b = 4415$ years for eight samples and 4370 years for the six samples left after discarding the two outliers.

The error limits on the weighted mean are given by

$$\bar{S} = \left\{ \frac{1}{1/S_1^2 + 1/S_2^2 + \dots} \right\}^{1/2} \tag{4.11}$$

and so $S_a \pm 30$ years, $S_b = 18$ for eight samples and ± 20 for six samples. The value for eight samples is low despite those samples not being a group; this is because S is based on *predicted* error limits.

We may note that for n samples having the same quoted error limit S, it follows from equation (4.11) that

$$\bar{S} = \frac{S}{n^{1/2}} \tag{4.12}$$

14. The archaeological implications (see Renfrew 1973) of calibration were more serious than a further lengthening of prehistoric time-scales because whereas from about 3000 BC onwards the chronology of the Near East is based on links with astronomically dated Egyptian history, for regions remote from it, such as western Europe, the chronology is based on radiocarbon. Even with uncalibrated dates there had been some difficulty in accepting the traditional interpretation of archaeological evidence in terms of outward diffusion from the Near East. With calibration that interpretation became untenable; for instance the first temples in Malta were shown to predate the pyramids by several centuries and the trilithons of Stonehenge (phase III) to be earlier than Mycenae. The beginning of settled farming communities in central Europe, already put 1500 years earlier by uncalibrated dates than had been assumed, were pushed back a further 700 years to c. 5000 BC or beyond.

15. There is also a fourth, more subtle aspect than the three that were mentioned earlier. The internationally recognized calibration curves, and some others, are based on wood spanning 20 years of growth (in order to obtain enough sample for high precision); this tends to smooth out any rapid fluctuations that may have been present. If these were large enough to be important, then for short-lived

samples such as seeds and grain the true calendar date spans are liable to be wider, and the ambiguities more numerous, than indicated by 20-year curves. Thus although short-lived samples have the advantage of avoiding uncertainty due to delay between fixation of carbon and archaeological utilization, they have the disadvantage of 'seeing' any fine structure that exists. Ideally the sample being dated has about the same growth period as the samples used for calibration.

However, for levels of precision attainable in the foreseeable future it has yet to be established that the effect is of consequence. Two sets of single-year data reported by Stuiver (1982), spanning a total of 250 years, reveal no evidence for any short-term variation beyond that attributable to the ± 12-year measuring precision; this is consistent with the effect of the 11-year sunspot cycle being rather small (see note 10 of Chapter 3). On the other hand, measurements throughout the third millennium BC using samples spanning a few years (Vogel *et al.* 1986) indicate occasional rapid changes of greater magnitude; even so, it would seem that use of a decadal calibration for single-year samples would barely introduce significant error.

Of course, in the opposite direction, when dating samples which have formed over a time substantially greater than the growth span of the calibration samples, e.g. peat, the calibration curve needs to be smoothed. Hundred-year averages have been published for the two internationally recognized curves (Stuiver and Pearson 1986; Pearson and Stuiver 1986).

16. MASCA: The Museum Applied Science Centre for Archaeology based at the University Museum, Philadelphia, Pennsylvania.

17. The probabilistic method used by Robinson has been described by Weniger (1986). A probability spectrum for the eruption of Thera has also been given by Klein (1988) on the basis that for a radiocarbon age of $(a \pm \sigma)$ the probability that the calendar date is D_i is given by

$$P(D_i) = \exp\{-(a_i - \bar{\alpha})^2/2\sigma^2\}/\sum_i \exp\{-(a_i - \bar{\alpha})^2/2\sigma^2\} \quad (4.13)$$

where a_i is the radiocarbon age corresponding to D_i.

A summary of various assessments of the conventional determinations relevant to the eruption of Thera, and archaeological comment, is contained in Aitken *et al.* 1988).

REFERENCES

Aitken, M. J. (1987) Archaeometrical dating: rapporteur review, in *Chronologies in the Near East* (eds. O. Aurenchel, J. Evin and F. Hours) *BAR* (International Series) **379**, 207–18.

Aitken, M. J., Allsop, A. L., Bussell, G.C. and Winter, M. (1989) Geomagnetic intensity variations during the last 4000 years, *Phys. Earth Planet. Int.* 56, 49–58.

Aitken, M.J., Michael, H. N., Betancourt, P. P. and Warren, P. M. (1988) The Thera eruption: continuing discussion of the dating, *Archaeometry* 30, 154–82.

Anderson, E. C., Libby, W. F., Weinhouse, S., Reid, A. F., Kirshenbaum A. D., and Grosse, A. V. (1947) Radiocarbon from cosmic radiation, *Science* 105, 576.

Arnold, J. R. and Libby, W. F. (1949) Age determinations by radiocarbon content: checks with samples of known age, *Science* 110, 678–680.

Bastin, B. and Gewelt, M. (1986) Analyse pollinique et datation ^{14}C de concretions stalagmitiques holocènes, *Géographie Physique et Quaternaire* 40, 185–196.

Baxter, M. S. (1983) An international tree-ring replicate study, *Proc. Groningen Conference on ^{14}C and Archaeology* (eds. W. G. Mook and H. T. Waterbolk), PACT Publication 8, 123–31.

Bruns, M., Levin, I., Munnish, K. O., Hubbertsen, H. W. and Fillipakis, S. (1980) Regional sources of volcanic carbon dioxide and their influence on ^{14}C content of present-day plant material, *Radiocarbon* 22, 532–6.

Burleigh, R., Matthews, K., and Leese, M. N. (1984) Consensus ^{13}C values, *Radiocarbon* 26, 46–53.

Chatters, R. M., Crosby, J. W. III, and Engstrand, L. G. (1969) *Fumarole Gaseous Emanations: Their Influence on Carbon-14 Dates*, Circular 32, College of Engineering, Washington State University.

Clark, R. M. (1975) A calibration curve for radiocarbon dates, *Antiquity* 49, 251–266.

Clark, R. M. and Renfrew, C. (1972) A statistical approach to the calibration of floating tree-ring chronologies using radiocarbon dates, *Archaemoetry* 14, 5–19.

Clark, R. M. and Sowray, A. (1973) Further statistical methods for the calibration of floating tree-ring chronologies, *Archaeometry* 15, 255–6.

Cowan, C., Alturi, C. R. and Libby, W. F. (1965) Possible anti-matter content of the Tunguska meteor of 1908, *Nature* 206, 861–5.

Damon, P. E., Long, A. and Wallick, E. I. (1972) Dendrochronology calibration of the carbon-14 time scale. *Proc. 8th Internat. Conf. Radiocarbon Dating* (eds. T. A. Rafter and T. Grant-Taylor), Royal Society of New Zealand, Wellington, New Zealand, pp. 44–59.

Damon, P. E., Donahue, D.J., Gore, B. H., Hatheway, A. L., Jull, A. J. T., Linick, T. W., Sercel, P. J., Toolin, L. J., Bronk, C. R., Hall, E. T., Hedges, R. E. M., Housley, R., Law, I. A., Perry, C., Bonani, G., Trumbore, S., Woelfli, W., Ambers, J. C., Bowman, S. G. E., Leese, M. N., and Tite, M. S., 1989, Radiocarbon Dating of the Shroud of Turin, *Nature* 337, 611–615.

Dauchot-Dehon, M., Van Strydonch, M., and Heylen, J. (1983) Institut Royal du Patrimoine Artistique radiocarbon dates IX, *Radiocarbon* 25, 867–74.

Ferguson, C. W., Huber, B. and Suess, H. E. (1966) Determination of the age of Swiss lake dwellings as an example of dendrochronologically-calibrated radiocarbon dating, *Zeitschrift für Naturforschung* 21A, 1173–7.

Gascogne, M. and Nelson, D. E. (1983) Growth mechanisms of recent speleothems from Castleguard Cave, Columbia Icefields, Alberta, Canada, inferred from a comparison of uranium-series and carbon-14 age data, *Arctic and Alpine Research* 15, 537–42.

Geyh, M. A. and Hennig, G. J. (1986) Multiple dating of a long flowstone profile, *Radiocarbon* 28, 503–9.

Gillespie, R. (1984) *Radiocarbon User's Handbook*, Oxford University Committee for Archaeology. Distributed by Oxbow Books, 10 St Cross Road, Oxford, UK.

Gillespie, R., Hedges, R. E. M. and Wand, J. O. (1984) Radiocarbon dating of bone by accelerator mass spectrometry, *Journ. Archaeol. Sci.* **11**, 165–70.

Gowlett, J. A. J. and Hedges, R. E. M. (eds.) (1986) *Archaeological Results from Accelerator Dating*, Oxford University Committee for Archaeology, Monograph 11. Distributed by Oxbow Books, 10 St Cross Road, Oxford, UK.

Harris, D. R. (1987) The impact on archaeology of radiocarbon dating by accelerator mass spectrometry, *Phil. Trans. Roy. Soc. Lond.* **A323**, 23–43.

Hassan, F. A. and Robinson, S. W. (1987) High-precision radiocarbon chronometry of ancient Egypt, and comparisons with Nubia, Palestine and Mesopotamia, *Antiquity* **61**, 119–35.

Hedges, R. E. M. and Moore, B. C. (1978) Enrichment of the C-14 and radiocarbon dating. *Nature* **276**, 255–7.

Hedges, R. E. M. (1987) Radiocarbon dating by accelerator mass spectrometry: some recent results and applications, *Phil. Trans, Roy, Soc. Lond.* **A323**, 57–73.

Henning, W., Bell, W. A., Billquist, P. J., Glagola, B. G., Kutschera, W., Liu, A., Lucas, H. F., Paul, M., Rehm, K. E. and L'Yntema, J. (1987) Calcium-41 concentration in terrestrial materials: prospects for dating Pleistocene samples, *Science* **236**, 725–7.

Houseley, R. A., Hedges, R. E. M., Law, I. A. and Bronk, C. (1990) Radiocarbon dating by AMS of the destruction of Akrotiri, *In Thera and the Aegean World III*, ed. C. Doumas (in press). Publisher: Thera and the Aegean World, 105–109 Bishopsgate, London.

International Study Group (1982) An inter-laboratory comparison of radiocarbon measurements in tree rings, *Nature* **298** 619–23.

Klein, J. (1988) Appendix to the Thera eruption: continuing discussion of the dating, *Archaeometry* **30**, 165–81.

Klein, J., Lerman, J. C., Damon, P.E. and Linick, T. (1980) Radiocarbon concentration in the atmosphere: 8000 year record of variation in tree-rings, *Radiocarbon* **22**, 950–61.

Klein, J., Lerman, J. C., Damon, P. E. and Ralph, E. K. (1982) Calibration of radiocarbon dates: tables based on the concensus data of the workshop on calibrating the radiocarbon time scale, *Radiocarbon* **24**, 103–50.

Kra, R. (1986) Standardizing procedures for collecting, submitting, recording and reporting radiocarbon samples, *Radiocarbon* **28**, 765–75.

Kruse, H. H., Linick, H. T. W. and Suess, H. E. (1980) Computer-matched radiocarbon dates of floating tree-ring series, *Radiocarbon* **22**, 260–6.

Leese, M. N. (1988) Methods for finding calendar date bands from multiple-valued radiocarbon calibration curves, in *Computer and Quantitative Methods in Archaeology* (eds. C. L. N. Ruggles and S. P. Q. Rahtz) *BAR* (International Series), **393**, 147–51.

Libby, W. R. (1955) *Radiocarbon Dating* (1st edn) University of Chicago Press, Chicago.

Libby, W. F. (1965) *Radiocarbon Dating* (2nd edn) University of Chicago Press, Chicago.

Libby, W. F., Anderson, E. C., and Arnold, J. R. (1949) Age determination by radiocarbon content: Worldwide assay of natural radiocarbons, *Science* **109**, 227–8.

Libby, L. M. and Lukens, H. R. (1973) Production of radiocarbon in tree rings by lightning bolts, *Journal of Geophysical Research* **78**, 5902–3.

Litherland, A. E. (1987) Fundamentals of accelerator mass spectrometry, *Phil. Trans. Roy. Soc. Lond.* **A323**, 5–21.

Long, A. and Rippeteau, B. (1974) Testing contemporaneity and averaging radiocarbon dates, *American Antiquity* **39**, 205–15.

Manning, S. W. (1988) The Bronze Age eruption of Thera: absolute dating, Aegean chronology and Mediterranean cultural interrelations, *Journal of Mediterranean Archaeology* **1**, 17–82.

Mellars, P. A. and Bricker, H. M. (1986) Radiocarbon accelerator dating in the Upper Palaeolithic, in *Archaeological Results from Accelerator Dating* (eds. J. A. J. Gowlett and R. E. M. Hedges), Oxford University Committee for Archaeology Monograph II, pp. 73–80. Distributed by Oxbow Books, 10 St Cross Road, Oxford, UK.

Michael, H. N. and Betancourt, P. P. (1988) Further arguments for an early date, *Archaeometry* **30**, 169–74.

Middleton, R., Fink, D., Klein, J. and Sharma, P. (1989) [41] Ca concentrations in modern bone and their implications for dating, *Radiocarbon* **31**(3), (in press).

Mook, W. G. (1984) Archaeological and geological interest in applying ^{14}C AMS to small samples, *Nucl. Instrum. Meth. Phys. Res.* **233**, 297–302.

Mook, W. G. and Waterbolk, H. T. (1985) *Handbook for Archaeologists No. 3: Radiocarbon Dating*, European Science Foundation, 1 quai Lezay-Marnesia, 67000 Strasbourg, France, 65 pp.

Muzzolini, A. (1982) Les datations au ^{14}C sur roches carbonatées en zone aride: corrections à appliquer et incertitudes, *Archaeometry* **24**, 85–96.

Nelson, D. E., Loy, T. H., Vogel, J. S. and Southon, J. R. (1986) Radiocarbon dating blood residues on prehistoric stone tools, *Radiocarbon* **28**, 170–4.

Olsson, I. V. (1979) The radiocarbon contents of various reservoirs, in *Proc. 9th Internat. Radiocarbon Conf.*, Berkeley (eds. R. Berger and H. E. Suess), pp. 613–18.

Olsson, I. U. (1983) Radiocarbon dating in the arctic region, *Radiocarbon* **25**, 393–4.

Olsson, I. U. (1987) Carbon-14 dating and interpretation of the validity of some dates from the Bronze Age in the Aegean. In *High, Middle or Low?*, part 2, pp. 4–38: Paul Astroms Forlag, Gothenburg.

Ottaway, B. (1973) Dispersion diagrams: a new approach to the display of carbon-14 dates, *Archaeometry* **15**, 5–12.

Pearson, G. W. (1986) Precise calendrical dating of known growth-period samples using a 'curve fitting' technique, *Radiocarbon* **28**, 292–9.

Pearson, G. W. (1987) How to cope with calibrations, *Antiquity* **61**, 98–103.

Pearson G. W., Pilcher, J. R., Baillie, M. G. L., Corbett, D. M. and Qua F. (1986) High-precision ^{14}C measurement of Irish oaks to show the natural ^{14}C variations from AD 1840–5210 BC, *Radiocarbon* **30**, 911–934.

Pearson, G. W. and Stuiver, M. (1986) High-precision calibration of the radiocarbon time scale, 500–2500 BC. *Radiocarbon*, **28**, 839–62.

Pearson, G. W., Becker, B. and Qua, F. (1989) High-precision ^{14}C measurement of German oaks to show the natural ^{14}C variations from 6102 to 5090 BC, *Radiocarbon* **31**(3), (in press).

Raisbeck, G. M. and Yiou, F. (1979) Possible use of [14] Ca for radioactive dating, *Nature* **277**, 42–4.

Ralph, E. K. and Stuckenrath, R. (1960) Carbon-14 measurements of known age samples. *Nature* **188**, 185–7.

Ralph, E. K., Michael, H. N. and Han, M. C. (1973) Radiocarbon dates and reality, *MASCA Newsletter* **9**, 1–20.

Renfrew, C. (1973) *Before Civilization: The Radiocarbon Revolution and Prehistoric Europe*, Jonathan Cape, London.

Saupé, F., Strappa, O., Coppens, R., Guillet, B., and Jaegy, R. (1980) A possible source of error in ^{14}C dates: volcanic emanations (examples from the Monte Amiata District, Provinces of Grosseto and Sienna, Italy), *Radiocarbon* 22, 525–31.

Scott, E. M., Aitchison, T. C., Harkness, D. D., Baxter, M. S. and Cook, G., T. (1989) An interim progress report on Stages 1 and 2 of the International Collaborative Programme, *Radiocarbon* 31(3), (in press).

Shackleton, N. J., Duplessy, J.-C., Arnold, M., Maurice, P., Hall, M. A. and Cartlidge, J. (1988) Radiocarbon age of last glacial Pacific deep water, *Nature* 335, 708–711.

Spaulding, A. C. (1958) The significances of differences between radiocarbon dates, *American Antiquity* 38, 32–7.

Stuiver, M., and Waldren, W. H. (1975) ^{14}C carbonate dating and the age of the post-Talayotic lime burials in Mallorca, *Nature* 255, 475–6.

Stuiver, M., and Polach, H. A. (1977) Discussion: Reporting of ^{14}C data. *Radiocarbon* 19, 355–63.

Stuiver, M. and Quay, P. D. (1981) Atmospheric ^{14}C changes resulting from fossil fuel CO_2 release and cosmic ray flux variability, *Earth Planet. Sci. Lett.* 53, 349–62.

Stuiver, M. (1982) A high precision calibration of the AD radiocarbon time scale, *Radiocarbon* 24, 1–26.

Stuiver, M. and Becker, B. (1986) High precision calibration of the radiocarbon time scale, AD 1950–2500 BC, *Radiocarbon* 28, 863–910.

Stuiver, M. and Pearson, G. W. (1986) High precision calibration of the radiocarbon time scale, AD 1950–500 BC. *Radiocarbon*, 28, 805–38.

Stuiver, M., Pearson, G. W. and Braziunas, T. F. (1986) Radiocarbon age calibration of marine samples back to 9000 Cal Yr BP, *Radiocarbon* 28, 990–1021.

Suess, H. E. (1955) Radiocarbon concentration in modern wood, *Science* 122, 415–17.

Suess, H. E. (1970) Bristlecone-pine calibration time 5200 BC to present, in *Radiocarbon Dating* (eds R. Berger and H. E. Suess), University of California Press, Berkeley, p. 777–84.

Suess, H. E. (1986) Secular variations of cosmogenic ^{14}C on earth: their discovery and interpretation, *Radiocarbon* 28, 259–65.

Suess, H. and Strahm, C. (1970) The neolithic of Auvernier, Switzerland, *Antiquity* 44, 91–9.

Taylor, R. E. (1987) *Radiocarbon Dating: An Archaeological Perspective*, Academic Press, Orlando, Fla. 32887.

Taylor, R. E., Slota, P. J., Henning, W., Kutschera, W. and Paul, M. (1989) Radiocalcium dating: potential applications in archaeology and paleoanthropology, in *Archaeological Chemistry IV* (ed. R. O. Allen), American Chemical Society, Washington DC, 321–35.

Van Strydonck, M., Dupas, M., Dauchot-Dehon, M., Pachiaudi, C. and Marechal, J. (1986) The influence of contaminating (fossil) carbonate and the variations of ^{13}C in mortar dating, *Radiocarbon* 28, 702–10.

Vogel, J. C., (1987) Calibration of radiocarbon dates beyond 10,000 BP, in *Chronologies in the Near East* (eds O. Aurenche, J. Evin and F. Hours) *BAR* (International Series), 379, 319–24.

Vogel, J. C., Fuls, A. and Visser, E. (1986) Radiocarbon fluctuations during the third millennium bc, *Radiocarbon* 28 935–8.

de Vries, H. (1958) Variations in concentration of radiocarbon with time and location on earth, *Proceedings, Nederlandsche Akademie van Wetenschappen*, Series B61, 1.

de Vries, H., Barendsen, G.W. and Waterbolk, H. T. (1958) Groningen radiocarbon dates II, *Science* **127**, 129–37.

de Vries, H. and Waterbolk, H. T. (1958) Groningen radiocarbon dates III, *Science* **128**, 1550–6.

Ward, G. K. and Wilson, S. R. (1978) Procedures for comparing and combining radiocarbon age determinations: a critique, *Archaeometry* **20**, 19–32.

Waterbolk, H. T. (1971) Working with radiocarbon dates, *Proceedings of the Prehistoric Society* **37**, 15–33.

Waterbolk, H. T. (1983) Ten guidelines for the archaeological interpretation of radiocarbon dating, in *14C and Archaeology* (eds W. G. Mook and H. T. Waterbolk), *PACT* **8**, 57–70 Council of Europe, Strasbourg.

Weniger, B. (1986) High-precision calibration of archaeological radiocarbon dates, *Acta Interdisciplinaria Archaeologica IV*, Nitra, Czechoslovakia pp. 11–53.

Wilson, S. R. and Ward, G. K. (1981) Evaluation and clustering of age determinations: procedures and paradigms, *Archaeometry* **23**, 19–39.

Zouridakis, N., Saliege, J. R., Person, A. and Filippakis, S. E. (1987) *Archaeometry* **29**, 60–8.

5 Potassium–argon; uranium series; fission tracks

These are primarily geological techniques but with increasing relevance to archaeology, particularly in respect of uranium-series dating of stalagmite calcite, and of bone, from Palaeolithic caves of the last 350,000 years. The other two techniques have been used for indirect dating of early hominids, particularly the Olduvai Man and earlier examples from East Africa in the age range of several million years. With technological advance the recent age limit for potassium–argon is being reduced so that relevance to archaeology is increasing, though still with limitation to circumstances in which there is chance association of human occupation with geological events, viz. volcanic eruptions. All three techniques, but particularly potassium–argon, have been important in establishment of the oxygen–isotope time-scale and magnetic reversal stratigraphy.

5.1 POTASSIUM–ARGON DATING

5.1.1 BASIC PRINCIPLE

In naturally occurring potassium there is a weakly radioactive isotope, potassium-40, with a half-life of 1250 million years.[1] When this decays two daughter products are formed: argon-40 and calcium-40. The former is a gas and it is the accumulation of this gas that is the basis of dating, as illustrated in Fig. 5.1.

The simplest scenario of application is where the human occupation level is bracketed between two lava flows. Retention of argon within potassium-bearing minerals of the lava commences on cooling from the molten state; it is assumed that while molten the retention is negligible. Thus the ages obtained for the two flows give upper and lower limits for the archaeological level. Other volcanic products may be dated too, e.g. crystal components of volcanic ash.

For a general account of the technique, see Faure (1986).

5.1.2 MEASUREMENT

The argon present is determined by means of a mass spectrometer, the gas being released by fusion of the sample. Although of comparable

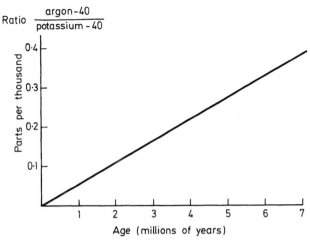

Fig. 5.1 Potassium–argon dating: basic concept. While molten, volcanic lava releases any argon–40, but after solidification there is accumulation due to its production from radioactive decay of potassium–40. Because the half-life of the latter is 1250 million years the production rate is effectively constant over archaeological times. The potassium–40 content of natural potassium is 0.0118% (atomic abundance).

high sensitivity to the accelerator-type facility used for AMS radiocarbon dating the high energy input is not necessary in this case; nevertheless an appropriate measurement installation represents a very substantial investment of resources. In the traditional approach the potassium content is measured by atomic absorption spectrometry, or some comparable technique; the ratio of argon content to potassium content then gives the age as indicated in Fig. 5.1.

Measurements are made on samples of the whole rock or, preferably, on several separate fractions of different minerals; the latter procedure can be effective in detecting the presence of older contaminating material. A few grams of separated mineral are normally required, less in the case of minerals rich in potassium; in the laser dating approach (see below) an age can be obtained from a single millimetre-sized grain.

In extending the technique to more recent samples the obvious limitation is the need for ultra-high sensitivity in argon mass spectrometry. Another limitation is contamination by argon–40 from the atmosphere; this occurs due to absorption within the sample material and on the walls of the measuring apparatus. The extent of atmospheric contamination can be determined, and corrected for [2] by measurement of argon–36. Using the most sensitive techniques ages have now been obtained for volcanic rocks from eruptions of less than 30,000 years ago (Gillot *et al.* 1982; Gillot and Cornette 1986); minerals of high potassium content are most often used in such work (e.g. potassium feldspars such as sanidine).

The argon–argon technique

An alternative way of evaluating the potassium content is by means of neutron irradiation in a nuclear reactor. This converts some of the potassium into argon-39 and this is measured in the mass spectrometer at the same time as the argon-40; the age is then derived from the ratio ($^{40}Ar/^{39}Ar$).

In measurement the argon is released from the sample by stepwise heating to successively increasing temperatures and an age determination made for the gas released at each step. For a well-behaved sample the age stays the same for all steps of gas release and a plateau is obtained as in the plot illustrated in Fig. 5.2(a). Also shown is the situation for a problem sample (Fig. 5.2(b)). One possible cause of the lower age obtained for the gas released in the early heating steps is that mineral alteration (or secondary heating) occurred during burial thereby allowing release of the less firmly held argon. Alternatively, it could be that the lower age

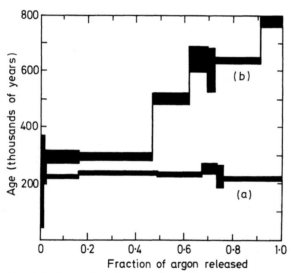

Fig. 5.2   Examples of age spectra obtained using the argon–argon technique (redrawn from Féraud *et al.* 1983). The argon is released in steps, by heating the sample to successively increasing temperatures; an age determination is made on each portion released. Argon that is less firmly held is released in the early steps. The plateau obtained for sample (a) gives confidence in its reliability, but this is not the case for sample (b). One possible explanation is that due to alteration associated with weathering some of the less firmly held argon has been lost during antiquity; in that case the true age would be 800,000 years. Alternatively, the absence of plateau could be due to incomplete removal of firmly held argon at time zero; in that case the true age for (b) would be about 290,000 years. The samples were from two basalt flows in Israel between which there was a palaeosol containing Upper Acheulean artefacts.

is correct and the higher ages obtained during the later steps are due to excess argon – previously accumulated gas that failed to escape while the rock was molten; however this circumstance is usually characterized by a U-shaped age spectrum.

Whatever the interpretation the absence of a plateau gives a warning of unreliability that is not available with the conventional approach to measurement.

Laser dating of single grains
By using an argon laser for heating the technique can be applied to single grains of the order of 1 mg or less (e.g. Layer *et al.* 1987; Bogaard *et al.* 1987). This grain-by-grain approach has the advantages that the labour of mineral separation is much reduced and that the presence of older contaminating grains can be detected.

5.1.3 AGE RANGE; ERROR LIMITS

The potassium-40 half-life of 1250 million years more than encompasses any possible archaeological application. With the technological developments mentioned above, the limitation in respect of recent samples has been substantially reduced, particularly for high-potassium rocks. Gillot *et al.* (1982) quote error limits of ±10,000 years for rocks of the last 30,000 years containing 1% potassium and proportionally smaller ones for higher potassium content; thus by using feldspar extracts containing about 10% potassium Gillot and Cornette (1986) achieve error limits (at the 95% level of confidence) of around ±1000 years for rocks in the age range 1000–30,000 years, there being confirmation of validity by means of historically dated and radiocarbon-dated samples. For such young material the error limits are dominated by uncertainty in the correction for atmospheric argon, and for a given potassium content their magnitude (in years) is independent of age.

5.1.4 ARCHAEOLOGICAL APPLICATION

The event dated is a volcanic eruption and the validity of the age obtained for any associated archaeology rests heavily on geological interpretation. The technique has been of prime importance in dating hominid remains in East Africa, and elsewhere. An early example was the dating (Evernden and Curtis 1965) of tuffs within Bed I at the Olduvai Gorge, Tanzania, where 'Zinjanthropus' was found, and other hominid remains subsequently; the age of close to 1.8 million years is the result of many determinations (see Curtis and Hay 1972; Johanson *et al.* 1987) and it is also relevant to magnetic reversal stratigraphy, the site giving its name to the *Olduvai* magnetic *event* (or *subchron*) on account of the relevant eruptions having occurred during a relatively short period (about

300,000 years) of normal polarity within the *Matuyama chron* of reversed polarity.

Another example is the dating of the KBS Tuff, Koobi Fora Formation, adjacent to Lake Turkana in northern Kenya and having hominids in stratigraphic proximity. Concordant ages at 1.88 ± 0.02 million years, based on both the conventional technique and the argon–argon technique (McDougall *et al.* 1980; McDougall 1981) have replaced an earlier estimate of about 2.6 million years (Fitch and Miller 1970) now thought to have been affected by contamination by inherited radiogenic argon – illustrative of the desirability of separate dating of more than one mineral (see Curtis 1975); the stratigraphically later Okote Tuff in this formation has been dated to 1.64 ± 0.03 million years (McDougall *et al.* 1985). Further north, in Ethiopia, hominid skull fragments have been shown to be at least 3.9 million years old by the dating of air-fall volcanic deposits (Hall *et al.* 1984); fission-track ages from zircons in the same deposit confirmed this great antiquity.

With the technological advances that allow measurement of young samples, more archaeological application is to be expected (e.g. Fig. 5.2). The technique is important archaeologically also for determining how far back in time thermoluminescence and other methods are valid; beyond 100,000 years the uncertainty in potassium–argon ages becomes progressively smaller in percentage terms, with reliability well attested.

5.2 URANIUM-SERIES DATING

In archaeological application this essentially means the use of thorium-230, with ancillary measurements.of protactinium-231 in some circumstances. The discussion following is primarily concerned with the former; some other variants of uranium-series dating are mentioned in section 5.2.6.

5.2.1 BASIS

Thorium-230
Natural uranium consists of two 'parent' radioactive isotopes: uranium-235 and uranium-238. Each has a chain of 'daughter' radioisotopes formed by successive radioactive decays; in the latter uranium-234 is the third daughter, followed by thorium-230; details are in Appendix A. It is only the long-lived components that are relevant to the present discussion, *i.e.*

Uranium-238   half-life: 45000 million years
Uranium-234   half-life: 245,000 years
Thorium-230   half-life: 75,400 years

Stalagmitic calcite is the principal archaeologically relevant material to which this technique is applied. The crystals of calcite are formed from carbonate in ground water in which there is usually uranium present (at trace impurity levels) but no thorium, because of its low solubility. Some of the uranium is incorporated in the calcite crystals, and so, through radioactive decay there is gradual accumulation of thorium-230. The initial build-up is at a uniform rate, as in the case of argon-40, but because thorium-230 is itself radioactive there is gradual levelling off, as indicated[3] in Fig. 5.3;

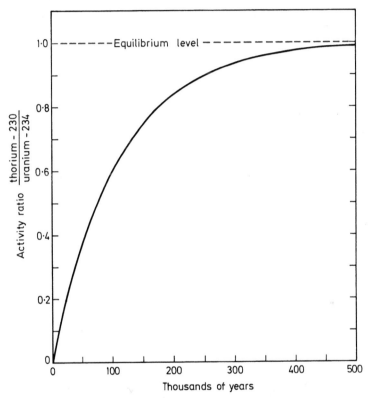

Fig. 5.3 Uranium-series dating, using build-up of thorium–230. At formation crystals of stalagmitic calcite contain uranium but no thorium. With time thorium–230 'grows-in', it being the radioactive daughter of uranium–234; eventually the decay-rate (*activity*) of the thorium–230 becomes equal to that of the uranium–234, but until this equilibrium situation is reached the growth is characterized by the 75,400-year half-life of thorium–230 so measurement of the activity ratio enables the age to be determined.

In the curve shown it is assumed that the initial activity of uranium–234 was equal to that of the parent uranium–238. Usually it is greater, gradually decaying to equality. This alters the shape of the curve somewhat and measurement of the (234/238) ratio in the sample is necessary to define the shape; this is important, except for young samples.

Whereas in Fig. 5.1 the vertical scale showed the weight-for-weight ratio, here activity ratio has been used.

eventually an equilibrium situation is reached in which the rate of decay of the thorium-230 is equal to its rate of production. In the age range during which the thorium-230 is increasing, measurement of the ratio of thorium-230 to uranium-234 allows the time that has elapsed since crystal formation to be evaluated.

Protactinium-231

The series (or 'chain') formed from the parent uranium-235, which has a half-life of 700 million years, has only one long-lived daughter, namely protactinium-231 with a half-life of 34,300 years. The basis of dating is the same as for thorium-230. Use of the two together is advantageous in establishing whether or not the samples concerned form a 'closed' system – see below.

In natural uranium the activity ratio of uranium-235 to uranium-238 is 1 : 22; hence the two associated series are known as the minor and major series respectively. As might be expected, dating based on the major series is possible with samples having much lower concentrations of uranium than is the case when using the minor series; there are other measurement problems too, particularly with archaeologically relevant samples.

5.2.2 MEASUREMENT

The established technique is by means of alpha spectrometry; this must be preceded by time-consuming chemical extraction of thorium and uranium. However, the apparatus is at least an order of magnitude less expensive than required for potassium–argon and can be set up by a competent physicist, chemist or geologist given good back-up facilities; but as with all dating methods considerable experience needs to be gained before reliable results are obtained. Discussion of experimental details and other aspects of the method will be found in Ivanovich and Harmon (1982).

The need for chemical separation is avoided if high-resolution gamma spectrometry is used (e.g. Yokoyama and Nguyen 1981); however, only the ratio between thorium-230 and uranium-238 can then be obtained so that it is necessary to make assumptions about the content of uranium-234, thereby introducing serious uncertainty. A much superior approach is the use of mass spectrometry (Edwards *et al.* 1987),though the same comments on cost, etc. as made in respect of potassium-argon apply; substantially better accuracy is obtainable than with either alpha or gamma spectrometry, and the required size of sample is much reduced.

5.2.3 AGE RANGE; ERROR LIMITS

For calcite samples of good integrity (see below) the age range that can be covered with thorium-230 using alpha spectrometry is roughly 5000–350,000 years. Younger samples can be dated if the uranium content is high, but an upper limit is imposed by the flattening of the dating curve (Fig. 5.3). At 350,000 years the thorium-230 activity is within 4% of the equilibrium value that an infinitely old sample would have, and consequently good experimental accuracy is needed to distinguish with confidence a sample of that age from one that is infinitely old, quite apart from difficulties due to poor sample integrity. If distinction is not possible then either a minimum age may be given or the best value quoted with an upper error limit of infinity; thus for a 350,000-year-old sample with a ±4% uncertainty in the activity ratio the age quoted will be 350^{+00}_{-80} ka. In any case except for young samples the error limits are likely to be unequal, e.g. 250^{+60}_{-40} ka, again because of the flattening of the dating curve.

Using mass spectrometry quite remarkable accuracy is attainable as well as an extended age range, at any rate for coral (Edwards *et al.* 1987). Even at the 95% level of confidence smaller error limits than ±1% of the age are possible for ages between 1000 and 100,000 years; if ±10% error limits are acceptable the age range extends forward to only 50 years ago and reaches back to 500,000 years.

For protactinium-231 the age range using alpha spectrometry is roughly 5,000–150,000 years.

5.2.4 SAMPLE INTEGRITY

Quite apart from any experimental uncertainties of measurement the reliability of the result rests very heavily on the degree to which the sample fulfils the assumptions on which the dating is based; essentially these are: (i) that at crystal formation the content of thorium-230 is zero; and (ii) that subsequently there has not been movement of uranium or thorium into or out of the sample. When these conditions are not fulfilled it is possible to attempt laboratory correction procedures, such as discussed by Schwarcz (1980:16), but inevitably the dates then obtained are of questionable reliability and in the words of that author '. . . the best procedure is to hunt for those sites and strata which provide the cleanest, most detritus-free [samples] . . .'.

Detrital contamination

When calcite is forming there is the possibility that dust from neighbouring sediment is blown on to it; there may also be contamination with detrital limestone. These effects are likely to upset the assumption that the thorium-230 content was zero at the time of crystal formation, thereby leading to an apparent age that is erroneously too ancient. There may also be contamination by bone fragments.

One indicator of contamination is the presence of thorium-232, the parent of the thorium series (see Appendix A); thorium is usually present in sediment as a trace impurity. An essential of the method is that there is not thorium in the water from which the calcite is formed, and this is ensured by the geochemical behaviour of thorium. Hence the presence of thorium-232 is an indication that contamination has occurred and if it is present it is likely to have been accompanied by some thorium-230; hence the ratio of thorium-230 to uranium-234 that is evaluated for the sample will be higher than the value corresponding to the accumulation of thorium-230 resulting from radioactive decay of the sample's own uranium-234. It is usual to quote the ratio (thorium-230/thorium-232) as indication of the degree of detrital contamination, the higher the value of the ratio the more reliable the sample; except for samples near the limits of the age range a value above 20 : 1 is usually considered satisfactory. If the value is lower correction may be attempted and a 'detritally-corrected' date quoted; however, as implied by the quotation above, such dates should be treated with caution.

'Closed' and 'open' systems

If some of the uranium has been leached out from the sample during antiquity, but the thorium has remained due to its lower solubility, then the measured ratio will be erroneously high and hence the evaluated age also. This is an 'open' system. In a severe case leaching can give rise to a (thorium-230/uranium-234) ratio that is greater than the equilibrium value of unity, thus giving a clear indication that something is amiss.

Evidence that the system has been 'closed' is most effectively provided by concordance of the age derived from thorium-230 with that derived from protactinium-231. However, the latter may not be available either because the sample is beyond its age range or because of the technical difficulties of measurement. Other indications concerning leaching are obtained from the (uranium-234/uranium-238) ratio which is liable to be anomalously low in old samples which have suffered leaching; also the overall uranium content is liable to be lower than in comparable samples which have not suffered leaching. But, as with all techniques, a more general indicator that something is wrong is an unacceptable spread in the ages obtained for coeval samples.

Recrystallization is liable to cause some mobilization of uranium and thorium, and hence effectively make the system open. There is also the possibility of secondary deposition – overgrowth – occurring in the pores of a porous calcite during a wet period subsequent to the original formation. The latter gives rise to ages that are erroneously too young; both can be recognized by microscopic examination in thin section.

5.2.5 ARCHAEOLOGICAL APPLICATION

Sample types

There is a wide range of materials to which the technique has been applied, both successfully and unsuccessfully; Schwarcz and Blackwell (1985) give a listing. In earth science application coral has been one of the most fruitful and reliable types, along with stalagmitic calcite. The predominant archaeological application, as discussed by Schwarcz (1980), has so far been to this latter material, mostly in Palaeolithic caves. Other cave possibilities are calcite encrustations on skeletal fragments, calcite infilling in bone and breccia and other localized accumulations, e.g. on cave walls. In all of these the required size of sample is a severe limitation unless measurement by mass spectrometry is available.

On open-air sites the most important sample type is the calcium carbonate precipitated by spring waters as they emerge from the ground or after they have travelled some distance from the point of emergence. Several important European Palaeolithic sites have been excavated in such spring-deposited carbonate, such as the Vértesszöllös, Tata, Ehringsdorf and Bilzingsleben (see Fig. 7.6). Among other sample types of possible archaeological relevance are carbonates deposited in lake sediment, concretions in arid soil, caliche and calcrete.

Speleothems and travertine

In European usage *travertine* refers to spring deposits and *speleothems* to those in caves; in North American usage either type tends to be called travertine. Speleothems take the form of stalactites (from the roof), stalagmites (from the floor), or flowstone sheets on the floor of the cave. Sometimes there is a succession of 'stalagmitic flows' between which there are layers of detrital sediment containing archaeological artefacts and bones; sometimes the latter are embedded in a flow. In the sediment layers there may be fragments of speleothem which can be used to give maximum ages for any accompanying artefacts and bones. Some of these fragments may be from stalactites which were cracked off the ceiling by frost action; hence their date is likely to correspond to a wet period preceding the last cold phase before the sediment was deposited. Speleothems are indicative of wet periods, i.e. interglacials and interstadials, and so the datings obtained are of palaeoclimatic significance (e.g. Schwarcz *et al.* 1982; Ivanovich, 1985; Hennig *et al.* 1985; Gordon *et al.* 1989).

Criteria for selection of samples from archaeological sites have been comprehensively discussed by Schwarcz (1980:10), who, after reviewing stratigraphic criteria, notes that 'the ideal material . . . [consists] . . . of coarse crystals . . . intimately intergrown, with no intergranular porosity or permeability, and free of any impurities such as detritus, organic matter, bone fragments, etc.', and then goes on to list the ways in which actual deposits fail to meet these requirements. A review of some applications has been given by the same author; the initial contribution made by this technique to the chronology of European hominid development has been put in context by Cooke *et al.* (1982). Extensive application continues, often in parallel with electron spin resonance dating (see Fig. 7.6 for instance).

Uranium–series dating has the strong advantage over electron spin resonance (and thermoluminescence) that it does not have any dependence on environmental radiation, the reliable assessment of which is difficult in the heterogeneous surroundings of most calcite deposits. However, except when measurement is by mass spectrometry, the amount of sample required (typically around 50 g, more if the uranium content is low, and vice versa) may be restrictive. Stalagmites grow over long periods and it may be desirable to use only the outer layers; note also (see section 7.4.1) the advantage of electron spin resonance in being able to deal with samples of about 1 g when there is calcite encrustation directly attached to a skull – arguments about the relationship of the skull to the flowstone stratigraphy are then avoided.

In practice the available samples may have characteristics that make them non-ideal for one or other of the techniques and trial of both is the prudent policy. If apparently reliable answers are obtained from both then a further indicator of credibility is the concordance (or otherwise) of the two results – because the various possible interferences are likely to affect the two to different degrees. With a succession of flowstone sheets a further test is provided by stratigraphy.

Bone and teeth

The uranium concentration in living bone is less than 0.1 ppm, but in fossil bone it is in the range 1–1000 ppm. If it is assumed that the uranium is taken up from ground water rapidly after burial, but that thorium, being insoluble, is not available, then dates may be evaluated on the same basis as for stalagmitic calcite (e.g. Szabo *et al.* 1969; Szabo and Collins 1975; Rae and Ivanovich 1986; Rae *et al.* 1987a, 1987b; Chen and Yuan 1988). However, if the uptake was gradual then there will be less thorium-230 in the bone than if the final concentration of uranium had been present throughout burial – and if the latter is assumed to have been the case the age obtained will be too recent. The uptake is conditioned by the chemical nature of the burial environment; due to changes in this there may have been periods when some of the uranium was leached out and since it is unlikely to have been accompanied by the less soluble thorium, such leaching will tend to make the calculated age erroneously old. The porous structure of bone makes it easily vulnerable to such open system effects, with consequent risk of unreliability in the answers obtained. Apart from leaching effects, there may also be chemical degradation of bone; this is liable to go on for many millennia, as will be mentioned again in section 7.4.3.

The same uptake uncertainties, etc. apply to tooth dentine; nevertheless Chen and Yan (1988) have obtained encouraging results for Chinese palaeolithic sites using dentine, and bone also in a few cases. In this work protactinium-231 was used as evidence in respect of closed/open-system situations, and where the former was indicated there was acceptable concordance with radiocarbon. It was noted that the closed-system situation was usually found for samples from caves where water seepage had ceased long ago, or where the teeth/bones were encased in impermeable carbonate; on the other hand, for many other sites, particularly open-air sites on river terraces, the samples exhibited discordance between the thorium and protactinium ages.

Studies of trace element distribution in bone cross-sections usually show a high degree of inhomogeneity (see Fig. 7.4 for example; also Matsu'ura 1978; Henderson *et al.* 1983; Williams and Potts 1988). In the absence of leaching during burial there is often a high concentration on the outer surface – as is the case in Fig. 7.4. On the basis that this uranium was taken up and fixed early in the burial period, and that thereafter no further uptake occurred in this layer, it might be expected that by restricting material for dating to the outer layer reliable results should be obtained. Initial results using the outer 0.5 mm for small bones and the outer 5 mm for large ones were highly encouraging (Rae and Ivanovich, 1986; Rae *et al.* 1987a, 1987b), particularly when burial had been in a relatively dry, stable environment; however, subsequent investigations have so far indicated that reliable results are not the general rule, particularly for deposits at open sites (Rae *et al.* 1989).

The success obtained in the ESR dating of tooth enamel, more compact than dentine, suggests that uranium-series dating might be reliable there also; the micro sampling made possible using mass spectrometry gives access to this.

Coral and mollusc shells

Although coral is not often of archaeological relevance, mention of it is appropriate because it is the material *par excellence* for uranium-series dating, it being a reliable closed system as long as material in which recrystallization from aragonite to calcite has occurred is avoided: living coral incorporates about 3 ppm of uranium and there is no change with age; a negligible amount of thorium-230 is incorporated; the initial (uranium-234/uranium-238) ratio is known for sea-water and hence the method based on that ratio is applicable also (see section 5.2.6). Uranium-series dating of coral reefs has been an important tool in the study of sea-level changes associated (in part) with variations in global ice volume such as discussed in section 2.3; the high-precision results obtainable with mass spectrometry are particularly important here (e.g. Edwards *et al.* 1987).

On the other hand, mollusc shells, like bone, are an open system and despite attempts at correction for uranium movement ages obtained are of questionable reliability, more so for aragonitic shells than for the calcite variety – which are less subject to uranium uptake; the uranium content of fossil aragonitic shells ranges from 0.1 to 50 ppm, whereas the content in living examples is an order of magnitude lower.

5.2.6 VARIANTS: IONIUM DATING; URANIUM-234; LEAD-210

There are a variety of other ways in which age information can be obtained from the uranium series, of which three are mentioned below; among publications dealing with this aspect are those by Broecker and Bender (1972), Ivanovich and Harmon (1982) and Schwarcz and Blackwell (1985).

Ionium dating. In earlier terminology thorium-230 was known as *ionium* and this name used to be associated with a technique for dating ocean sediment. Because of its low solubility thorium tends to be precipitated from sea-water whereas the parent uranium remains dissolved. Hence in the sediment there is thorium-230 and being 'unsupported' it decays according to its 75,400-year half-life; thus the ratio of thorium-230 to the long-lived thorium-232 (also precipitated) decreases with depth into the sediment and is a measure of the time that has elapsed since deposition.

Uranium-234. In well-mixed ocean water the activity ratio between this daughter and parent uranium-238 is close to 1.14/1; this is also the ratio in living corals but subsequently there is a gradual change to the equilibrium value of unity; this allows dating in the range 50,000–1.5 million years, but unfortunately the material concerned is rarely of archaeological significance.

Lead-210. This radioisotope, half-life 22 years, can be used in the age range 1–400 years for the dating of sediments; it has also been used in the authentication of oil paintings (Keisch 1968).

5.3 FISSION-TRACK DATING

The preceding techniques are radiometric in the strict sense of the word, i.e. the dating clock is based on the build-up of a daughter product, as with potassium–argon and uranium series, or the gradual disappearance of a radioactive parent, as with radiocarbon. In this section and the next two chapters we turn to techniques in which the dating clock is based on the cumulative effect of nuclear radiation on crystal structure.

As with potassium–argon the main involvement of fission-track dating in archaeology has been through application to volcanic material with which hominid remains have been associated; however, there has also been some direct application to archaeological objects (see Wagner 1978). Geological use was initiated in the early 1960s and a comprehensive account has been given by the researchers concerned (Fleischer *et al.* 1975); there are a number of later reviews (e.g. Naeser and Naeser 1984).

5.3.1. BASIS

When uranium-238, the parent of the major series in natural uranium (see Appendix A), undergoes spontaneous radioactive decay there is a small probability that instead of emitting an alpha particle, its nucleus will split into two roughly equal smaller nuclei. These fission fragments recoil from each other and for uranium atoms located in a number of minerals (e.g. zircon) and glasses(e.g. obsidian) the fragments cause substantial disruption in the structure of the mineral (or glass), leaving tracks that are around 0.01 mm long. These damage tracks can be made visible under the microscope by prior etching with an appropriate chemical reagent, the damaged regions being less resistant to attack; the etching also reveals other imperfections in the structure but these are distinguishable.

Heating anneals the tracks and it is such an event in antiquity that sets the clock to zero; for zircon an hour at around 800 °C is required, but for obsidian a lower temperature is sufficient. Thereafter the number of tracks regrows with time and hence can be used for dating that heating event. Obviously it is also necessary to know the amount of uranium present and the rate at which its atoms undergo spontaneous fission, which like other forms of radioactive decay is an immutable process totally uninfluenced by temperature or other environmental conditions.

Fission tracks can be observed in upwards of 100 minerals and glasses but only a few are suitable for dating, of which zircon is the one used routinely; other minerals include mica, sphene and apatite, though attempts to date the apatite component of bones and teeth have not so far been successful. Obsidian, which is a volcanic glass, was specifically mentioned above because it has been used in direct archaeological application (see section 5.3.4).

5.3.2 MEASUREMENT

The basic requirements for fission-track dating are chemical facilities, an optical microscope (with magnification in the range of ×500 to ×2500) and a nuclear reactor. Hence, given access to the latter the outlay is small; however, experience in observation and understanding in interpretation are as critically important as in other techniques, if not more so.

The basis of age evaluation is a comparison of the number of tracks per cm^2 found in the sample, ρ_s, with the number of extra tracks, per cm^2, ρ_i, induced by exposure in a nuclear reactor.[4] The former are the result of spontaneous fission of uranium-238 during antiquity and the latter are essentially a measure of the natural uranium in the sample; hence the ratio (ρ_s/ρ_i) is proportional to the time that has elapsed since the sample was last heated. Derivation of an age in years can be achieved either through knowledge of relevant nuclear data[5] or by simultaneous measurement of a known-age standard (or a substandard calibrated against it).

The sample is prepared for track counting by embedding in resin, followed by polishing and etching; a reagent such as sodium hydroxide is used for zircon, and hydrofluoric acid for obsidian. As may be imagined, counting the tracks is tedious and a track density of 100 per cm² is the routine lower limit. With volcanic glasses care is necessary to avoid counting gas bubbles and other irregularities.

Fading

Particularly with glass there is some loss of tracks with time and even if correction is made the age obtained is liable to be a minimum estimate. When fading has occurred the tracks remaining are smaller than fresh tracks and it is possible to relate the percentage that have disappeared to the diminution in size.

Alternatively the *plateau correction technique* is used. There is a range of stabilities in freshly created tracks and those of poor stability are of course the ones that fade; they are also the ones that disappear first if the sample is subjected to thermal annealing at successively higher temperatures, or at a fixed temperature for successively longer times. Thus the sample is split into two portions, the 'natural' track density, ρ_s, being measured in one, and the extra track density, ρ_i, due to nuclear reactor exposure being measured in the other; then both portions are subjected to progressive annealing and the ratio (ρ_s/ρ_i) plotted against temperature, or time. If the ratio gradually rises to a constant value then this is indicative that at the onset of this plateau the annealing has been sufficient to remove the same percentage of tracks from the irradiated portion as faded from the 'natural' portion during antiquity; hence the plateau value of (ρ_s/ρ_i) gives the corrected age.

A more stringent variant of the plateau method is to accept the plateau value only if the size distributions of ρ_s and ρ_i have become the same (e.g. Westgate 1988).

5.3.3 AGE RANGE; ERROR LIMITS

Though there are some samples for which fading gives an upper limit to the attainable age it is the lower limit that is restrictive as far as archaeology is concerned, simply due to sparsity of tracks. Taking 100 tracks per cm² as the routine lower limit to what is measurable, the minimum age attainable with a sample having a uranium content of 5 ppm is 20,000 years.[6] The uranium content of obsidian usually lies in the range 1–10 ppm, and hence in order to use the technique in later times than palaeolithic it is necessary for the operator to have enough patience to count much lower track densities than 100 per cm². This is done by the procedure of repeated grinding and etching, thereby exposing fresh areas for counting. The classic example of this is the dating of an obsidian knife-blade, which was known to have been heated in antiquity because of its distorted shape; altogether 36 fresh surfaces were counted yielding only a total of 17 tracks in 5.6 cm² of effective surface and giving an age of 3700 (±900) years (Fleischer *et al.* 1965); by a similar procedure an age as young as 520 (±110) years has been obtained, for glass glaze on a bowl fragment (Watanabe and Suzuki 1969). Thus the lower limit is essentially dependent on the enthusiasm of the operator, though of course uncertainty in identification is also a factor.

For zircon the uranium content is in the range 100–1000 ppm and the corresponding lower limit ages are 1000–100 years. Using zircon grains extracted from hearths and pottery, fission track ages in the range 700–2300 years have been reported (Nishimura 1971; see also Wagner and Reimer 1972).

Certain nineteenth- and early-twentieth-century glasses – to which uranium was added as a colourant – have uranium contents as high as a few per cent, and dating of several of these, for which the year of manufacture was known, has given a striking demonstration of the validity of the method (see Brill 1964). For a 1% content the limit of about 100 tracks per cm² is reached in only 10 years.

As with all methods based on radioactivity a limit to the precision attainable is set by random fluctuations in the decay process. If 100 tracks are counted then the date can never be more precise than ±10% of the age. However, there are usually other uncertainties that are dominant, such as that associated with the fading correction. Also, because the rate at which spontaneous fission occurs is very low it is difficult to measure accurately and this is a limitation if the method is regarded as a true absolute technique (i.e. independent of other dating methods); however, it is usual to side-step this uncertainty by means of a known-age standard.

5.3.4 ARCHAEOLOGICAL APPLICATION

Various applications have already been mentioned in section 5.3.3. Another has been the dating of obsidian flakes in Ecuador (Miller and Wagner 1981); whereas several flakes gave ages, after correction for fading, of the order of 2 million years, some gave only 2000 years – indicative of heating at the time of active obsidian flake production on the site. This illustrates the need for a heating event that is associated with the archaeology, and uncertainty about this association may account for the paucity of direct applications to archaeological artefacts, another factor being the tediousness of the counting procedure.

Indirectly, as with potassium–argon, there has been an important contribution to hominid chronology through the dating of volcanic minerals from layers in stratigraphic association. An early example was concerned with Olduvai Man (Fleischer 1965); others include dating of the Hadar formation in Ethiopia (Aronson *et al.* 1977), of the Zhoukoutien Man site in China (Guo *et al.* 1980), of the Hueyatlaco archaeological site in

Mexico (Steen-Mcintyre *et al.* 1981), of the KBS Tuff in Kenya (Gleadow 1980), and of 3.8–4.0-million-year-old sediments in Ethiopia (Hall *et al.* 1984) as mentioned in section 5.1.4. As with laser dating of single grains (section 5.1.2) the technique has the strong advantage of utilizing only a few grains thereby minimizing contamination risks.

Provenance studies
Identification of the source of obsidian is important in mapping neolithic trade routes, and geological age is one of several characteristics that have been used in this (e.g. Durrani *et al.* 1971; Bigazzi and Bonnadonna 1973).

5.3.5 ALPHA-RECOIL TRACKS
A severe limitation in application of fission-track dating to archaeology is the low rate at which fission occurs – so that there are usually too few tracks to get a date. Emission of alpha particles is many orders of magnitude more frequent and these too leave a track, as has been observed in geological samples of mica (Huang and Walker 1967); however, the tracks are very much shorter and consequently rather difficult to identify with reliability. In a preliminary investigation using mica extracted from pottery, hearths and burnt stones of the American South-west, Garrison *et al.* (1978) observed that the track density increased linearly with time elapsed since firing, absolute dating not being attempted.

NOTES

1. This is the value recommended by the International Subcommission on Geochronology (Steiger and Jäger 1977); for some earlier results a value lower by 2.7% was used. See also Appendix, Section A.2.
2. In the atmosphere the ratio of argon-40 to argon-36 is 296 : 1. Since argon-36 is present only because of atmospheric contamination, the amount of contaminating argon-40 is equal to 296 times the amount of argon-36. The contaminating argon-40 is referred to as *atmospheric argon-40* in contrast to the sample-generated *radiogenic argon-40*, the latter being denoted by Ar*. Correction for atmospheric argon can also be made in the argon–argon technique, though it is more complex because in this case there is production of argon-36 from calcium during exposure in the nuclear reactor; correction then involves measurement of argon-37, which is produced likewise (Hall and York 1984).
3. The growth in Fig. 5.3 follows the equation

$$r = \text{(activity ratio)} = 1 - \exp(-\lambda t) \tag{8.1}$$

where t is the age in kiloyears and $\lambda = (0.693/75.4)$ per kiloyear
In practice the measured activity ratio, r', between uranium-238 and uranium-234 is not equal to unity and the correct equation is then

$$r = r' \{1 - \exp(-\lambda t)\} + \left(\frac{\lambda}{\lambda - \lambda'}\right)(1 - r')\{1 - \exp(\lambda' - \lambda)t\}$$

$$(8.2)$$

where $\lambda' = (0.693/245)$ per kiloyear, the half-life of uranium-234 being 245 kiloyears.

4. For obsidian and other glasses ρ_s and ρ_i are measured using separate portions of the sample; this is the *population method*. For zircon, because of non-uniformity in uranium content, it is necessary to make an implicit measurement of ρ_i using the same portion as used for ρ_s; this is done by means of the external detector method (see Naeser and Naeser, 1984). Measurement of ρ_i after removal of ρ_s by annealing is unreliable because of associated changes in characteristics.

5. For samples in which the track density is far from saturation,

$$\text{Age} = \left(\frac{\rho_s}{\rho_i}\right)\left(\frac{\phi I \sigma}{\lambda}\right) \qquad (1.3)$$

where ρ_s is the track density that has accumulated from spontaneous fission during antiquity, ρ_i is the track density resulting from induced fission due to a thermal neutron fluence ϕ, σ is the fission cross-section, and I is the isotopic ratio of uranium-235 to uranium-238; whereas the latter is responsible for the tracks from spontaneous fission, the former contributes the tracks due to induced fission. Reliable measurement of λ is difficult and there has been appreciable variation in the value used by different authors for dating; one approach is by counting the track density in high-uranium glass of known date of manufacture.

6. Based on the rule of thumb (Wagner, 1976) that the product of (% of uranium) × (age) must exceed 10. There is also an upper limit to the track density that can be counted – reached when this product exceeds 100,000 – but this is only relevant in geological application.

REFERENCES

Aronson, J. L., Schmitt, T. J., Walker, R. C., Baieb, M., Tiercelin, J. J., Johanson, D. C., Naeser. C. W. and Nairn, A. E. M. (1977) New geochronology and paleomagnetic data for the hominid-bearing Hadar Formation of Ethiopia, *Nature* **267**, 323–7.

Bigazzi, G. and Bonnadonna, F. (1973) Fission track dating of the obsidian of Lipari Island (Italy), **Nature** 242, 322–3.

Bogaard, P., Hall, C. M., Schmincke, H. -U. and York, D. (1987) [40]Ar/[39]Ar laser dating of single grains: ages of Quaternary tephra from the east Eifel volcanic field, FRG, *Geophys. Res. Lett.* **14**, 1211–14.

Brill, R. H. (1964) Applications of fission-track dating to historic and prehistoric glasses, *Archaeometry* 7, 51–7.

Broecker, W. S. and Bender M. L. (1972) Age determinations on marine strandlines, in *Calibration of Hominoid Evolution* (eds W. W. Bishop and J. A. Miller), Scottish Academic Press, Edinburgh and University of Toronto Academic Press, pp. 19–36.

Chen, T. and Yuan, S. (1988) Uranium-series dating of bones and teeth from Chinese palaeolithic sites, *Archaeometry* 30, 59–76.

Cooke, J., Stringer, A., Currant, A., Schwarcz, H. P. and Wintle, A. (1982) A review of the chronology of the European middle Pleistocene hominid record, in *Yearbook of Physical Anthropology* 25, 19–65.

Curtis, G. H. (1975) Improvements in potassium–argon dating, *World Archaeology* 7, 198–209.

Curtis, G. H. and Hay, R. L. (1972) Further geological studies and potassium–argon dating at Olduvai Gorge and Ngorongoro Crater, in *Calibration of Hominid Evolution*, (eds W. W. Bishop and J. A. Miller), Scottish Academic Press, Edinburgh, pp. 289–302.

Durrani, S. A., Khan, H. A., Taj, M. and Renfrew, C. (1971) Obsidian source identifications by fission track analysis, *Nature* 233, 242–5.

Edwards, R. L., Chen, J. H. and Wasserburg, G. J. (1987) Precise timing of the last interglacial period from mass spectrometric determination of thorium-230 in corals, *Science* 236, 1547–53.

Evernden, J. F. and Curtis, G. H. (1965) The potassium–argon dating of Late Cenozoic rocks in East Africa and Italy, *Current Anthropol.* 6, 343–85.

Faure, G. (1986) *Principles of Isotope Geology* (2nd edn), Wiley, New York.

Féraud, G., York, D., Hall, C. M., Goren, N. and Schwarcz, H. P. (1983) $^{40}Ar/^{39}Ar$ age limit for an Acheulian site in Israel, *Nature* 304, 263–5.

Fitch, F. J. and Miller, J. A. (1970) Radioisotope age determination of Lake Rudolf artefact site, *Nature* 226, 226–8.

Fleischer, R. L. (1965) Fission-track dating of Bed I, Olduvai Gorge, *Science* 148, 72–4.

Fleischer, R. L., Price, P. B., Walker, R. M. and Leakey, L. S. B. (1965) Fission track dating of a mesolithic knife, *Nature* 205, 1138.

Fleischer, R. L., Price, P. B. and Walker, R. M. (1975) *Nuclear Tracks in Solids:Principles and Applications*, University of California Press, Berkeley 605 pp.

Garrison, E. G., McGimsey, C. R. and Zinke, O. H. (1978) Alpha-recoil tracks in archaeological ceramic dating, *Archaeometry* 20, 39–46.

Gillott, P. Y., Chiesa, S., Pasquare, G. and Vezzoli, L. (1982) <30,000-yr K/Ar dating of the volcano-tectonic horst of the Isle of Ischia, Gulf of Naples, *Nature* 299, 242–4.

Gillot, P. -Y. and Cornette, Y. (1986) The Cassignol technique for potassium–argon dating, precision and accuracy; examples from the Late Pleistocene to Recent volcanics from southern Italy, *Chemical Geology* 59, 205–22.

Gleadow, A. J. W. (1980) Fission track age of the KBS tuff and associated hominid remains in northern Kenya, *Nature* 284, 225–30.

Gordon, D., Smart, P. L., Ford, D. C., Andrews, J. N., Atkinson, T. C., Roe, P. J. and Christopher, N. S. J. (1989) The dating of Late Pleistocene interglacial and interstadial periods in the United Kingdom from speleothem growth frequency, *Quaternary Research* 31, 1–13.

Guo, S. L. *et al.* (1980) Fission track dating at Zhoukoutien, *Kexue Tongbao* 25, 384 (in Chinese).

Hall, C. M. and York, D. (1984) The applicability of dating to young volcanics, in *Quaternary Dating Methods*, (ed. W. C. Mahaney), Elsevier, Amsterdam, Oxford, New York, Tokyo pp. 67–74.

Hall, C. M., Walter, R. C., Westgate, J. A. and York, D. (1984) Geochronology, stratigraphy and geochemistry of Cindery Tuff in Pliocene hominid-bearing sediments of the Middle Awash, Ethiopia, *Nature* **308**, 26–31.

Henderson, P., Marlow, C. A., Molleson, T. I. and Williams, C. T. (1983) Patterns of chemical change during bone fossilization, *Nature* **306**, 358–60.

Hennig, G., Grün, R. and Brunnacker, K. (1985) Speleothems, travertines and palaeoclimates, *Quaternary Research* **20**, 1–29.

Huang, W. H. and Walker, R. M. (1967) Fossil alpha particle recoil tracks, *Science* **155**, 1103–4.

Ivanovich, M. (1985) Application of uranium series dating to palaeoclimatic studies *Modern Geology* **9**, 249–60.

Ivanovich, M. and Harmon, R. S. (eds) (1982) *Uranium Series Disequilibrium: Applications to Environmental Problems*, Oxford University Press.

Johanson, D. C., Masao, F. T., Eck, G. G., White, T. D., Walter, R. D., Kimbel, W. H., Asfaw, B., Manega, P., Ndessokia, P. and Suwa, G. (1987) New partial skeleton of Homo habilis from Olduvai Gorge, Tanzania, *Nature* **327**, 205–9.

Keisch, B. (1968) Dating works of art through their natural radioactivity: improvements and applications, *Science* **160**, 413–16.

Layer, P. W., Hall, C. M. and York, D. (1987) The derivation of $^{40}Ar/^{39}Ar$ age spectra of single grains of hornblende and biotite by laser step heating, *Geophys. Res. Lett.* **14**, 757–60.

McDougall, I. (1981) $^{40}Ar/^{39}Ar$ age spectra from the KBS Tuff, Koobi Fora Formation, *Nature* **294**, 120–4.

McDougall, I., Maier, R., Sutherland-Hawkes, P. and Gleadow, A. J. W. (1980) K–Ar age estimate for the KBS tuff, East Turkana, Kenya, *Nature* **284**, 230–4.

McDougall, I., Davies, T., Maier, R. and Rudowski, R. (1985) Age of the Okote Tuff complex at Koobi Fora, Kenya, *Nature* **316**, 792–4.

Matsu'ura, S. (1978) Uranium analysis of fossil bones using fission track techniques and its application to archaeological science, *Quat. Res.* (Japan) **17**, 95–104.

Miller, D. S. and Wagner, G. A. (1981) Fission-track ages applied to obsidian artefacts from South America using the plateau-annealing and the track-size age-correction techniques, *Nuclear Tracks* **5**, 147–55.

Naeser, N. D. and Naeser, C. W. (1984) Fission-track dating, in *Quaternary Dating Methods* (ed. W. C. Mahaney), Elsevier, Amsterdam, Oxford, New York, Tokyo pp. 87–100.

Nishimura, S. (1971) Fission track dating of archaeological materials from Japan, *Nature* **230**, 242–3.

Rae, A. M. and Ivanovich, M. (1986) *Applied Geochemistry* **1**, 419–26.

Rae, A. M., Ivanovich, M., Green, H. S., Head, M. J. and Kimber, R. W. L. (1987a) A comparative study of bones from Little Hoyle Cave, South Wales, UK, *Journ. Archaeol. Sci.* **14** , 243–50.

Rae, A. M., Ivanovich, M. and Schwarcz, H. P. (1987b) Absolute dating by uranium series disequilibrium of bones from the cave of La Chaise-de-Vouthon (Charente), *Earth Surface Processes and Land Forms* **12**, 543–50.

Rae, A. M., Hedges, R. E. M. and Ivanovich, M. (1989) *Applied Geochemistry* **4**(3), Further studies in uranium series dating of fossil bone, in press.

Reynolds, T. E. G. (1985) The Early Palaeolithic of Japan, *Antiquity* **59**, 93–6.

Schwarcz, H. P. (1980) Absolute age determination of archaeological sites by uranium series dating of travertines, *Archaeometry* **22**, 3–24.

Schwarcz H. P., Gascogne, M. and Harmon, R. S. (1982) Applications
  of U-series dating to problems of Quaternary climate, in *Uranium-series
  Disequlibrium: Applications to Environmental Problems* (eds M. Ivanovich and
  R. S. Harmon), Oxford University Press, pp. 326–50.
Schwarcz H. P. and Blackwell, B. (1985) Uranium-series disequilibrium dating,
  in *Dating Methods of Pleistocene Deposits and their Problems* (ed. N. W. Rutter)
  Geoscience Canada Reprint Series 2 pp. 9–18.
Steen-Mcintyre, V., Fryxell, R. and Malde, H. E. (1981) Geologic evidence for
  age of deposits at Hueyat Laco archaeological site, Valsequillo, Mexico, *Quat.
  Res.* 16, 1–17.
Steiger, R. H. and Jäger, E. (1977) Subcomission on geochronology: convention
  in the use of decay constants in geo- and cosmochronology, *Earth Planet. Sci.
  Lett.* 36, 359–62.
Szabo, B. J., Malde, H. E. and Irwin-Williams, C. (1969) Dilemma posed
  by uranium-series dates on archaeologically significant bones from Valsequillo,
  Puebla, Mexico, *Earth Planet, Sci. Lett.* 6, 237–44.
Szabo, B. J. and Collins, D. (1975) Ages of fossil bones from British
  interglacial sites, *Nature*, 254, 680–2.
Wagner, G. A. (1976) Radiation damage dating of rocks and artefacts,
  Endeavour 35, 3–8.
Wagner, G. A. (1978) Archaeological applications of fission-track dating,
  Nuclear Track Detection 2, 51–64.
Wagner, G. A. and Reimer, M. (1972) Dating error, *Nature* 237, 57.
Watanabe, N. and Suzuki, M. (1969) Fission track dating of archaeological
  glass materials from Japan, *Nature* 222, 1057–8.
Westgate, J. A. (1988) Isothermal plateau fission-track age of the Late Pleistocene
  Old Crow tephra, Alaska, *Geophysical Research Lett.* 15, 376–9.
Williams, C. T. and Potts, P. J. (1988) Element distribution maps in fossil
  bones, *Archaeometry* 30, 237–47.
Yokoyama, Y. and Nguyen, H. -V. (1981) Datation directe de l'Homme
  de Tautavel par la spectrometrie gamma, non destructive, du crane humain
  fossile Arago XXI, *C. R. Acad. Sci. Paris* 292, 741–4.

6 Luminescence dating

6.1 THERMOLUMINESCENCE (TL)

This technique was first developed for the dating of pottery (and other forms of baked clay – bricks and tiles, etc.), but subsequently it has been extended to types of sample that enable it to reach back well beyond the limit of radiocarbon. Burnt flint in particular is useful in this context, as also is stalagmitic calcite; these have the prospect of reaching to about half a million years, perhaps more. Another development has been to wind- and water-borne sediment, this being of substantial importance in Quaternary geology also; the event dated is the last exposure to sunlight. Burnt stones, volcanic glass and lava are also suitable, given always that the date of last heating is the relevant one for archaeology.

Although thermoluminescence (TL) has a substantially wider age range than radiocarbon it usually gives poorer precision; so when radiocarbon is available, and the samples are reliable, that technique is to be preferred. However, this advice needs qualification: first, over the last 1000 years the accuracy is comparable and over the last 300 years that of TL is far superior (due to distortion in the radiocarbon time-scale); secondly, beyond the limit of calibration (presently around 10,000 BC) radiocarbon does not give an age in calendar years and the use of truly absolute techniques, although less precise, then makes good sense.

A companion technique dealt with later in the chapter is *optical dating* (utilizing *optically stimulated luminescence* (OSL) which is primarily applicable to sediment; the term *luminescence dating* comprises the two. *Electron spin resonance* (ESR), covered in Chapter 7, is a closely allied technique. All three have the same basic mechanism for recording the passage of time: unlike radiocarbon, the observed signal increases with age.

Focusing now on TL we shall begin by describing its essential features in terms of dating pottery and then indicate the modifications appropriate for other types of sample.

6.1.1 THE PHENOMENON; THE AGE EQUATION

If a ground-up sample of ancient pottery is heated rapidly to 500 °C there is a weak emission of light, measurable by means of a sufficiently sensitive *photomultiplier* – see Fig. 6.1, curve (a). For a second heating of the same sample the emission – curve (b) – consists only of a red-hot glow. The extra light that is emitted in the first heating is TL; it comes from minerals in the pottery, principally quartz and feldspar grains, and it results from the cumulative effect of prolonged exposure to the weak flux of nuclear radiation emitted by radioactive impurities in the pottery and the surrounding burial soil. These impurities are potassium-40, thorium and uranium, at concentrations of a few parts per million; they have long half-lives (1 billion years or more) and so the radiation flux is constant over time periods relevant to archaeology.

Of course the minerals have been exposed to nuclear radiation from natural radioactivity ever since they were formed, and so when the potter took his raw clay the minerals in it carried a strong geological TL. However, the act of firing 'drained' all previous TL, thereby setting the clock to zero. From cooling onwards the archaeological TL began to accumulate at a nearly constant rate; hence the measured TL today is proportional to the age. Because TL is observed only when the sample is heated the

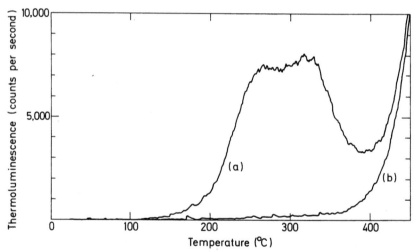

Fig. 6.1   Thermoluminescence glow-curve observed from small sample taken from a terracotta statue (measurement by D. Stoneham). Curve (a) shows the light emission observed during the first heating (at a rate of 20 °C/sec), and curve (b) the light observed during a second heating. The latter is the red-hot glow, or incandescence, that occurs whenever a sample is heated, but during the first heating there is in addition substantial emission of TL – resulting from exposure during antiquity to the weak flux of ionizing radiation emitted by natural radioactivity in the clay and soil. (From Aitken 1985.)

term *latent TL* is sometimes used when referring to the accumulation process.

The amount of TL is also proportional to the radiation flux and to the sensitivity of the minerals in acquiring TL. The former is referred to as the *annual dose* of radiation,[1] or *dose rate*, and calculated from radioactive analysis of the pottery and soil (or measured directly). The sensitivity is measured by exposing portions of the self-same sample to the radiation from a calibrated radioisotope source. In principle the age is then calculated from the basic equation

$$\text{Age} = \frac{\text{Archaeological TL}}{(\text{Annual dose}) \times (\text{TL per unit dose})} \qquad (6.1)$$

In practice there are many complications and several dozen measured quantities, rather than three, go into the calculation. A full account of these has been given elsewhere (Aitken 1985; Fleming 1979); in this chapter we shall attempt only to give some outline of the problems, enough to establish that any facile approach is likely to be unreliable.

6.1.2 THE MECHANISM RESPONSIBLE
The details of the mechanism by which TL is produced in any given mineral are not well understood, and in general it is only for crystals grown in the laboratory with strict control of impurities that these details can be elucidated. The situation is very different from that in radiocarbon dating; there the essential mechanism is the radioactive decay of the carbon–14 nucleus and this occurs at the same rate whether the sample is wood, shell or human bone. In TL dating different minerals have different mechanisms, and even for the same mineral the sensitivity of each sample must be measured individually because it will be influenced by the actual impurity content and thermal history.

However, the main features of TL dating can be discussed usefully in terms of a simple model. It is convenient to base this on the ionic crystal shown in Fig. 6.2, though it should be realized that other types of insulator, such as covalent solids and glasses, also exhibit TL; metals do not. An ionic crystal (e.g. calcium carbonate) consists of a lattice of positive and negative ions; however, there can be defects in this regular order such as those due to rapid cooling from the molten state, damage caused by nuclear radiation and the presence of impurity atoms. There are many types of defect that can occur, of which three simple ones are shown. A defect due to one of the negative ions being absent from its proper place, that is, a negative-ion vacancy, acts as an electron *trap* because the local deficit of negative charge attracts a 'free' electron if it diffuses into the vicinity. Free, or 'ionized', electrons result from the action of nuclear radiation in detaching them from their parent nuclei.

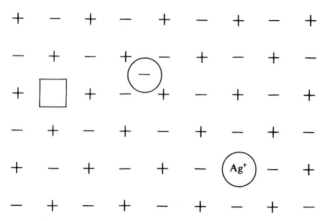

Fig. 6.2 Simple types of defect in the lattice structure of an ionic crystal. From left to right: negative-ion vacancy, negative-ion interstitial, substitutional impurity centre. (From Aitken 1985.)

On an archaeological time-scale the number of traps remains constant, but the number of electrons in them – the trap population – increases with time (being proportional to the radiation dose). Once in a trap an electron remains there until 'shaken out' by the vibrations of the crystal lattice. As the temperature is raised these vibrations get stronger, and the probability of eviction increases so rapidly that within quite a narrow temperature range the situation changes from that of the electrons being firmly trapped to that of being free to diffuse about the crystal. A variety of fates awaits a diffusing electron. It can be retrapped and re-evicted; it can be trapped at a different type of defect better able to shield it from the lattice vibrations, that is, a deeper trap; or it can recombine with an ion from which an electron has previously been detached. This recombination can be of two types – radiative (i.e. with emission of light) or non-radiative. Ions or atoms at which radiative recombination can occur are called *luminescence centres* and the light emitted is, of course, the TL. The colour of the emitted light is a characteristic of the luminescence centre – e.g. blue–violet for a silver impurity, orange for manganese.

In summary, the steps are as follows:

1. Ionization of electrons by nuclear radiation.
2. Immediate capture of some of these at traps, where they remain stored as long as the temperature is not raised.
3. Eviction from the traps due to heating during the measurement process, centuries later; eviction occurs at a temperature characteristic of each type of trap.
4. Combination, almost instantaneously, of some of these evicted electrons with luminescence centres, accompanied by emission of

light. The amount of light is proportional to the number of trapped electrons, which in turn is proportional to the amount of nuclear radiation to which the crystal has been exposed (and therefore to the time that has elapsed since the traps were last emptied).

Item (2) requires qualification. There is a finite time for which an electron remains trapped – this lifetime depending upon vulnerability to lattice vibrations of the type of trap concerned. Even at normal temperatures there is always a small probability of escape, but this may be so slight that the lifetime is millions of years; such traps are said to be 'deep' and the characteristic temperature at which rapid eviction occurs is correspondingly high – upwards of 300 °C. In any crystal there are usually several different types of trap, each with a different characteristic temperature; for the shallower ones lifetimes may be only an hour or less (with characteristic temperatures below 100 °C). Obviously, in dating it is only traps having lifetimes of a million years and upwards, roughly corresponding to characteristic temperatures of 300 °C or more, that are of interest. In ancient pottery there is usually a variety of minerals, each with a variety of traps; as a result, the TL glow-curve, such as illustrated in Fig. 6.1, is continuous, being composed of a number of components each corresponding to a particular trap type. Note that in the glow-curve of archaeological TL there is no signal below about 200 °C; this is because the lifetimes of the associated traps are too short; for a sample recently irradiated with an artificial source there would usually be a strong signal in this region.

The energy-level diagram

A convenient way to represent the TL process is shown in Fig. 6.3. A trap is characterized by the energy E which an electron must acquire from the lattice vibrations in order to escape and diffuse around the crystal; while diffusing they are described as being 'in the conduction band' and from there some of them reach luminescence centres as already mentioned in (4) above. For some minerals (feldspars and zircon, for instance) there is also the possibility of direct transitions from trap to nearby centre without entry into the conduction band. Such transitions occur for an activation energy substantially lower than E, and as a result the lifetime is much less than corresponds to E. This leakage of electrons, which occurs only for some of the traps, is termed *anomalous fading*;[2] loss from a trap having low E is *thermal fading*.

6.1.3 MEASUREMENT OF TL (see Fig. 6.4)

Although the TL exhibited by some bright geological minerals (which have been accumulating latent TL for millions of years) can be seen with the naked eye, the level of TL emitted by archaeological samples is very faint. Not only is it necessary to use a highly sensitive photomultiplier

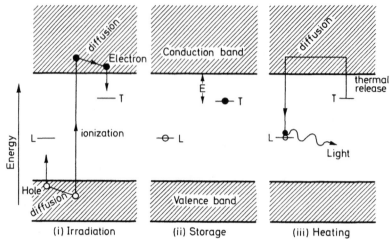

Fig. 6.3 Energy-level representation of TL process. (i) Ionization due to exposure of crystal to nuclear radiation, with trapping of electrons and 'holes' at defects, *T* and *L* respectively. (ii) Storage during antiquity; the lifetime of the electrons in the traps needs to be much longer than the age span of the sample in order that leakage is negligible. This lifetime is determined by the depth *E* of the trap below the conduction band and for dating purposes we are interested in those deep enough (~1.5 eV) for the lifetime to be the order of a million years or more. (iii) To observe TL the sample is heated and there is a certain temperature at which the thermal vibrations of the crystal lattice causes eviction. Some of these evicted electrons reach luminescence centres and if so, light is emitted in the process of combining into those centres. Alternatively, the electron may recombine at a non-luminescence centre (a 'killer' centre) or be captured by a deeper trap. (From Aitken 1985.)

for detection but it is vital also to discriminate against two other types of light emission. The more basic of these is the red-hot glow from the sample and from the heater plate on which it is carried; this is *incandescence* and referred to in technical jargon as 'black-body' radiation. Unless colour filters are interposed in front of the photomultiplier so that only blue and violet light are transmitted this glow would completely swamp the TL signal; so by means of filters it is kept down to a level such as illustrated by curve (b) of Fig. 6.1, which is subtracted off from curve (a) in order to obtain the net signal which represents TL.

The second, known as *spurious TL*, is less basic but more insidious because of its variability, even from portion to portion of the same sample; this precludes subtracting it off. It arises from a variety of causes, e.g. from chemical change (*chemi*-TL), from grinding the pottery into powder (*piezo*- and *tribo*-TL) or merely pouring the grains in the course of preparation (*tribo*-TL). These are all *non-radiation-induced* forms of TL and as such are not dependent on age – hence the term 'spurious'.

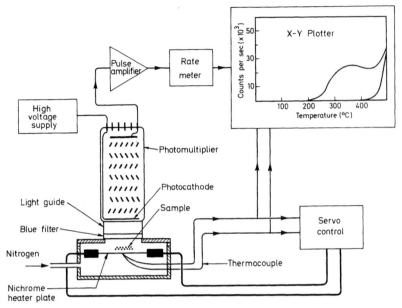

Fig. 6.4 Diagrammatic illustration of apparatus for TL measurement. (From Aitken 1985.)

Suppression is achieved primarily by filling the TL oven with an inert gas such as nitrogen, argon or helium, and ensuring that the oven contains less than a few parts per million of oxygen and water vapour (hence the need to evacuate the oven before admitting the inert gas); an additional defence against spurious TL is by pre-treatment, e.g. washing the grains in dilute acid before measurement.

Another important requirement in laboratory procedure is that as soon as processing begins, and particularly when the constituent grains are exposed, all operations must be carried out in subdued red light. Exposure to light causes most minerals to lose some of their latent TL (i.e. to be 'bleached'); sunlight, daylight and fluorescent white light are particularly effective; incandescent bulb light is not so serious.

6.1.4 THE PLATEAU TEST
The need to avoid interference by spurious TL cannot be stressed too strongly. Inattention to this aspect can result in an age of several thousand years being obtained for a sample that was fired only recently – a very serious mistake in the context of authenticity testing. Because some samples are more prone to spurious TL than others it is not adequate to rely on the practical precautions taken for suppression; it is essential also to apply the *plateau test*, illustrated in Fig. 6.5. In this test the shape

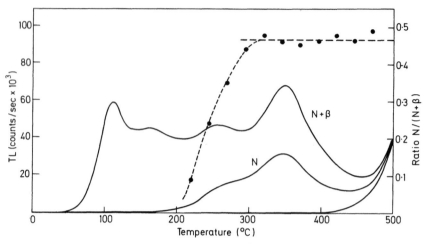

Fig. 6.5   The plateau test. Curve *N* is the 'natural' glow-curve from one
portion of the sample, and curve *N* + β is the 'natural + artificial' glow-curve
obtained from another portion to which an artificial dose of beta radiation has
been administered; the thermal signal is also shown. The dashed line represents
the ratio of the two glow-curves; the plateau level of 0.47 indicates that the dose
equivalent to the natural TL is 0.47/(1 − 0.47), i.e. 0.89 times the artificial dose
used. (From Aitken, 1985.)

of the glow-curve for a portion carrying only the archaeological TL
is compared with that for a portion carrying *artificial* TL in addition
– as a result of irradiation by means of a radioisotope source. These
shapes should match in the region, above about 300 °C, where the light
is from traps that have lifetimes substantially longer than the age of the
sample. Hence in this region the ratio of the two glow-curves, plotted
against temperature, should remain constant, i.e. give a flat plateau. For
a sample that is afflicted by spurious TL it is usually the case that the
natural glow-curve is more strongly affected than the artificial, hence
destroying the plateau – the ratio continues to increase with glow-curve
temperature, never reaching a steady level.

The plateau test was initially introduced as a stability check. Because
lifetime varies very sharply with glow-curve temperature the existence of
a plateau region shows that throughout that region the lifetimes must be
long compared to the sample's age. This then is the region from which
the TL levels must be taken for insertion into equation (6.1).

Absence of a plateau region can also be indicative that the grains
have become contaminated during preparation, e.g. by soil that was
adhering to the surface when processing began, by detergent or by a
bright mineral such as calcium fluoride (likely to be in the laboratory for
dosimetry purposes). A more fundamental reason for absence of plateau

is inadequate firing in antiquity, or no firing at all. Partial firing will have drained the TL up to a certain temperature beyond which there will be geological TL and the glow-curve ratio (i.e. geological TL/artificial TL) for this usually increases continuously with glow-curve temperature. This is because a longer electron lifetime is associated with a higher glow-curve temperature and, although it may never reach the geological age, the degree of electron leakage becomes less. For the same reason there will be no plateau from a sample which has not been fired at all. Of course the term 'geological' is being used here to signify a sample having an age of 10 million years or more; a plateau can be expected from volcanic rocks of Quaternary age.

We have dealt at some length with this aspect of the measurement process because the plateau evidence regarding reliability represents a strong advantage that TL dating has over, say, radiocarbon dating. In the latter the measurement produces a number representing the carbon-14 content of the sample. Unlike a glow-curve, a number has no structure and there is no intrinsic evidence of, say, whether or not the sample has been contaminated with extraneous carbon of a different age.

The *age plateau* is a more sophisticated version which takes into account additional subtleties of TL behaviour such as discussed in section 6.2. For the age plateau the age is calculated from the data for each glow-curve temperature.

6.2 PALAEODOSE AND ANNUAL DOSE

6.2.1 PALAEODOSE

In Fig. 6.5 the archaeological TL from one portion of the sample (often referred to as the 'natural') was compared with the TL from another portion to which a known dose of radiation had been administered in addition to the 'natural' dose. The plateau obtained, as well as indicating the temperature region over which the glow-curve shapes are the same, also gives the ratio between the two. If the artificial dose is equal to the natural dose then the ratio (natural TL/natural-plus-artificial TL) is 0.5; if it is twice the natural dose then it is 0.33, etc. In the example of Fig. 6.5 the ratio is 0.47 and the artificial dose was 10 Gy; it follows that the archaeological dose that has been received by the sample since its last firing, the *palaeodose*, is 8.9 Gy. In terms of a palaeodose the basic age equation (6.1) may be rewritten as

$$\text{Age} = \frac{\text{Palaeodose}}{\text{Annual dose}} \tag{6.2}$$

The symbol P is used to denote palaeodose; alternative names are *accrued dose, accumulated dose, archaeological dose,* all denoted by *AD*, *equivalent dose, ED, total dose, TD*. Strictly, equivalent dose should be

reserved for an evaluation based on the assumption that the growth of
TL with dose is uniform;[3] it is then denoted by Q.

6.2.2 NATURAL RADIOACTIVITY: ANNUAL DOSE

For most pottery the latent TL is produced in roughly equal proportions
by the nuclear radiations from potassium, thorium and uranium. There are
also minor contributions from rubidium and from cosmic radiation. The
isotope of potassium that is radioactive is potassium-40, which is present
in natural potassium with an atomic abundance of about 0.01%. It emits
beta particles (electrons) having an energy which allows penetration of a
few millimetres of pottery. Potassium-40 also emits gamma radiation; this
is more lightly ionizing and it penetrates soil (or pottery) to a distance of

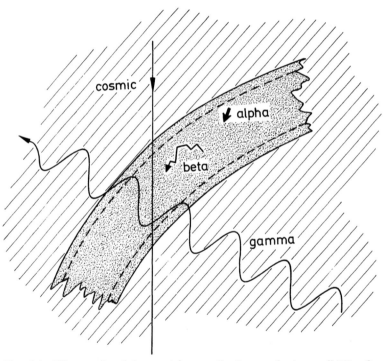

Fig. 6.6 Whereas the alpha-particle contribution to the 'natural' TL of a pottery
fragment is entirely from thorium and uranium impurities carried by the clay of
the fragment, the gamma-ray contribution is almost entirely from the surrounding
burial soil, because of the greater penetration of this type of radiation. Beta particles
have a penetration depth of a few millimetres, and as long as a 2 mm
surface layer is discarded the beta contribution is entirely of internal origin. For
'typical' pottery and soil the relative contributions (to fine grains – see Table 6.1)
are: alpha, 45%; beta, 30%; gamma, 21%; cosmic 3%. The relative contributions
from the three principal radioactive impurities are: potassium, 21%; thorium, 37%;
uranium, 39%.

about 30 cm. From thorium and uranium, in addition to beta and gamma radiation, there is alpha radiation. This consists of heavily ionizing particles with penetration ranges in pottery of between 0.01 and 0.05 mm (i.e. 10–50 μm). For more detail see the Appendix.

Because of its greater penetration the TL contribution from gamma radiation is almost entirely from radioisotopes in the soil, as illustrated in Fig. 6.6. The alpha particle contribution is entirely internal and so too the beta contribution as long as the outer 2 mm of the sample are discarded (i.e. sawn off during preparation for measurement); in this outer layer the beta dose is transitional between pottery and soil. The fuller form of equation (6.2) is

$$\text{Age} = \frac{P}{D'_\alpha + D_\beta + D_\gamma + D_c} \tag{6.3}$$

where D'_α and D_β are the internal annual dose contributions and D_γ is the external contribution along with D_c from cosmic radiation. Here D'_α is the *effective* annual dose from alpha particles; this is equal to kD_α, where D_α is the actual annual dose. The *k-value*[4] is always less than unity and usually in the range 0.1–0.3. The poor effectiveness of alpha particles is because the ionizaton density they produce is so great that the TL traps lying in the central core of their tracks get saturated; consequently a much higher proportion of the ionization energy goes to waste than in the case of beta or gamma radiation.

A simple example
Table 6.1 gives 'typical' values for the annual dose components, and assumes a typical value of 0.15 for k. Using these values for the example of Fig. 6.5 the age obtained is

$$\text{Age} = \frac{8.5}{(2.36 + 1.58 + 1.24)} \tag{6.4}$$
$$= 1.64 \, \text{ka}$$

where ka indicates *kiloan* (1000 years). Hence, for a measurement made in 1990, the corresponding date of firing is AD 350; the likely error limits for a TL date are discussed in section 6.5. This example is for the fine-grain technique of sample preparation as discussed in section 6.4.2.

Of course the radioactivities of actual samples and soils differ widely from these typical values; they are given only as a basis for discussion and a yardstick of comparison.

6.2.3 MOISTURE CONTENT
Water in the pores of pottery or in the interstices of soil absorbs part of the radiation that would otherwise reach the mineral grains responsible

Table 6.1 Annual radiation doses for 'typical' pottery and soil[a]

	Alpha	Effective alpha[b]	Beta	Gamma	Effective totals
Potassium	—	—	0.83	0.24	1.07
Rubidium	—	—	0.02	—	0.02
Thorium	7.39	1.11	0.29	0.51	1.91
Uranium	8.34	1.25	0.44	0.34	2.03
Cosmic	—	—	—	0.15	0.15
	15.73	2.36	1.58	1.24	5.18

[a] The values are quoted in gray per 1000 years (Gy/ka). The values given correspond to pottery and soil having 1% potassium, 0.005% rubidium, 10 ppm natural thorium and 3 ppm natural uranium.

[b] The effective alpha contribution assumes a value of 0.15 for k, the alpha effectiveness in inducing TL relative to the effectiveness of the beta and gamma radiation. This contribution is appropriate when the 'fine-grain' technique is being used.

for the TL; if the effect is ignored there may be appreciable underestimate of the age. Alternatively, one can think of water as decreasing the amount of radioisotope per unit mass compared to the dry situation, e.g. if the concentration of thorium measured for a dried pottery sample is 10 ppm then for an assumed wetness in the ground of 10% the corresponding concentration is 9.1 ppm. The actual calculation is more complicated,[5] but the real difficulty in making correction is that, although the degree of wetness 'as found' can be measured, it is the average wetness over the whole burial period that is relevant, and uncertainty about this is usually a limitation in reducing the error limits on the age below ±5%. Of course, for arid environments that have always been arid there is no problem; similarly for many sites in north-west Europe there is a fair degree of certainty that pottery and soil have always been fully saturated – though the possibility of interference by change in water-table is sometimes present. Estimation of how near to saturation soil and pottery will be in any given situation is a matter for a soil specialist, and also a matter of knowing various parameters such as pore-size distribution. However, too much effort in this direction is vitiated by uncertainty about the situation during the burial period, whether due to climatic change or due to natural or human interference with the site's drainage and so forth.

Although uncertainty about wetness may be an ultimate barrier to high accuracy its importance should not be overemphasized. It does lead to some widening of error limits on the age, but not usually a dramatic widening. Its effect is limited by the porosities of sample and soil concerned; for pottery having a compact fabric the porosity may be as low as 5% though for cruder pottery it may be as high as 25%; for soils, values in the range 10–40% are likely. Thus reliable correction is more important for samples such as burnt flint and calcite for which the annual dose is predominantly due to gamma radiation from the soil than for compact pottery – for which 70–80% of the annual dose is internal.

6.3   ON-SITE PROCEDURES

For a TL date of good accuracy and reliability close collaboration between archaeologist and laboratory scientist is necessary at the stage of sampling. Ideally the scientist is present on the site at this stage, and if this is not possible then the archaeologist needs to make himself fully cognizant of the requirements. Besides the obvious one that the samples must be securely related to the archaeology and the need for wetness assessment, the dominant on-site consideration concerns assessment of the gamma component of the annual dose. In Table 6.1 this 'soil gamma dose', 'external dose' or 'environmental dose' amounts to 25% of the total annual dose. For other techniques and types of sample it is more important still; thus in the quartz inclusion technique the gamma contribution may be around 50%; for burnt flint and stalagmitic calcite it may be as high as 80% as mentioned above.

Before embarking on TL dating for a particular site it is common sense to establish that there is a good case for application of this technique – which is an expensive one, the cost per date being comparable with radiocarbon. First and foremost, is the site within the age range of the available types of sample? In respect of a specific site it is good sense to arrange preliminary measurements on pilot samples (and soil) such as might be available from earlier excavations. Secondly, is the likely accuracy of TL (error limits of between ±5% and ±10% of the age) good enough to be useful? A related question is whether there are satisfactory radiocarbon samples; if so, TL is only likely to do better for sites of the last 1000 years – and, of course, increasingly for sites beyond the range of radiocarbon calibration and the limit of radiocarbon applicability.

6.3.1 ACCEPTABILITY OF CONTEXTS

The ideal situation is where the sample has been surrounded by homogeneous soil to a distance of 30 cm (this being the distance from which gamma rays can reach the sample). The gamma dose can then be evaluated by laboratory analysis of a soil sample – though on-site measurements are also advisable when the external dose is dominant. If the surroundings are not homogeneous – as for the sherd at the bottom of the pit in Fig. 6.7 – then on-site measurements by capsule or gamma spectrometer (see below) are essential; of course if laboratory analyses indicate that all

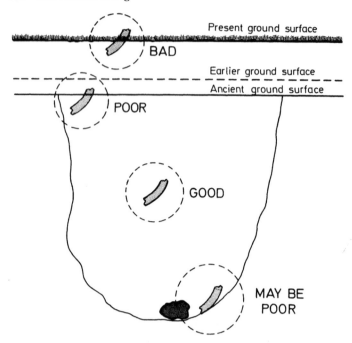

Present ground surface

BAD

Earlier ground surface

Ancient ground surface

POOR

GOOD

MAY BE
POOR

Fig. 6.7 Good and bad situations for TL samples. Gamma rays reach the sample from a distance of up to about 0.3 m; hence for a reliable assessment of the gamma contribution to the annual dose to be made the sample should be in a uniform surround of soil, such as obtains in the middle of a pit or ditch. The situation for the sample at the bottom will be poor if the subsoil, or the lump of rock, has an appreciably different level of radioactivity to that of the filling of the pit.

materials within 30 cm of the sample have the same radioactivity then effectively the surroundings are homogeneous.

Samples that have not been covered to a depth of 30 cm for the major part (say two thirds) of the burial period are in a much worse situation and good accuracy is not then possible; likewise samples that are not in their original situation. The accuracy obtainable then depends on the relative importance of the gamma contribution: if the radioactivity of the soil is much weaker than that of the sample then the uncertainty introduced into the age may be no more than ±5–10%, but for a burnt flint weak in radioactivity no worthwhile age can be obtained in such adverse circumstances. In the case of pottery the technique used is highly relevant; as mentioned above the quartz inclusion technique has a strong dependence on external dose, but for inclusions of alkali feldspar and zircon the dependence is much weaker than indicated by Table 6.1.

6.3.2 SAMPLING REQUIREMENTS

In general terms the aim should be to collect between six and twelve samples from each archaeological level; a variety of fabrics is advantageous. The *minimum* acceptable size of a sample is about 1 cm in thickness by 3 cm across. Detailed collection instructions should be obtained from the laboratory involved; these vary according to sample type and laboratory measurement procedure (for an example, see Aitken 1985). Unless on-site measurements are being made by the laboratory then it is important to collect specimens of the soil and rock type that surround each sample – up to a distance of about 30 cm – and to provide a sketch; between an egg-cupful and a mugful is required, depending on technique.

If the laboratory requires data on 'as dug' water content then samples and soil specimens should be tightly sealed in a plastic bag or other watertight container immediately on retrieval. For semi-transparent samples such as flint avoid unnecessary exposure to light, particularly direct sunlight. For sediment dating (see section 6.7.5) stringent precautions against exposure to light should be taken and for optical dating special cylinders are needed; alternatively it may be possible to collect the sediment as a lump so that the light-exposed surface can be cut off in laboratory darkness.

6.3.3 CAPSULE BURIAL

Some varieties of the mineral fluorite (calcium fluoride) have extremely high TL sensitivity, likewise some artificial *phosphors* such as calcium sulphate doped with dysprosium. The sensitivity is so high that an accurately measurable TL signal is induced by a few months' exposure to a typical soil gamma dose. Measurement in this way is termed *thermoluminescence dosimetry* (TLD); this and other applications of TLD are widely used in environmental and health hazard monitoring in connection with nuclear power and radiotherapy, etc.

For burial on an archaeological site the phosphor is contained in a capsule such as shown in Fig. 6.8. It is inserted[6] into a hole (usually made with an auger) that is at least 30 cm long and in a situation as similar as possible to that from which the sample was obtained; after insertion the hole is refilled using the soil that came out of it. It is usual for the burial period to be about a year, but there is no disadvantage in it being longer (except for the delay in finalizing the date) and if necessary it can be shorter. The advantage of a year or more is that any seasonal variations of soil wetness are averaged.

Another convenient means of insertion is by packing the capsule, which can be plastic, into a steel tube, the latter being driven into the ground to the required depth and left there until retrieval.

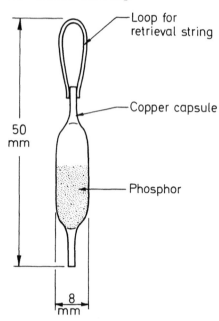

Loop for
retrieval string

Copper capsule

50
mm

Phosphor

8
mm

Fig. 6.8 Capsule for on–site burial; only gamma rays from the soil (and
also cosmic radiation) reach the phosphor because alpha and beta particles are
stopped by the 0.7 mm copper wall. Before insertion the capsule is heated to at
least 300 °C for a few minutes to set the TL of the phosphor to zero; this can be
done in a gas flame, temperature-sensitive paint being a useful indicator. (From
Aitken, 1985.)

6.3.4 THE PORTABLE GAMMA SPECTROMETER

There are often circumstances that make it impractical to leave capsules
buried on site and in such cases a gamma spectrometer can be used, the
measurement time being less than an hour (per context). Even when
capsule burial is possible it is advantageous to use the spectrometer too
if the gamma dose is likely to be dominant. The spectrometer gives
the individual components from potassium, thorium and uranium and
this may be useful data in checking for leaching effects[7] and radioactive
disequilibrium; also the spectrometer is able to exclude gamma radiation
from contaminating radioisotopes (such as caesium-137) which result from
nuclear power plant accidents.

A disadvantage compared to a capsule is the appreciable size of the
housing that carries the scintillation crystal (sodium iodide), photomultiplier
and preamplifier; this necessitates a substantially larger auger hole. In the
commercial instrument commonly used in archaeology the diameter is
64 mm, the length 27 cm and the weight 1 kg; it is connected by cable
to an electronic package weighing 5 kg and powered by eight 1.5 V dry
batteries.

The gamma scintillometer

This instrument has about the same physical size but the measurement time is much shorter, 5–10 minutes. On the other hand, it does not separate the separate components of the gamma dose, giving only the total; hence there is more risk of interference from contaminating isotopes.

6.4 LABORATORY MEASUREMENTS

6.4.1 MICRODOSIMETRY

In the baked clay matrix of pottery there are crystalline inclusions sometimes ranging in size from a few micrometres to a few millimetres; these were either present in the raw clay or added by the potter to improve refractory properties. The TL sensitivity of these inclusions is at least an order of magnitude higher than that of the clay matrix in which they are embedded and they are responsible for the major part of the TL signal. However, the quartz and feldspar inclusions have negligible amounts of thorium and uranium, or at any rate a very much lower content than the clay matrix in which they are embedded. Because alpha particles have such a short range (10–50 μm) the core of an inclusion greater than 10 μm across tends to be shielded from them; for inclusions upwards of a few hundred micrometres the dosage of alpha radiation becomes relatively unimportant and the beta and gamma components are the main part of the annual dose. Hence in large quartz inclusions the annual dose for the 'typical' pottery of Table 6.1 is nearer to 3 Gy/ka than the 5 Gy/ka obtained when the alpha-particle contribution is included – as pertains in the case of fine grains less than 10 μm across; the situation is different in large inclusions of alkali feldspar, as will be discussed in section 6.4.4. In following the argument of this paragraph the reader should keep in mind that 'dose' equals energy deposited *per unit weight*.

In order to get correct evaluation of the palaeodose corresponding to the full 5 Gy/ka, the grains of less than 10 μm must be extracted from the pottery and used for the appropriate TL measurements; this is done by the fine-grain technique of Zimmerman (1971a), now to be outlined. The alternative quartz inclusion technique of Fleming (1970) will be mentioned later, along with two other coarse-grain methods: the alkali feldspar technique of Mejdahl (1983, 1985) and zircon dating as originated by Zimmerman (1971b; Sutton and Zimmerman 1976).

6.4.2 THE FINE-GRAIN TECHNIQUE

The first step in all techniques is to remove a 2 mm layer from each surface of the fragment by sawing with a diamond-impregnated wheel. This outer layer is discarded because:

(a) the beta dosage in it is transitional between that corresponding to the sample radioactivity and that corresponding to soil radioactivity;

(b) there may be a reduced level of TL in the outer surface because of the effect of sunlight;

(c) soil contamination must be rigorously avoided because of its high level of geological TL.

From sawing onwards all operations have to be carried out in subdued red light to avoid 'bleaching' effects. The fragment is then squeezed in a vice and the rubble so produced is washed in acetone, yielding a suspension of a wide range of sizes. Grains in the size range 1–8 μm are separated by making use of the fact that the settling time is determined by diameter; the limits correspond to settling times of 20 and 2 minutes respectively, for a 6 cm column. After resuspension of these fine grains in acetone they are allowed to deposit on 1 cm diameter aluminium discs, the acetone being lost by evaporation. Usually sixteen such discs are prepared; each disc carries a few milligrams of sample, and the disc-to-disc scatter in TL reproducibility should be not more than ±5%. Such discs are a convenient way of handling the fine grains, both for artificial irradiation and for measurement of TL, the disc being placed on the heater plate: the layer of grains is remarkably robust.

Palaeodose evaluation

One group of discs is used for measurement of the natural TL, thereby obtaining a good average; the TL from another group is measured after exposures to beta particles or gamma radiation; a third group is measured after exposures to alpha particles. The derivation of the palaeodose from these measurements is illustrated in Figs 6.9 and 6.10. An important point of procedure is that there should be a delay of some weeks or even months between irradiation and measurement, or storage for a week at 100 °C, in order to allow disappearance of anomalously fading[2] components of the artificial TL; additional pre-heat procedures may also be employed.

6.4.3 RADIOACTIVITY MEASUREMENTS (FOR ANNUAL DOSE)

There are various options available, all having advantages and disadvantages. One is to determine the potassium, thorium and uranium contents by neutron activation analysis (requiring access to a nuclear reactor) and then obtain the annual dose components by reference to nuclear data tables; potassium can also be determined by flame photometry, X-ray fluorescence or atomic absorption techniques. However, most laboratories employ techniques that are more direct, namely *alpha counting* and *beta TLD*.

Alpha counting

The rubble obtained from 'vicing', after further crushing to a fine powder, is spread on a scintillation screen which is placed on top of the photomultiplier (see Fig. 6.11). Each alpha particle striking the screen produces a scintillation and this is detected by the photomultiplier, an electronic pulse being produced

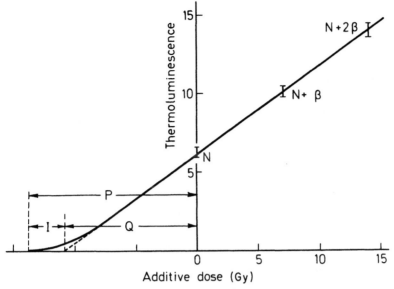

Fig. 6.9 The additive method for evaluation of the equivalent dose, Q (often referred to as *ED*). At least two levels of additive dose (which can be administered either with beta or with gamma radiation) should be used in order to check for linearity of response above the level of the natural TL. The palaeodose, *P*, that the sample has received during antiquity is usually greater than Q because of initial supralinearity of response. Evaluation of the correction, *I*, for this is as shown in Fig. 6.10. (From Aitken 1985.)

and registered by a suitable counting device. About 1 g of sample is needed to give full coverage of the screen, and for the 'typical' compositions of Table 6.1 about 1000 counts per day are obtained; the background count rate for an inert sample is about 1 count per day.

The beta and gamma components of the annual dose from thorium and uranium can also be derived from the alpha count rate but this may introduce additional uncertainty, particularly for the gamma component from uranium, and so beta TLD for the beta component and on–site evaluation for the gamma component are preferred. In any case for potassium, which has no alpha activity, these other techniques are essential, unless chemical evaluation is being used.

Beta TLD
In this case the beta component is measured directly using a TL dosimetry phosphor (usually fluorite or calcium sulphate) as in the case of the capsule technique for gamma dose. In the device shown in Fig. 6.12 about 1 g of powdered sample is needed. A storage time of a few weeks is required to obtain an accurately measurable TL signal; the tray

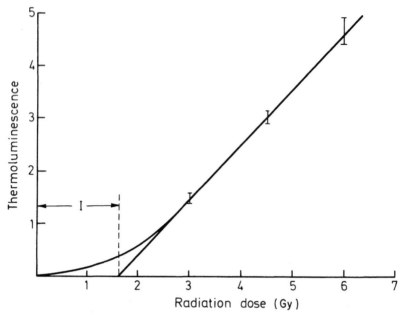

Fig. 6.10 Second-glow growth characteristic for evaluation of supralinearity correction, *I*. This is obtained with portions from which the natural TL has been drained by heating in the course of the first-glow measurement. To avoid interference by pre-dose effects a fresh portion is used for each measurement. As with first-glow measurements of Fig. 6.9 each data point is the average of several measurements. (From Aitken 1985.)

containing the phosphor is then placed directly on the heater plate of the standard TL oven.

6.4.4 INCLUSION TECHNIQUES (COARSE-GRAIN DATING)
Quartz
Quartz inclusions do not usually carry any significant amount of radioactivity, and as already noted in section 6.4.1 the beta and gamma components of the annual dose are dominant for inclusions of 100 μm and upwards. The alpha component is not negligible but it can be made so by etching the grains with concentrated hydrofluoric acid (for about an hour); this removes the outer layer of each grain. It is only this outer layer that has received alpha dosage from the clay matrix and so its removal leaves a core for which the appropriate age equation is

$$\text{Age} = \frac{P}{0.90D_\beta + D_\gamma + D_c} \tag{6.5}$$

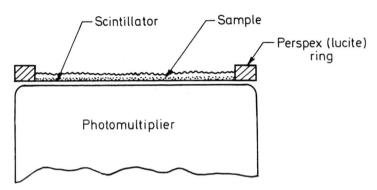

Fig. 6.11 Basic form of 'thick source' alpha counting. The scintillator consists of a monograin layer of zinc sulphide on the upper surface of a Sellotape screen which is carried by the Perspex ring. The scintillations produced in the zinc sulphide by alpha particles are detected by the photomultiplier and recorded electronically. Scintillation screens can also be purchased ready made as zinc sulphide incorporated into plastic. (From Aitken, 1985.)

The factor 0.90 allows for attenuation of the beta particles from the matrix; this is for grains in the size range 90–125 μm, the factor becoming smaller for larger grains.

Using the data of Table 6.1 we may note firstly that the total annual dose is now (1.42 + 1.24) = 2.7 Gy/ka instead of the value of 5.2 Gy/ka appropriate to fine grains; hence the expected value of the palaeodose for quartz inclusions from this sample is 4.4 Gy rather than the fine-grain

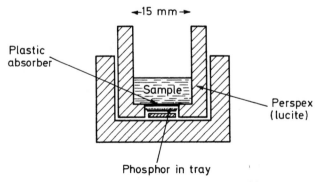

Fig. 6.12 Dosimetry unit for measurement of beta activity (Bailiff 1982). After a few weeks' exposure the TL acquired by the phosphor is measured by placing the copper tray directly on the heater plate of the standard TL oven. The plastic absorber stops alpha particles from reaching the phosphor.

Table 6.2 Dating of mineral fractions from Viking pottery fragment[a]

Mineral and grain size (mm)	Annual dose (Gy/ka)			Palaeodose (Gy)	Age (years)
	Sample (beta)	Grain (beta)	Total[b]		
Quartz					
0.3–0.5	2.98	0	3.76	3.36	894
Plagioclase					
0.5–0.8	2.69	0.28	3.75	3.57	952
Alkali–feldspar					
0.1–0.3	3.26	0.51	4.55	4.05	890
0.5–0.8	2.69	1.76	5.23	4.60	880
0.8–1.0	2.42	2.03	5.23	5.08	971
1.0–2.0	1.93	2.77	5.48	5.00	912

Average 920
(standard deviation ±40)

[a] From Mejdahl (1983).
[b] The gamma–plus–cosmic annual dose was 0.78 Gy/ka

value of 8.5 Gy. Secondly, the gamma component contributes 46% of the total, instead of 24%; hence reliable assessment of the external dose becomes substantially more important.

Grains in the required size range are obtained by sieving and the quartz fraction by appropriate mineralogical techniques. For measurement of palaeodose the portions may be carried either on 1 cm diameter stainless steel discs (lightly coated with silicone oil to ensure adherence) or in planchets.

Not all quartz is free of radioactivity and consequently it is advisable to check this by alpha counting and potassium analysis, making an appropriate correction for this intragrain contribution if necessary. This internal radioactivity is liable to be in the form of microinclusions of radioactive minerals such as monazite and zircon (Spooner and Hutton 1988).

Historically the quartz inclusion technique was the first by which absolute TL dates were obtained; it was developed by Fleming (1966, 1970) following on from work by Ichikawa (1965).

Alkali feldspar; the isochron technique
Alkali feldspar inclusions commonly have potassium contents in the range 5–10%; the upper limit is 14% which is the potassium content of orthoclase. For grains having a diameter in excess of 0.1 mm the internal beta contribution becomes increasingly important and this can be used advantageously. Table 6.2 shows an example in which from one

fragment of pottery separate dates have been obtained using alkali feldspar grains of various sizes, quartz grains, and plagioclase feldspar grains, the latter being much lower in potassium content than alkali feldspar grains. The agreement between the six dates so obtained is highly satisfactory. The separate mineral fractions are obtained by density separation using heavy liquids.

The attraction of alkali feldspar dating is that the relative importance of the external contribution to the annual dose is reduced, as also is dependence on wetness assessment. In fact use of an *isochron technique* allows the age to be calculated without knowledge of the external contribution; this is a form of *subtraction dating*.[8]

Zircon dating; zoning and autoregeneration
Grains of this mineral are present to a limited extent in most pottery, bricks and tiles. It has particular interest for TL dating because of its high content of thorium and uranium, ranging from 10 to 100 times that of typical clay. As a result the intragrain component of the annual dose is high enough for the gamma component to become almost insignificant thus very substantially weakening dependence on environmental radioactivity – and opening up the possibility of dating potsherds from excavations of long ago; dependence on wetness is made almost negligible too. The intragrain component becomes dominant for much smaller grains than in the case of feldspar because it is due to alpha particles, which have a very much shorter range.

Unfortunately it is technically rather difficult, not least because of the need to extract and identify uncracked grains as required for measurement, about fifty per potsherd, in subdued orange light (to avoid bleaching). Many grains exhibit *zoning*, that is, there are zones of high radioactivity and there are zones of high TL sensitivity; since these do not coincide alpha particles from the former do not reach the latter and as a result the palaeodose is anomalously low. For this reason the autoregeneration technique is used – called the 'natural method' by Sutton and Zimmerman (1976) who carried out the pioneer work. After measurement of the archaeological TL from a group of grains they are stored for about 6 months. The radioactivity is high enough for a just-measurable signal to regrow in this time and the age is given by

$$\text{Age} = \frac{(\text{Archaeological TL})}{(\text{Regrown TL})} \times (\text{storage time}) \qquad (6.7)$$

Correction needs to be made for the small contribution to the archaeological TL from extragrain radioactivity. Like feldspar zircon is prone to anomalous fading[2] and thermal treatment to avoid interference from this effect is necessary. The validity of the technique has been demonstrated (Templer and Smith 1988) but at the time of writing routine utilization is not yet in operation.

6.5 ACCURACY AND ERROR LIMITS; DATE CITATION; AGE RANGE

6.5.1 GENERAL

Estimation of accuracy is a particularly tedious aspect of TL dating, but it has to be faced because if a date is to be useful some realistic estimate of error limits needs to be given; inexperienced practitioners tend to be over-optimistic about accuracy and ultimately this leads to disillusion on the part of the archaeologist. A dozen or so quantities and components enter into the calculation of a date, and the error limits quoted need to reflect the combined effect of uncertainties in these, appropriately weighted.

Not all sources of inaccuracy are quantifiable, and to assess whether such sources are causing significant interference it is necessary to look at the coherence of a group of dates for samples known to be contemporary or to make comparison with other dating evidence. An unfortunate characteristic of TL dating is the variability of relevant parameters and circumstances from region to region, or even from site to site within the same region. Thus to demonstrate experimentally on a particular site that TL dating 'works' to the degree of accuracy predicted from the quantifiable uncertainties does not prove anything about its performance on a site where conditions are different; however, accumulated evidence from a wide variety of sites has established the general validity of the technique to within the predicted error limits. The formalized procedure for prediction was proposed early in the development of TL dating (Aitken and Alldred 1972; Aitken 1976) and this has been adopted by the majority of laboratories.

6.5.2 RANDOM AND SYSTEMATIC UNCERTAINTIES

In this standard procedure distinction is made between random and systematic uncertainties. The former include measurement errors and other errors likely to be different from sample to sample. The latter arise from errors that would affect all samples, such as those due to uncertainties in basic radioactive source calibrations, and errors that would affect all contemporary samples from a given site, such as those arising from uncertainty about wetness. Whereas the overall random error limit on a date can be reduced by averaging the results for a number of contemporary samples, this is not so for the systematic uncertainty.[9] Because of this the latter is the ultimate barrier to better accuracy, and at present it is difficult to see real prospects of reducing the overall error limit (at the 68% level of confidence) to below ±5% of the age, except in particularly advantageous circumstances. More typically the error limit

Table 6.3 Dating[a] of the church of Santa Maria Foris Portas, Lombardy, Italy

---

Age (years) of individual samples, with predicted overall error limits

$$1158 \pm 92 \qquad 1167 \pm 94 \qquad 1126 \pm 99 \qquad 1174 \pm 94$$
$$1168 \pm 97 \qquad 1152 \pm 90 \qquad 1127 \pm 85 \qquad 1183 \pm 99$$

Weighted average[b]	1157
Predicted random error limits	± 27
Predicted overall error limits	± 90

Citation

Aitken and Alldred system[c]   AD 828 (± 7, ± 90, Mi TL Cal(a–h))

Ancient TL system[d];   TL Context Date[e]
828 AD $\pm$ 90 (Mi 85 TL fg) Cal (a–h) tile SMFP

---

[a] The data have been taken from *Ancient TL* Date List[10] no. 1 (October 1987); report by Martini, Sibilia and Spinolo.
[b] See note 9.
[c] The first error limit quoted is the standard error, obtained by dividing the root–mean–square deviation (σ_{n-1}, on a hand calculator) of the individual ages by the square root of the number of samples; 'Mi' refers to Milan where the laboratory concerned is located; 'Cal' is the laboratory reference.
[d] '85' refers to the year in which the determination was made; 'fg'– fine grain technique; 'SMFP' – archaeological reference.
[e] For sites earlier than Neolithic the age is given instead, counting the year of determination as zero.

is in the 7–10% range; a $\pm 7\%$ error limit corresponds to ± 70 years at AD 1000, ± 210 years at 100 BC, ± 350 years at 3000 BC, etc. Note, however, that there are some types of pottery fabric which have such poor TL characteristics that a reliable date cannot be obtained.

6.5.3 DATE CITATION; PUBLICATION

Table 6.3 shows an example of citation format together with individual sample dates on which the average date for the context is based; it may be noted that the predicted overall error limits are substantially larger than the predicted random error limits, and also that the actual scatter of ages is somewhat less than might be expected from the latter – experienced TL laboratories tend to be cautious. The wider error limits should be used in comparisons between dissimilar sites or between different techniques; use of the random error limits is only justified in TL comparisons between sites for which the effect of systematic errors is likely to be the same.

Date lists are published from time to time as supplements to *Ancient TL*.[10]

6.5.4 AGE RANGE

TL dating can reach back to the earliest pottery and beyond. How much beyond depends on the mineral being used and for quartz the onset of saturation – a flattening off of the growth curve – is liable to occur around 30,000–50,000 years; for pottery of high radioactivity saturation may be reached sooner. The limit for other minerals is not well determined though it appears that for alkali feldspar there is limitation at around 500,000 years due to inadequate stability of the storage traps (Mejdahl 1988); a similar limit has been noted for stalagmitic calcite (see later for further discussion of non-pottery minerals).

At the recent end of the age range limitation is due to dimness of the true TL signal; even when the latter is measurable there is risk of spurious TL making a significant contribution to the total. In practice, pottery that is only several hundred years old, depending on level of radioactivity and TL sensitivity, may be dated using the techniques so far described. However, there is also the remarkable quartz pre-dose technique[11] and this allows measurement down to a few decades.

6.6 AUTHENTICITY TESTING

The burial environment of an art ceramic of questionable authenticity is unknown by definition and, because of the consequent uncertainty in gamma dose, the error limits on the age obtained are typically ±25%. However, this does not matter when it is a question of deciding between an age of less than 100 years and one of upwards of several hundred. On the other hand, absolute reliability is essential because the results of the test may alter the value of an object from an astronomical figure to a negligible one, and vice versa; hence several years' experience is necessary and tests must be conducted with meticulous care. Reputable art dealers have doubtful pieces tested as a matter of routine; at time of writing the usual fee for such a service is about $250. Examples of pieces tested have been discussed by Fleming (1975).

Technique
The sample is obtained by drilling a small hole, 4 mm across by 4 mm deep, in an unobtrusive location using a tungsten carbide bit; this yields about 100 mg of powder, sufficient for an abbreviated version of the fine-grain technique. For porcelain (Stoneham 1983) it is necessary to use thin 0.5 mm slices cut from a 3 mm core extracted by means of a diamond–impregnated corer; the palaeodose is evaluated by means of the pre–dose technique.[11]

It is also possible to test the authenticity of bronze heads, etc. which have a core of clay; this core will have been heated in the casting process, and a sample for TL is extracted through a convenient hole in the bronze.

Radioactivity measurements are made using alpha counting for thorium and uranium, and chemical analysis (flame photometry) for potassium. Because of the restricted amount of sample available the scintillation screen used for alpha counting has a much smaller diameter than the one shown in Fig. 6.9, typically 15 mm.

6.7 BEYOND POTTERY

6.7.1 GENERAL

Pottery was not made much before 10,000 years ago and it is earlier, in the Palaeolithic, beyond the 40,000-year range of radiocarbon that TL makes its most important contribution to archaeology. In this section we deal with burnt flint, burnt stones, volcanic lava, unburnt stalagmitic calcite and unburnt sediment. With these two latter the question arises as to how well the TL clock was set to zero at $t=0$.

This section occupies a disproportionately small fraction of the chapter, given the importance of materials other than pottery. The reason is that the basic notions of TL dating were developed for pottery; pottery can be regarded as the proving ground for TL before it set off into the unknown. Of course in considering application in the Palaeolithic, besides the materials now to be discussed there was baked clay in the form of hearths and ovenstones, and occasionally figurines; for TL these are equivalent to pottery.

6.7.2 BURNT FLINT

Flint is the specific name given to the nodules and bands of *chalcedony* that occur in chalk, but as is common it should here be taken to refer to other occurrences of chalcedony too, *i.e.*, to *chert* in general. Chalcedony is a form of quartz and similar TL properties are to be expected; in fact these are usually superior and it is an excellent material for dating. However, there are two serious limitations. First, the external gamma contribution to the annual dose is usually dominant, thereby accentuating dependence on environment. Secondly, on Middle and Lower Palaeolithic sites there is usually a paucity of flints that are sufficiently well burnt and not too small.

Flint implements (blades, scrapers, arrowheads, etc.) were in widespread use by Palaeolithic man, and in addition to the implements themselves, there remain some of the flakes, chips and cores associated with manufacture. Some of these artefacts were heated accidentally by falling into the fire, some were heated deliberately in order to improve the 'knapping' properties.

Sufficiency of heating; size

It is essential that the heating was sufficient to set the TL clock to zero by erasure of the geological TL. Depending on the duration of heating a temperature in the range 300–400 °C is required, the higher the better though excessive heating is liable to produce flint which shatters into small pieces when processing begins. The critical test for sufficiency of heating is through measurement of the TL plateau (see section 6.1.4) and as this is intrinsic to the dating procedure there is no point in considering ancillary techniques. It seems that visual appearance (reddening, vitreous lustre, potlids, crackling, etc.) is not always a reliable guide to adequacy of heating, and in collecting for dating the policy should be to collect too many rather than too few and hope that on trial in the laboratory enough will be found satisfactory; upwards of half a dozen are desirable though some dating indication can be obtained from one or two if necessary.

Even more so than with pottery it is important to saw off and discard the outer 2 mm on commencement of processing for TL measurement; the size and shape must be such that after sawing a disc remains which is at least 5 mm thick and 30 mm across. Unfortunately the bigger the flint the longer must have been the duration of heating in order to reach the necessary temperature. The requirement for removal of a 2 mm layer is accentuated for flint because it is translucent and if there has been exposure to light since excavation the TL of the surface layer is liable to have been reduced by 'bleaching', thereby yielding an age which is erroneously too recent. Also, because flint is usually much weaker in radioactivity than its burial soil it is essential to avoid the beta transition layer (see section 6.4.2).

In pyrotechnological studies of flint the actual temperature of heating is of interest for its own sake and an estimate can be made by measurement of TL sensitivity change on reheating (Valladas 1983); ESR is also powerful in this context (e.g. Robins *et al.* 1981).

Sample preparation

After sawing off the surface layer – in subdued red light as for all subsequent operations – the flint is squeezed in the jaws of a vice, as for pottery, or crushed in a hydraulic press. The resulting grains are then washed in dilute acid (hydrochloric or acetic) and the desired grain size (coarse: 90–125 μm, or fine: 1–8 μm) separated for TL measurement, being deposited on discs in the same ways as for pottery.

The brutality of the crushing is liable to give rise to spurious TL unless strict precautions are taken (see section 6.1.3). Because of the difficulty of suppressing this parasitic interference in early days of flint dating (Goksu and Fremlin 1972) the TL measurements were made on slices cut with a saw; however, with slices there are severe complications of interpretation.

Radioactivity

As with quartz from pottery the radioactivity of flint is low but by no means negligible. Typically the effective annual dose from alpha and beta radiation is in the range 0.05–1 Gy/ka, so since the soil gamma dose rate is usually between 0.5 and 1.5 Gy/ka we see there is a range of circumstances extending from the internal dose being negligible to it being dominant. If the latter then the possibility of non-uniform distribution of radioactivity needs to be considered. As in the case of zircon and calcite, if there is zoning into some regions which are high in thorium and uranium and other regions that are high in TL sensitivity the age obtained may be erroneously too recent. However, there is no evidence of non-uniformity of radioactivity – from fission-track mapping – and routine comparison of the coarse-grain palaeodose with the fine-grain palaeodose gives some check on this possibility. Unlike the case of quartz inclusions from pottery, the two should be the same if there is unformity.

However, usually the gamma dose is dominant, often being as much as 80% of the total annual dose; hence reliable assessment is critical (see section 6.3). This includes estimation of average wetness during the burial period; the possibility of radon escape and radioactive disequilibrium[7] due to leaching needs also to be considered. In the flint itself there is negligible uptake of water and because of its compact structure there is little scope for radon escape and so forth; hence, assuming continued absence of indication of non-uniformity, best accuracy is to be expected when uncommonly the internal dose is dominant.

Age range

The upper limit on the age that can be reached is set by the onset of saturation; this varies from type to type usually occurring in the region of 100–500 Gy. For an annual dose of 1 Gy/ka the corresponding age limits are 100,000–500,000 years; obviously in the circumstance of lower radioactivity there is the possibility of reaching a million years. The stability of the TL signal appears to be adequate for this; in any case the plateau test gives a check of adequate stability for the case of each sample being dated.

At the other end of the time-scale the limit is set by the intensity of the TL. Flints burnt more recently than several thousand years ago are liable to have TL that is too weak for reliable measurement; obviously for young ages high radioactivity is advantageous.

Light exposure

Although it might be expected that flint would be insufficiently transparent for there to be negligible bleaching of the signal beyond the depth of the surface layer that is discarded in sample preparation, there have been some instances of evidence to the contrary. Hence flints should be transferred to a black bag as soon as excavated, any exposure to direct sunlight being avoided. Of course flints will have been in the sun during their utilization by ancient man but at that time there was no accumulated TL to be bleached; in principle there was the possibility of light-induced TL being acquired at that stage but experimental studies indicate any such effect to be insignificant.

Application to a problem in hominid evolution

Published results at present extend from flints burnt only 2000 years ago at the Alice Boer site in Brazil (Beltrao *et al.* 1982) to flints burned about 250,000 years ago at the Lower Palaeolithic site of Bélvèdere in The Netherlands (Huxtable and Aitken 1986; Aitken *et al.* 1986).

As an illustration of the importance of the technique in Palaeolithic studies, Fig. 6.13 shows the results obtained at two cave sites in Israel (Valladas *et al.* 1987; Valladas *et al.* 1988); these are directly relevant to the question of whether in south-west Asia anatomically modern humans

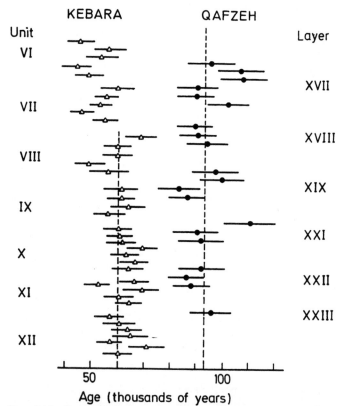

Fig. 6.13 Burnt flint dates for two caves in Israel. A Neanderthal skeleton was recently found in Unit XII of Kebara Cave and 'Proto–Cro-Magnon' remains have been found at Qafzeh throughout the layers shown. (Derived from Valladas *et al.* 1987, 1988.)

('proto–Cro–Magnons') were well installed, *c.* 100,000 years ago, long before the arrival of the Neanderthals (*Homo sapiens neanderthalensis*) or whether the former evolved from a Neanderthal population *c.* 40,000–50,000 years ago. At Kebara, Unit XII contained the skeleton of an adult Neanderthal and at Qafzeh, layers XVII–XXIII contained a number of proto–Cro–Magnon skeletons. The dating of the latter layers, to 92,000 ± 5000 years ago, indicated that these early modern humans were already present in the area during oxygen isotope Stage 5; together with the Kebara dating of about 60,000 years these results give strong support to the prior arrival of the modern humans. Electron spin resonance dating of animal tooth enamel from the relevant layer of Qafzeh is in agreement (see section 7.4.3).

6.7.3 BURNT STONES AND OTHER FIRED MATERIAL

Burnt stones
In pre-pottery cultures it was common practice to use 'pot-boilers' for cooking. Stones, or balls of clay if stones were not plentiful, were heated in a fire and then placed in the food container, which might be a skin bag or a stone trough. Because the stones tended to shatter when placed in the water reuse was not convenient; consequently burnt fragments are plentiful on such sites and often there are large mounds of them, for instance, on sites of the first millennium BC in the Orkney Islands (TL dates by Huxtable *et al.* 1976). A particularly intriguing application has been to the vitrified forts of Scotland (Sanderson *et al.* 1988; Strickertson *et al.* 1988). These hilltop ramparts were evidently fired to surprisingly high temperatures, presumably by enemy action, and had formerly been assumed to be of the first millennium *BC*; however, the spread in TL ages is from 2000 BC to AD 1000, thus stimulating substantial reappraisal of the archaeological evidence.

In burnt stones there are a variety of minerals that may be encountered and hence a corresponding variation in TL characteristics. Large grains are more likely than in pottery and hence problems of radioactive inhomogeneity are accentuated. However, in some cases this can be put to good use as is illustrated in the dating of granite stones from Scandinavian sites (Mejdahl 1983); large grains of alkali feldspar have an annual dose that is dominated by potassium within the grain thereby weakening dependence on external radioactivity and wetness – see section 6.4.4.   –

Volcanic products
Though primarily concerned with geology such material is occasionally relevant to archaeology. This may be when layers of ash or lumps of lava are associated with an occupation layer or when a volcanic explosion has caused destruction of human habitation such as at Pompeii – accurately dated by historical recording of course. An earlier example was the cataclysmic eruption of the Thera volcano on the Aegean island of Santorini which

destroyed the highly developed Minoan civilization on that island around 1750–1500 BC; however, the likely error limits, of around ±250 years, would more than encompass the conflicting alternatives indicated by other evidence (see section 2.3.6).

Lava from the Chaîne des Puys, France, has been successfully dated by Guerin and Valladas (1980) using plagioclase feldspar extracted from it; they suggest that the useful age range for this mineral is 3000–30,000 years. Quartz is not present in most lava but has been used for dating other volcanic products (Miallier *et al.* 1983); also, quartz pebbles trapped in lava have been used (Valladas and Gillot 1978). Dating of airborne volcanic ash samples in the age range 450–13,000 years has been achieved using the glass component (Berger and Huntley 1983). An indirect way of dating volcanic eruptions is by means of the soil or rock over which the molten lava has flowed and solidified; for soil, standard pottery techniques can be used (e.g. Huxtable *et al.* 1978).

Metallurgical slag; glass

Although slag is of prime importance in archaeometallurgy, successful dating has not yet been achieved, the microdosimetry being extremely complex (Elitzsch *et al.* 1983).

Glass from ancient windows and vessels has so far resisted attempts at dating also (Sanderson *et al.* 1983), one difficulty being very low TL sensitivity.

6.7.4 UNBURNT MATERIALS: CALCITE, SHELL, BONE AND TEETH

Of these, only the first (in stalagmitic form in palaeolithic caves, i.e. speleothems) is suitable because for the others decomposition occurs when the sample is heated for measurement; the technique of the next chapter, ESR, is applicable and for calcite too, with advantages over TL. For either technique one critical question in respect of any unheated material is whether at crystal formation the latent signal was zero. For both techniques it is certainly low enough to be unimportant in the age range of applicability; for TL it is essential to interpose the correct colour filter in front of the photomultiplier in order to reject light from specks of limestone, carrying geological TL, which are presumed to have been incorporated in the calcite during formation (Debenham *et al.* 1982).

The age range for dating calcite is roughly 5,000–500,000 years, the latter limit being imposed by signal instability. A difficulty with old samples is interference by recrystallization when effectively the TL clock gets reset; to some extent this can be recognized in visual inspection; this effect also upsets the other techniques for dating calcite – uranium series and ESR, though with the latter a signal indicative of recrystallization may sometimes be apparent.

With either TL or ESR there is considerable difficulty in making a reliable evaluation of the annual dose. This arises from non-uniformity of the radioactivity within a cave. The calcite is usually much weaker than the sediment present and although dosimetry capsules may be left in drilled holes close to the prospective samples it is likely that there has been dose-rate variation during the past due to movement of sediment and growth of further stalagmites. A secure circumstance in this respect is when a fragment of calcite is well buried in sediment and there is evidence that that has been the case for the lifetime of the calcite. Another advantage of this situation is that the annual dose is likely to be dominated by the gamma component, hence making irrelevant the possibility of zoning effects which are observed in some calcite samples (see Walton and Debenham 1982); if the annual dose is predominantly internal, there is risk that zoning will cause the apparent age to be erroneously too recent.

6.7.5 UNBURNT SEDIMENT

Eviction of an electron from a trap (see Fig. 6.3) can also be through the direct action of light. This is the zeroing event that allows dating of the deposition of sediment. The prime material here is *loess*, the name given to layers of silt-sized sediment (2–60 μm) which extend from north-west Europe across northern Asia to China as well as occurring in the Americas and many other parts of the world. Before deposition this sediment is carried by the wind and therefore well exposed to sunlight. After deposition the light is cut off by subsequent sediment and the TL then reaccumulates in the same way as in pottery after firing.

Although loess is primarily of geological interest it is present on many Palaeolithic sites. There are other forms of windblown (*aeolian*) deposit too, such as sand-dunes, which are relevant to archaeology. Also, sediment in glacial lakes, and on the ocean floor, can be dated in this way, the exposure to sunlight occurring while the sediment is suspended prior to deposition. The range of depositional circumstances for which exposure to light is sufficient is not well defined, and even for a long exposure an unbleachable residual remains – see Figs 6.14 and 6.15. Although the latter can be evaluated by long exposure to a solar simulator in the laboratory, direct measurement of the additional residual due to insufficient exposure is not possible; however, there are techniques[12] for circumventing this difficulty.

Quartz is more slowly bleached than feldspar, and except for the traps responsible for the 325 °C peak quartz is only bleached effectively by ultraviolet; consequently quartz in waterborne sediment is not at all well zeroed because there is poor penetration of ultraviolet through water.

Age range

Uncertainty about the residual signal is the limitation at the most recent end of the range; in round terms the limit can be taken as 5000–10,000 years, less for feldspar than for quartz. The furthest age that can be reached with quartz is limited by the onset of saturation; as with pottery dating

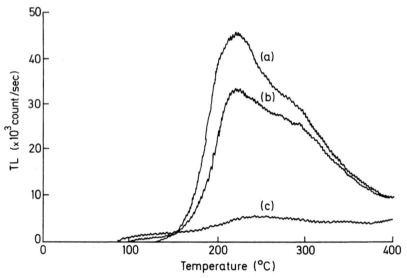

Fig. 6.14 'Bleaching' of TL due to exposure to light. Curve (a) is the natural TL; curve (b) after exposure to sunlight for 1 hour; curve (c) after exposure to simulated sunlight for 24 hours. (From Aitken, 1985.)

this depends on the quartz concerned and on the annual dose; in round terms the limit should be put at about 50,000 years, more if the annual dose is low as pertains in quartz-rich sand-dunes for instance.

Otherwise the limitation is the stability of the signal. There may be a limit of around 100,000 years for fine-grain polymineral samples

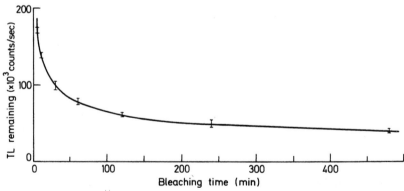

Fig. 6.15 Thermoluminescence remaining after bleaching for various times. Data are for the level of natural TL (at a glow-curve temperature of 280 °C) of fine grains of loess from the Palaeolithic site at Biache, France. Bleaching was by means of a 300 W solar simulator set at half-power, giving an irradiance that was approximately half that of natural sunlight. The unbleached level, not shown, was about four times the TL remaining after 5 minutes of bleaching (the highest point shown). (Measurements by V. Griffiths.)

(Debenham 1985), but substantial extension beyond this seems to be possible if appropriate thermal pre-treatment is used (Zöller *et al.* 1988); for coarse-grain alkali feldspar extension to around 500,000 years seems to be feasible (Mejdahl 1988).

Sampling
Strict precautions against exposure to light need to be taken during sampling. If the sediment is consolidated the sample can be obtained as a lump and then in the subdued lighting of the laboratory the exposed surfaces can be scraped away. Alternatively, the sample can be obtained by forcing a cylinder into an exposed section of sediment, having first scraped off the surface layer and then kept light on it to a minimum while the cylinder is being put in position.

In sediment dating sample and soil are one and the same, and if on-site radioactivity measurements are made with a gamma spectrometer (see section 6.3.4) these can be used to determine the alpha and beta components of the annual dose in addition to the gamma component. However, if radon escape is occurring this is not a reliable procedure and laboratory measurements in addition are advisable. Most other aspects – technique of measurement (fine-grain, inclusion, etc.) and wetness correction – are as for pottery.

6.8 OPTICAL DATING

For this the signal used is *optically stimulated luminescence* (OSL), i.e. the luminescence that follows eviction of an electron from a trap by the direct action of light; alternative terminology is *photo-stimulated luminescence* (PSL). This is the logical signal to use for dating unburnt sediment since the traps responsible for the signal are those that are easily bleachable, i.e. easily set to zero by exposure to sunlight. The technique was pioneered by Huntley *et al.* (1985) using an experimental arrangement similar to that indicated in Fig. 6.16; a critical feature is the colour filters in front of the photomultiplier which must discriminate against the green laser light used for excitation by many orders of magnitude while allowing through the blue-violet light which constitutes the luminescence signal. Subsequently it has been shown that longer wavelengths can be used for excitation, even infrared in the case of feldspars, and that a high-power xenon arc lamp can be substituted for the laser (Hütt *et al.* 1988). Use of a longer wavelength makes it easier to separate the wanted signal from the unwanted excitation light.

Suitable signals can be obtained from various minerals, including quartz, feldspar and zircon. Exposure to sunlight reduces the signal to a minute percentage of its initial value in a matter of minutes rather than the hours that are required in the case of the TL signal. Hence it is to be expected that in most circumstances of sediment deposition there will be

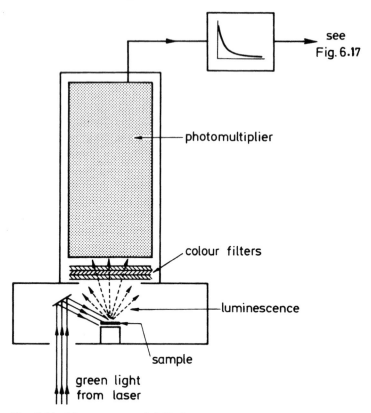

see
Fig. 6.17

photomultiplier

colour filters

luminescence

sample

green light
from laser

Fig. 6.16 Measurement of OSL for optical dating. The colour filters give severe discrimination against the green laser light and enable a rather weak blue–violet luminescence signal from the sample to be detected by the photomultiplier.

no residual to worry about and that quite short pre-depositional exposures will be acceptable. However, it seems that although the signal level may be zero at deposition there is a tendency for it to recuperate subsequently, this recuperation not being due to exposure to radiation (Aitken and Smith 1988); the effect is not strong but in some circumstances it may be the limiting factor in reaching ages of less than 1000 years; otherwise the limitation is due to the weakness of the signal. As regards the upper limit to the age range the same considerations apply as for TL dating of sediment.

Because of the rapidity of bleaching of the OSL signal meticulous precautions against exposure to light have to be taken in sampling and during mineral separation. Otherwise procedures are somewhat similar to those of TL dating, though a disadvantage of the technique is the need, following artificial irradiation, to remove unstable components of the signal; this is done by means of a 'pre-heat' before measurement, e.g. 1 hour at 160 °C.

In principle this technique can be used on burnt materials too, though it has yet to be seen whether it is advantageous in this respect. The elimination of the need to heat the sample to at least 400 °C as required for TL suggests the possibility of application to biogenic materials such as bone, teeth and shell.

Optically stimulated phosphorescence (OSP – see Fig. 6.17)
This is an allied technique in which instead of measuring the prompt luminescence occurring during exposure to the exciting light, the luminescence occurring immediately following shut-off of the latter is measured, i.e. the phosphorescence. The advantage is that it is no longer necessary to discriminate against the exciting light, so allowing greater flexibility in choice of wavelengths both for excitation and for detection. Its use for dating has been demonstrated (Wheeler 1988) but the sensitivity appears to be lower than for OSL.

Phototransferred thermoluminescence (PTTL)
Some of the electrons evicted by light from deep storage traps are retrapped in shallow traps. If the sample is then heated thermal eviction from these

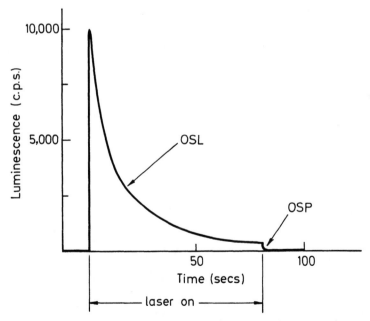

Fig. 6.17 The OSL signal decreases with continued exposure because the population of trapped electrons is rapidly depleted (i.e. the sample is 'bleached'); when the laser beam is shut off there is a weak phosphorescence (OSP) which disappears after a few seconds.

shallow traps gives rise to a TL signal – as illustrated for quartz in Fig. 6.18. This PTTL is proportional to the electron population of the deep traps and hence it can be used to evaluate the palaeodose – and age. Its feasibility for pottery dating has been demonstrated by Bowman (1979); because the signal ultimately derives only from light-sensitive traps, and because measurement is made after shut-off of the excitation light, it has the same advantages as OSP in respect of unburnt sediment (Mobbs 1979).

NOTES

1. The term *dose* refers to the ionization energy deposited per unit weight of sample; the unit of measurement is the *gray* (abbreviation Gy). It is defined as the deposition of 1 joule of energy per kilogram but it needs to be thought of on a much smaller scale than kilograms, e.g. as 1 microjoule per milligram.

   Formerly the unit used was the *rad*, defined as 100 erg per gram. One rad equals 0.01 Gy, i.e. 1 centigray (cGy). The former unit *röntgen* (R) was in respect of radiation exposure; in air exposed to 1 R of X-rays the absorbed dose is approximately 0.87 rad. The *sievert* (Sv) and *rem* are used in radiation hazard assessment; these take into

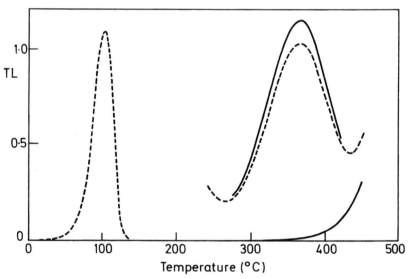

Fig. 6.18 Phototransfer in quartz. The solid curve shows the TL peak from a portion of quartz extracted from sand from a Palaeolithic dune in Morocco. The dashed curve shows the glow-curve obtained from a second portion which has been exposed to ultraviolet illumination before measurement. The 110 °C peak appears because there has been transfer of electrons from deep traps to shallow traps.

account the biological effectiveness of the radiation being measured; for an effectiveness of unity, 1 Sv = 1 Gy and 1 rem = 1 rad.

The dose received by a sample is not evaluated by direct measurement of the energy deposited but by comparison of the TL induced by the laboratory radioisotope source with the TL induced by a central calibrated source. Ultimately the calibration of this source is based on a national/international standard for which direct measurements in terms of energy deposited are made.

2. From laboratory experiments it is possible to determine the storage lifetime for electrons on the assumption that an activation energy E is needed for eviction (see Fig. 6.3). On this basis calculated lifetimes are upwards of a million years for traps responsible for the TL in the high-temperature region of the glow-curve – certainly from 350 °C but from a lower temperature for some minerals. This seems to be valid for some minerals (e.g. quartz, flint, calcite), but there are others for which some samples show loss of TL in the high-temperature region of the glow-curve even for a short delay between artificial irradiation and measurement; for some the loss is appreciable only if the delay extends to months but for others it can be serious in a matter of hours. Furthermore, in some cases the loss may be by a uniform percentage across the glow-curve and its occurrence will not then be detected by the plateau test; in other cases the percentage varies, so that the plateau is destroyed and the sample is rejected.

This *anomalous fading* has been observed in feldspar, zircon and apatite for instance (Wintle 1973) though it must be emphasized that there are some sources of these minerals (perhaps the majority) that are not afflicted in this way. The presence of grains from an afflicted source means that the date obtained is liable to be erroneously too young. This is because whereas the unstable component will have faded from the archaeological TL it will still be present in an immediately measured artificial TL. In order to guard against the effect some laboratories insert a long delay, weeks or months, between irradiation and measurement; recently it has been demonstrated (Clark and Templer 1988) that by storing at elevated temperature (e.g. 100 °C) the delay can be shortened (e.g. to a week) and a correct date obtained. The alternative practice is to test for anomalous fading by storage and to reject all samples that show evidence for it. Whatever the approach it is a phenomenon that cannot be ignored.

3. If the TL is exactly proportional to dose the sample is said to be linear. For many minerals the growth of TL in the low dose region is faster than linear; this is *supralinearity* and allowance is made by means of the supralinearity correction I which is added to Q in order to obtain P (see Fig. 6.9).

At high dose levels the growth may become *sublinear* due to onset of saturation (i.e. all available traps are filled). It is then necessary to make an exponential fit to the additive growth characteristic.

4. For experimental evaluation of alpha effectiveness it is better to use either the *a-value* or the *b-value* system, but because these are conceptually more difficult they will not be used in this book. It may be useful to note that for a given sample the *a*-value is approximately equal to the *k*-value, and that $b = 13a$.

5. In calculating the effect of moisture content on annual dose a complication is that water absorbs more than its fair share of radiation on a weight-for-weight basis and to a degree dependent on the type of radiation. The absorption coefficient for water is 50% higher than for pottery in the case of alpha radiation, 25% higher for beta radiation and 14% higher for gamma radiation. Consequently, if the dose rates have been evaluated from measurements on dry material, the actual values to be used in the age equation are given by

$$D'_\alpha = \frac{(D'_\alpha)_{dry}}{1 + 0.015FW} \tag{6.7}$$

$$D_\beta = \frac{(D_\beta)_{dry}}{1 + 0.0125FW} \tag{6.8}$$

$$D_\gamma = \frac{(D_\gamma)_{dry}}{1 + 0.0114FW_1} \tag{6.9}$$

where W refers to the porosity of the sample, W_1 to that of the soil and F to the fractional uptake of water averaged over the burial period. Porosity is defined as a percentage, i.e. (saturated weight of water/dry weight) × 100; hence the actual weight of water is $(FW/100)$ per gram of dry weight. Except in extreme conditions it is usual to assume that $F = (0.8 \pm 0.2)$. If $W = W_1 = 10\%$ this leads to a contribution of barely more than ±3% (of the age) to the age error limits of a pottery sample of typical composition, but for a sample for which the annual dose is predominantly from the soil and $W_1 = 40\%$ the wetness contribution to the error limits is liable to be more important than all others, reaching ±7% of the age. If uncertainty about past climate allows a no more precise value for F than (0.5 ± 0.5) these contributions become ±6% and ±19% respectively.

6. Before insertion the capsule is heated to above 300 °C to remove existing TL from the phosphor. On retrieval it is sent to the laboratory for measurement; on the day of retrieval another capsule – the 'travel monitor' – is set to zero by heating and then placed alongside the retrieved

capsule for transportation, which can be by mail. Measurement should be within a few weeks of retrieval, the sooner the better.

Of course for short burials the travel dose becomes relatively more important and there is greater reliance on the travel monitor. The travel dose is usually just due to the natural gamma radiation environment (comparable to the gamma level in the soil) but there is sometimes a contribution from security X-ray checks; the travel monitor copes with these too. The X-ray dose is negligible in checks which are film-safe. The cosmic ray dose during high-altitude flights is usually unimportant too.

Apart from it not being necessary, it is not practical to attempt any shielding of the capsules during transportation; to achieve substantial attenuation of the natural gamma dose the container would need to have a wall of several centimetres of lead.

7. In some soils there is downward leaching of uranium and also of potassium; this is more sensitively detected by a spectrometer than by a total dose-rate device such as a scintillometer. Also by comparison of the portable spectrometer with laboratory measurement of uranium, indication can be obtained of the extent to which the uranium is in equilibrium (see Appendix). Loss of the gas radon is one cause of disequilibrium, both in sample and in soil, and it can result in the measured annual dose being at variance with that actually experienced by the sample. A high-resolution germanium gamma spectrometer is a powerful, though expensive, laboratory tool in this context; alpha spectrometry can also be used.

8. The idea of subtraction dating can be illustrated (using the data of Table 6.2) by subtracting the palaeodose for quartz from that for the largest alkali feldspar fraction, i.e. (5.00 - 3.36) = 1.64 Gy; likewise the total annual dose, i.e. (5.48 - 3.76) = 1.72 Gy/ka. Dividing the two gives an age of 950 years. Since the external contribution was the same for both annual doses it subtracts out and hence the age is independent of it.

Subtraction dating has also been demonstrated using quartz inclusions versus fine grains (e.g. Fleming and Stoneham 1973).

9. The best value for the age, Y, of a context is obtained by weighting the individual ages according to

$$Y = \frac{\Sigma\, Y_i/\sigma_i^2}{\Sigma\, 1/\sigma_i^2} \tag{6.10}$$

and the error limit on this average is given by

$$\sigma^2 = \sigma_s^2 + \sigma_r^2 \tag{6.11}$$

where

$$\sigma_s = \frac{\sum(\sigma_i)_s/\sigma_i^2}{\sum\sigma_i^{-2}} \tag{6.12}$$

and

$$\sigma_r^{-2} = \sum(\sigma_i)_r^{-2} \tag{6.13}$$

where $(\sigma_i)_s$ and $(\sigma_i)_r$ are respectively the systematic and random error limits on the age Y_i. The overall error limit for a sample is obtained from

$$\sigma_i^2 = (\sigma_i)_r^2 + (\sigma_i)_s^2 \tag{6.14}$$

10. *Ancient TL* is a specialist newsletter/journal published by I. K. Bailiff, Department of Archaeology, University of Durham, DH1 3EB, UK.

11. Pre-dose dating is a different concept. Instead of being based on the size of the natural TL glow-curve observed from a sample it utilizes change of TL sensitivity – the degree of *sensitization* – in the 110 °C peak in quartz. The remarkable properties of this peak were investigated and developed as a dating tool by Fleming (1973), with later refinements by others. It is a powerful technique for pottery of the last 1000 or 2000 years, being limited by the early onset of saturation – usually at around several gray.

    Because of its short lifetime (about an hour) the 110 °C peak is not present in the natural TL glow-curve of a sample. However, exposure of the sample to a small *test-dose* (around 0.01–0.1 Gy) allows measurement of its initial sensitivity, S. If the sample is now heated to 500–600°C, this *thermal activation* causes a strong increase in the subsequent response, S_N, to the test-dose. The increase is proportional to the total dose received since the pottery was last fired, i.e. to the palaeodose; the latter is evaluated by comparison of $(S_N - S_0)$ with the increase resulting from thermal activation of a calibrating beta dose.

12. In the *partial bleach method* (also called the 'R-Γ' method, being method (c) of Wintle and Huntley 1980), the glow-curves of some portions are measured after artificial irradiation as in the additive dose procedure (see Fig. 6.9) while for another set of portions a short bleach is administered between irradiation and measurement, giving a partially bleached growth line as illustrated in Fig. 6.19. On the basis that the amount of TL removed by the short bleach is

a given fraction of the bleachable TL, the intercept of the two lines indicates the equivalent dose.

With this method it does not matter if the bleaching prior to deposition was incomplete as long as it was more complete than that effected by the short laboratory bleach. If it was less complete, then the short laboratory bleach will be able to reach components of the natural TL that were acquired prior to deposition – hence causing the equivalent dose to be an overestimate. This circumstance is termed 'overbleaching'. It can be checked for by repeating the evaluation using different bleaching times; the same value of equivalent dose will be obtained for times that are short enough to avoid overbleaching.

The *regeneration method* is illustrated in Fig. 6.20. If the bleaching prior to deposition was not sufficient to remove the bleachable component completely there will be no plateau between natural TL and regenerated TL, because bleachability is dependent on glow-curve temperature. The same applies if the additive dose method is used; in that case shorter laboratory bleaching times are tried.

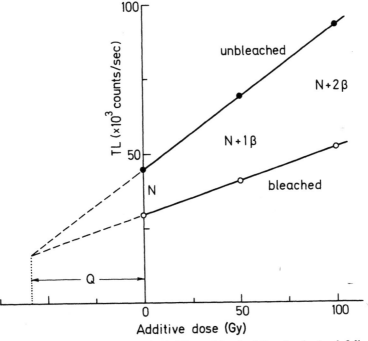

Fig. 6.19 Partial bleach method. The unbleached line is obtained following the same procedure as in the additive dose method (see Fig. 6.9). For the bleached line portions are exposed to sunlamp illumination before measurement; the bleaching caused by this illumination must be less than the bleaching prior to deposition; Q is the equivalent dose.

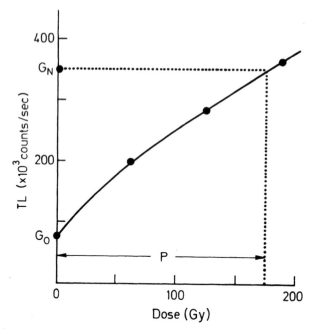

Fig. 6.20 The regeneration method. Several portions are used for measurement of the natural TL, G_N; the remaining portions are given a long bleach and the level of residual TL, G_0, checked with one of them; the rest are irradiated to various doses and the growth characteristic regenerated. The value of the palaeodose, P, is read off as indicated.

REFERENCES

Aitken, M. J. (1976) Thermoluminescent age evaluation and assessment of error limits: revised system, *Archaeometry* **18**, 233–8.

Aitken, M. J. (1985) *Thermoluminescence Dating*, Academic Press, London, Florida, 359 pp.

Aitken, M. J. and Alldred, J. C. (1972) The assessment of error limits in thermoluminescent dating, *Archaeometry* **14**, 257–67.

Aitken, M. J., Huxtable, J. and Debenham, N. C. (1986) Thermoluminescence dating in the palaeolithic: burned flint, stalagmitic calcite and sediment, *Assoc. Fr. Etude Quat. Bull.* **26**, 7–14.

Aitken, M. J. and Smith, B. W. (1988) Optical dating: recuperation after bleaching, *Quaternary Science Reviews* **7**, 387–94.

Bailiff, I. K. (1982) Beta TLD apparatus for small samples, *PACT* **6**, 72–5.

Beltrao, M. C., Danon, J., Enriquez, C. R., Poupeau, G. and Zuleta, E. (1982) Datations par thermoluminescence des silex brulés du site archeologique Alice Boer (Bresil), *C.R. Acad. Sci. Paris* **295**, 629–32.

Berger, G. W. and Huntley, D. J. (1983) Dating volcanic ash by thermoluminescence *PACT* **9**(2), 581–2.

Bowman, S. G. E. (1979) Phototransferred thermoluminescence in quartz and its potential use in dating, *PACT* 3, 381–400.

Clark, P. A. and Templer, R. H. (1988) Thermoluminescence dating of materials which exhibit anomalous fading, *Archaeometry* 30, 19–36.

Debenham, N. C. (1985) Use of UV emission in TL dating of sediments, *Nuclear Tracks and Radiation Measurements* 10, 717–24.

Debenham, N. C., Driver, H. S. T. and Walton, A. J. (1982) Anomalies in the TL of young calcites *PACT* 6, 555–62.

Elitzsch, C., Pernicka, E. and Wagner, G. A. (1983) Thermoluminescence dating of archaeometallurgical slags, *PACT* 9, 271–86.

Fleming, S. J. (1966) Study of thermoluminescence of crystalline extracts from pottery, *Archaeometry* 9, 170–3.

Fleming, S. J. (1970) Thermoluminescent dating: refinement of the quartz inclusion method, *Archaeometry* 12, 133–45.

Fleming, S. J. (1973) The pre-dose technique: a new thermoluminescence dating method, *Archaeometry* 15, 13–30.

Fleming, S. J. and Stoneham, D. (1973) The subtraction technique of thermoluminescent dating, *Archaeometry* 15, 229–238.

Fleming, S. J. (1975) *Authenticity in Art*, Institute of Physics, London and Bristol, 164 pp.

Fleming, S. J. (1979) *Thermoluminescence Techniques in Archaeology*, Clarendon Press, Oxford, 257 pp.

Godfrey-Smith, D. I., Huntley, D. J. and Chen, W.-H. (1988) Optical dating studies of quartz and feldspar sediment extracts, *Quaternary Science Reviews* 7, 373–80.

Goksu, H. Y. and Fremlin, J. H. (1972) Thermoluminescence from unirradiated flints: regeneration thermoluminescence, *Archaeometry* 14, 127–32.

Guerin, G. and Valladas, G. (1980) Thermoluminescence dating of volcanic plagioclases, *Nature* 286, 697–9.

Huntley, D. J., Godfrey-Smith, D. I. and Thewalt, M. L. W. (1985) Optical dating of sediments, *Nature* 313, 105–7.

Hütt, G., Jaek, I. and Tchonka, J. (1988) Optical dating: K-feldspars optical response stimulation spectrum, *Quaternary Science Reviews* 7, 381–6.

Huxtable, J., Aitken, M. J., Hedges, J. W. and Renfrew, A. C. (1976) Dating a settlement pattern by thermoluminescence: the burnt mounds of Orkney, *Archaeometry* 18, 5–17.

Huxtable, J., Aitken, M. J. and Bonhommet, N. (1978) Thermoluminescence dating of sediment baked by lava flows of the Chaîne des Puys, *Nature* 275, 207–9.

Huxtable, J. and Aitken, M. J. (1985) TL dating results for the palaeolithic site Maastricht-Belvedere, Mededelingen Rikjks Geologische Dienst 39, 41–44.

Ichikawa, Y. (1965) Dating of ancient ceramics by thermoluminescence, *Bull. Inst. Chem. Res. Kyoto Univ.* 43, 1–6.

Mejdahl, V. (1983) Feldspar inclusion dating of ceramics and burnt stones, *PACT* 9, 351–64.

Mejdahl, V. (1985) TL dating based on feldspars *Nuclear Tracks and Radiation Measurements* 10, 133–6.

Mejdahl, V. (1988) Long-term stability of the TL signal in alkali feldspars, *Quaternary Science Reviews* 7, 357–60.

Miallier, D., Fain, J., Sanzelle, S., Daugas, J. P. and Raynal J. P. (1983) Dating of the Butte de Clermont basaltic maar by means of the quartz inclusion method, *PACT* 9, 487–98.

Mobbs, S. F. (1979) Phototransfer at low temperatures, *PACT* 3, 407–13.

Robins, G. V., Seely, N. J., Symons, M. C. R. and MacNeil, D. A. C. (1981) Manganese (II) as an indicator of ancient heat treatment in flint, *Archaeometry* 23, 103–8.

Sanderson, D. C. W., Warren, S. E. and Hunter, J. R. (1983) The TL properties of archaeological glass, *PACT* 9, 287–298.

Sanderson, D. C. W., Placido, F. and Tate, J. O. (1988) Scottish vitrified forts: TL results from six study sites, *Nuclear Tracks and Radiation Measurements* 14, 307–16.

Spooner, N. A. and Hutton, J. T. (1988) A source of variability in the thermoluminescence of quartz, *Ancient TL* 6, 5–6.

Stoneham, D. (1983) Porcelain dating, *PACT* 9, 227–39.

Strickertsson, K., Placido, F. and Tate, J. O. (1988) Thermoluminescence dating of Scottish vitrified forts, *Nucl. Tracks and Radiation Measurements* 14, 317–20.

Sutton, S. R. and Zimmerman, D. W. (1976) Thermoluminescent dating using zircon grains from archaeological ceramics, *Archaeometry* 18, 125–34.

Templer, R. H. and Smith, B. W. (1988) Auto-regenerative TL dating with zircon inclusions from fired materials, *Nuclear Tracks and Radiation Measurements* 14, 329–32.

Valladas, H. (1983) Estimation de la temperature de chauffe de silex prehistorique par leur thermoluminescence, *C.R. Acad. Sci. Paris* 296, 993–6.

Valladas, G. and Gillot, P. Y. (1978) Dating of the Olby lava flow using heated quartz pebbles: some problems, *PACT* 2, 141–50.

Valladas, H., Joron, J. L., Valladas, G., Arensburg, B., Bar-Yosef, O., Belfer-Cohen, A., Goldberg, P., Laville, H., Meignen, L. and Rak, Y. (1987) Thermoluminescence dates for the Neanderthal burial site at Kebara in Israel, *Nature* 330, 159–60.

Valladas, H., Reyss, J. L., Joron, J. L., Valladas, G., Bar-Yosef, O. and Vandermeersch, B. (1988) Thermoluminescence dating of Mousterian 'Proto-Cro-Magnon' remains from Israel and the origin of modern man, *Nature* 331, 614–16.

Walton, A. J. and Debenham, N. C. (1982) Dating of paleolithic calcite by TL: observation of spatial inhomogeneity, *PACT* 6, 202–8.

Wheeler, G. C. W. S. (1988) Optically stimulated phosphorescence and optically transferred TL as a tool for dating, *Quaternary Science Reviews* 7, 407–10.

Wintle, A. G. (1973) Anomalous fading of thermoluminescence in mineral samples, *Nature* 245, 143–4.

Wintle, A. G. and Huntley, D. J. (1980) Thermoluminescence dating of ocean sediments, *Canadian Journal of Earth Sciences* 17, 348–60.

Zimmerman, D. W. (1971a) Thermoluminescent dating using fine grains from pottery, *Archaeometry* 13, 29–52.

Zimmerman, D. W. (1971b) Uranium distributions in archaeologic ceramics: dating of radioactive inclusions, *Science* 174, 818–19.

Zöller, L., Stremme, H. and Wagner, G. A. (1988) Thermoluminineszenz-datierung an loss-palaoboden-sequenzen von nieder-, mittel-und oberrhein/bundesrepublik Deutschland, *Chemical Geology* (Isotope Geoscience Section) 73, 39–62.

7 Electron spin resonance

This technique represents an alternative way of evaluating the dosage of nuclear radiation that has been received by a sample – in the terminology of the last chapter this is the *palaeodose*, though for ESR it is common to use *accumulated dose, AD,* or *total dose, TD*. In respect of *annual dose* (dose-rate) the same considerations apply as for TL, though with some change of emphasis because of the different sample types to which ESR is applied. Notable among these are tooth enamel, mollusc shells and coral which are unsuitable for TL owing to decomposition on heating; ESR also holds advantages in respect of calcite; the technique can also be used for quartz though having lower sensitivity than with TL.

Besides familiarity with the basic concepts of annual dose and radioactivity (section 6.2) it is assumed that the reader has assimilated the notion of palaeodose as a measure of the trapped electron population that has built up since time zero, and that

$$\text{Age} = \frac{\text{Palaeodose}}{\text{Annual dose}} \tag{7.1}$$

For most of the samples to which ESR is applied time zero corresponds to formation of the crystals concerned.

In writing this chapter substantial help has been obtained from the comprehensive review by Grün (1989), kindly made available to me by the author. In addition to this there are extensive accounts by Hennig and Grün (1983), Ikeya (1985a, 1986) and Nambi (1985), as well as the *Proceedings* of the first and second international symposia on ESR dating (Ikeya and Miki 1985; McLaughlin, Scharmann and Regulla 1989). There are also many papers on ESR dating in the *Proceedings* of successive specialist seminars on TL and ESR dating, of which the last were published in *Nuclear Tracks and Radiation Measurements*, volume 14 (1988) and *Quaternary Science Reviews*, volume 7 (1988).

There are approximately fifty laboratories involved in ESR dating and of these about half are located in Japan, presumably stemming from the pioneering work there of Ikeya. Equipment is expensive, upwards of $100,000; many science laboratories have ESR facilities but not necessarily of a type suitable for dating.

Sometimes ESR is referred to as EPR – *electron paramagnetic resonance*, which in French becomes RPE – *résonance paramagnetique électronique*.

7.1 ESR MEASUREMENT

7.1.1 THE PHENOMENON

With TL (and with OSL) eviction of electrons from traps is an integral part of the measurement process; with ESR eviction does not occur and the presence of electrons is detected by their response to high-frequency electromagnetic radiation in the presence of a strong, steady magnetic field which is slowly changed. For a given frequency there is a certain value of magnetic field at which the electrons resonate. The occurrence of this is detectable because when they are in resonance there is absorption of electromagnetic power; the greater the number of electrons the greater the absorption; hence the latter is a measure of age. The gradual build-up of population of trapped electrons occurs through exposure to nuclear radiation, as in TL.

7.1.2 DETECTION

As the magnetic field is changed and a resonance value approached there is a gradual increase in absorption until, at the resonance value,[1] the maximum is reached – see Fig. 7.1(a). For precision of measurement it is better to obtain the data in the form shown in Fig. 7.1(b). This shows how the value of the tangent to the absorption curve varies as the magnetic field goes through the resonance, i.e. it is a plot of the change in absorption for a small change in magnetic field; the conversion is obtained electronically by superimposing a weak alternating magnetic field on the steady field. The vertical distance between the two peaks is a measure of the strength of the resonance which in turn is a measure of the trapped electron population and the age (see Fig. 7.2).

For measurement the sample is contained in a quartz tube of about 5 mm diameter. This must be precisely positioned between the poles of the magnet producing the strong steady field; measurement takes a few minutes.

In most crystals there are ESR signals other than those due to trapped electrons; fortunately these usually occur at different values of magnetic field, though overlap sometimes occurs. Obviously, for dating, it is necessary to identify the age–dependent resonances, i.e. those due to trapped electrons (though there are also some other resonances which are age dependent); if there are several types of trapping site in a crystal, then there will be one resonance corresponding to each.

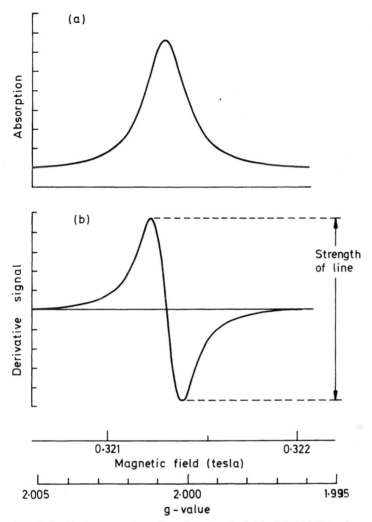

Fig. 7.1 (a) At a certain value of magnetic field, 0.32134 T in the example shown, the natural frequency of trapped electrons at a particular crystal defect is equal to the frequency of the applied electromagnetic power; there is then resonance and absorption of power is a maximum. (b) For measurement purposes it is advantageous to obtain, by electronic processing, the *first derivative* of the absorption; this is the slope of the tangent to the absorption curve. The *g*-value is always the same for a given defect, even though a different applied frequency may be used.

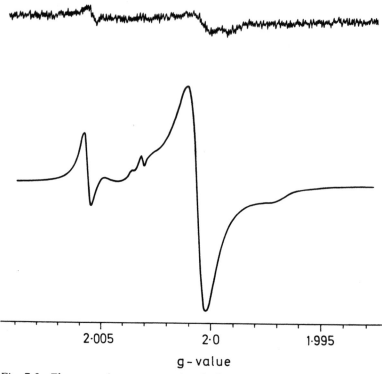

g - value

Fig. 7.2   Electron spin resonance signals from young calcite (above) and older calcite (below). The upper spectrum is amplified × 10. (After Grün 1989.)

g-value

For a given type of trap the ratio between electromagnetic frequency and the resonance value of the magnetic field is fixed. It is convenient to specify this ratio in terms of the *g-value*[1] and sometimes only the *g*-value is shown on the horizontal axis of plots such as Figs 7.1 and 7.2. For the types of trap relevant to dating the *g*-value is close to 2.

7.1.3 SAMPLE PREPARATION

The sample needs to be powdered before measurement and for some materials this may induce a 'crushing signal' originating in the surface of the grains – similar to one type of spurious TL. However, there are treatments by which this can be removed, e.g. for calcite, by etching in weak acetic acid. Although heating is not part of the measurement process it may be advantageous to 'pre-heat' the sample after artificial irradiation in order to remove unstable signals. For calcite a pre-heat of 2 hours at 120 °C removes a signal at $g = 2.0023$ which interferes with the stable dating signal at $g = 2.0007$ (Smith *et al.* 1985).

For most types of material the outer 2 mm is removed before crushing in order to avoid various surface effects. Ideally about 5 g of sample are obtained, about ten portions each of between 0.05 and 0.5 g usually being used for evaluation of palaeodose; for teeth substantially less may be acceptable −0.01–0.2 g per portion corresponding to a 2 g total, inclusive of 1 g for radioactivity determination; if need be a single portion can be used for all data points – a strong advantage over TL.

As a general rule ESR signals are not bleached by light and use of subdued red illumination used in TL is not necessary. However, there are signals in some minerals which are bleachable – hence giving the possibility of dating unburnt sediment, with predepositional exposure to sunlight being the zeroing event as for TL. Obviously, if such signals are being utilized strict precautions against inadvertent bleaching must be enforced during sample preparation and thereafter.

7.2 STABILITY

7.2.1 LIFETIME AND AGE RANGE
Because many ESR applications are concerned with the Middle and Lower Palaeolithic, practitioners are concerned to push back the age limit to a million years and beyond. Sometimes the limit is due to saturation and whether or not the sample has reached this state is indicated in the course of palaeodose determination. It is much more difficult to know if the limit of stability has been reached, i.e. that the age of the sample is approaching the lifetime of the trapped electrons. In TL this is likely to cause failure of the plateau test (see Fig. 6.5), but in ESR this test is only available for some sample types (see Miki and Ikeya 1985; Molodkov and Hütt 1985).

An evaluation of the stability of a particular signal can be made by measuring the lifetime for a series of elevated temperatures (in the range 150–200 °C) so as to reduce the lifetime to a span of days rather than millions of years. Then on the basis of the Arrhenius equation[2] the lifetime at typical burial temperature is found by extrapolation; however, this gives only a rough estimate. A more reliable approach is based on measurement of equilibrium levels in very old samples.[2]

The lifetime is strongly dependent on burial temperature; the age limit for a given signal will be substantially less in equatorial regions than in polar regions. In general age limits are not well defined; mention of some individual age limits is made in section 7.4.

7.2.2 RECRYSTALLIZATION
In unheated biogenic materials it is not surprising to find that changes in crystal structure occur in the course of time; there is then risk of a substantial underestimation of age, because the new product starts from

zero again (though there is a possibility that some of the electrons from the old structure will be retrapped in the new one). If the *g*-value of the signal from the new product is different to that from the parent then it may be recognizable that recrystallization has occurred; also, in such a case, if some of the parent remains then the palaeodose evaluated from its signal should be correct, though obviously the *strength* of the signal will be lowered.

The possibility of detecting the occurrence of recrystallization represents an advantage over TL; of course if the *g*-value of the product is the same as that of the parent the recrystallization will go undetected (unless by visual inspection), and an apparent age that is erroneously too small will be obtained.

Recrystallization is likely to affect also the uranium and thorium contents, as noted below.

7.3 RADIOACTIVITY AND ANNUAL DOSE

7.3.1 URANIUM UPTAKE

As will be discussed in section 8.3.2, the uranium content of bone can be used as a relative dating method in some burial conditions; the content in old bone may be several hundred times that in modern bone, likewise in teeth. In the context of ESR dating this means that the annual dose is not constant and the average value appropriate for insertion in equation (7.1) has to be based on an assumption about the rapidity with which the uranium was acquired. In the *early uptake model* (EU) it is assumed that the uptake occurred rapidly after death; in the *linear uptake model* (LU) it is assumed that the uranium content has increased at a uniform rate, from zero at death to the present-day level. On the basis of these two models, alternative ages are usually quoted. If the internal component of the annual dose is dominant the EU age will be substantially less than the LU age.

These models are particular forms of the open-system situation, and as already discussed there is upset to uranium-series dating too. However, the underestimate in that technique is greater than for ESR and so discordance between the two is an indication that the sample is not a closed system. Further, by complex mathematical analysis based on comparison of the apparent ages given by the two techniques, it is possible to infer the form which the uptake must have taken and hence make an estimate of the true age (Grün *et al.* 1988a).

7.3.2 RADIOACTIVE DISEQUILIBRIUM

Apart from any movement of uranium there is an intrinsic effect in most biogenic samples that causes the annual dose to change. This is the actual effect on which uranium-series dating is based, i.e. the radioactive 'grow-in' of thorium-230 and subsequent members of the uranium decay series (see Appendix). Most of this occurs during the first 100,000 years and during this period the internal component of the annual dose roughly doubles; as long as the parent uranium remains fixed (i.e. there is neither uptake nor leaching) exact allowance can be made by computation.

Besides such disequilibrium effects in the sample itself there is also the possibility of non-constancy of the external component of the annual dose, as for all TL and ESR samples.

Radon in caves; plate-out
In caves that are not ventilated there is substantial build-up of the radioactive gas radon due to its emanation from uranium in sediment deposits. This may make a significant contribution to the annual dose through gamma radiation. A further effect from radon is 'plate-out' of non-gaseous radioactive decay products on to surfaces. The dosage from these is partly gamma radiation, but there is also a strong component of beta radiation; this affects only the outer 2 mm of the surface, but by discarding that layer anomalous enhancement of the palaeodose can be avoided.

7.3.3 ALPHA PARTICLE EFFECTIVENESS (k-VALUE); ZONING
As with TL (see section 6.4) the energy deposited by alpha particles is less effective than that from beta and gamma radiation in causing accumulation of trapped electrons. Measurement of the effectiveness is technically more difficult than in the case of TL and it is not usually made routinely; instead the established value for the particular signal concerned is used.

Mention was made in section 6.6 of possible upset to TL dating due to zoning of thorium or uranium, there being the risk that regions of high radioactivity might be also regions of lower than average TL sensitivity; the age obtained would then be erroneously too small because alpha particles would not penetrate beyond the low-sensitivity region. The same applies with ESR, but here there is at present no way of mapping ESR sensitivity variations (in TL it is done by photography using an image intensifier); of course, radioactivity mapping can be accomplished using induced fission tracks. However, even if zoning occurs to some extent it is unlikely to lead to significant error unless the annual dose is dominated by the internal contribution − which is not usually the case.

7.4 APPLICATIONS

7.4.1 STALAGMITIC CALCITE (SPELEOTHEMS)
Beginning with the work of Ikeya (1975) in Akiyoshi Cave, Japan, the dating of calcite is the most highly developed archaeologically relevant

application of ESR. As indicated in Chapter 5, *speleothems* comprise secondary carbonates precipitated in caves, i.e. stalagmites, stalactites and flowstones; these occur in limestone regions and caves in such regions often contain Palaeolithic occupation levels closely associated with flowstone floors and stalagmites. As already noted in section 6.7.4 a major problem arises from the non–uniformity of the gamma radiation in caves because of the usually much higher levels of radioactivity in sediment than in calcite; a comprehensive on–site assessment by laboratory specialists is essential if reliable dating is to be achieved.

The generally favoured signal for dating is at $g = 2.0007$ (see Fig. 7.2); typically this has an age range of 10,000 to about 1 million years, depending on sensitivity, annual dose and temperature. There is also an age-dependent signal at $g = 2.0058$, which requires prior heating for a day at 160–190 °C for its utilization; however, although this can reach substantially further back in time the validity of its utilization is the subject of controversy, overestimation of palaeodose being alleged. However, not all speleothems have these signals; sometimes other age-dependent signals are present, sometimes there are no age-dependent signals at all. There may also be a signal from humic acid present in the calcite which grows with artificial irradiation; however, as this signal is sometimes present in zero-age samples it cannot be used for dating.

Palaeolithic occupation has been dated in a number of caves, mainly in France and Italy, for example (Yokoyama *et al.* 1983) Caune de l'Arago, Grotte du Lazaret, Grotte Vallonet and Abri Pie Lombard. In Greece the dating of samples from Petralona cave has raised considerable controversy (Ikeya 1980; Hennig *et al.* 1981; Poulianos *et al.* 1982; Xirotiris *et al.* 1982); among the samples dated was about 1 g obtained from the calcite encrustation on the hominid skull found on the site; this gave an age of 198,000 ± 40,000 years. As there was some doubt about the stratigraphy of the find spot the direct association of the sample with the skull was of considerable importance.

7.4.2 SPRING-DEPOSITED TRAVERTINE

Like speleothems, this is a carbonate precipitate, but it occurs on open-air sites and usually has a high concentration of organic components. The ESR signals are similar to those of speleothems, the signal at $g = 2.0007$ giving the same age range of roughly 10,000–1 million years. Many samples are not suitable for dating but by using crusts the success rate can be improved.

Palaeolithic sites dated by ESR, usually with uranium-series dating in parallel, include El Kown, Syria (Hennig and Hours 1982), various sites in Hungary (Hennig *et al.* 1983); Ehringsdorf (Grun *et al.* 1988b) and Bilzingsleben in East Germany (Schwarcz *et al.* 1988a). The latter site is of considerable interest because of the presence there of cranial fragments of a hominid attributed to *Homo erectus*, perhaps an early form of *Homo sapiens*. Two travertine samples gave ESR ages of *c*. 400,000 years, as did extensive measurements on enamel from rhinoceros teeth found in the hominid-bearing layer, hence indicating occupation during isotope Stage 11, though the error limits did not allow exclusion of Stage 9; the floral and faunal evidence indicated occupation during an interglacial (i.e. an odd-numbered isotope stage – see section 2.3).

7.4.3 TOOTH ENAMEL; BONE

In contrast to living tooth enamel, which contains very little organic matter and no amorphous phase, bone and dentine have a mineral content of only about 50%. As a result, changes in the ultrastructure go on for many millennia after death, even hundreds of millennia, before mineralization is complete. For these reasons Grün and Schwarcz (1987) suggest that a reliable ESR signal cannot be obtained from bone, only from enamel. Ikeya (1985b) suggests that even with enamel fluorinization might lead to an underestimation of palaeodose, but the former authors argue that only a decrease in signal strength will occur (see section 7.2.2).

Tooth enamel

The mineral concerned is hydroxyapatite and the signal used is at $g = 2.0018$, having an estimated lifetime of the order of 10 million years. It is highly sensitive so that samples only a few hundred years old can be dated, and for old samples the size can be as small as 10–100 mg.

Evaluation of annual dose is the main problem in obtaining reliable ages, and for some situations it is highly complex. The simplest from the technical point of view is when a separated enamel layer of low uranium content is found in sediment, though there is then less certainty in palaeontological classification and the possibility of reworking from older deposits must be considered. The annual dose is dominated by beta and gamma radiation from the sediment, the alpha contribution being eliminated by removal of a 20–100 μm layer with a diamond drill; measurement of overall thickness is necessary in assessing attenuation of the beta radiation within the enamel.

If the sample is a complete tooth or an enamel layer with dentine or cement attached it is likely that the beta contribution from the dentine/cement will be a substantial component of the annual dose. The uranium concentration in the dentine/cement of fossil teeth is liable to be in the range 10–1000 ppm, about ten times higher than in the enamel. In recent teeth the uranium concentration is only a fraction of a part per million and so in determining the average annual dose the important question is the rapidity with which uptake occurred (see section 7.3.1); a further complication is non-uniformity of the radioactivity; it seems that

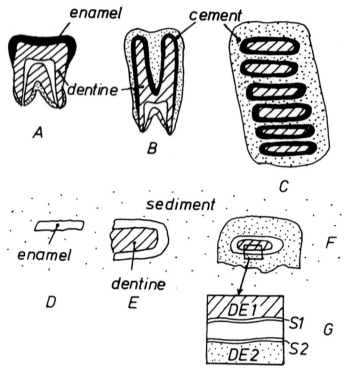

Fig. 7.3 Types of mammal teeth (A – human, B – camel, C – elephant) and some possible environments. In G, the sources of annual dose external to the enamel (central layer), are marked DE1 (dentine) and DE2 (sediment); S1 and S2 indicate removal of the enamel surface so as to avoid the alpha-particle contribution from DE1 and DE2. (From Grün *et al.* 1987.)

the uranium migrates into the tooth as some kind of saturation front (see Fig. 7.4).

There is advantage in having a large tooth (e.g. from a hippopotamus) if the comparative simplicity of a separated enamel layer is not available; this gives the possibility of a lower uranium content in the central regions, thereby reducing the importance of uncertainty about rapidity of uranium uptake. Figure 7.5 illustrates this for a mammoth tooth from northern Canada; there is not a great difference in age between evaluations based on the assumptions of EU and LU so that the tooth can be placed confidently in the warmth of isotope Stage 5.

On the other hand, for the hominid site at Bilzingsleben for which the travertine dating has already been mentioned in section 7.4.2, the tooth samples were small fragments of enamel with dentine attached on one side. The uranium concentrations in the dentine were in the range 25–45 ppm (whereas less than 3 ppm in the enamel) and consequently beta radiation

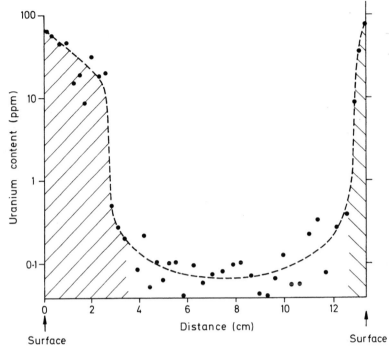

Fig. 7.4 Diffusion of uranium into the dentine of a mammoth tooth (from Grun and Invernati 1985). A section of the tooth (13 cm across) was obtained by a saw-cut made perpendicular to the length of the tooth; the uranium concentration was then mapped by means of induced fission tracks. The figure gives the uranium content along a thin layer of dentine; a similar enrichment near the outside surfaces was found in other layers of dentine and in the layers of cement. In the enamel the concentration was lower by a factor of 10 but the same pattern was evident. The tooth was about 150,000 years old.

from the dentine contributed an appreciable proportion of the annual dose, with the result that ages calculated on the EU model were about 30% less than on the basis of LU (see Fig. 7.6); the latter were consistent with the travertine ages, and it has been found on other sites too that there is usually better agreement using the LU model (Zymela *et al.* 1988). As already mentioned, in cases where uranium-series measurements can be made on the same samples as the ESR measurements it is possible to estimate the uptake history (Grün *et al.* 1988a).

In application to the enamel from six teeth of large mammals at the site of Qafzeh Cave, Israel, for which the TL burnt flint dates (92,000 ± 5000 years ago) have already been discussed in section 6.7.2, the average ages obtained were 96,000 years on the EU model and 115,000 years on the LU model (Schwarcz *et al.* 1988b). Uranium-series

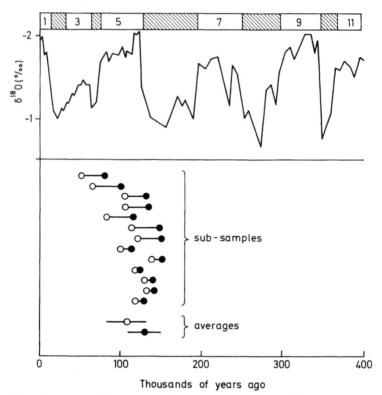

Fig. 7.5 (Lower) Electron spin resonance ages obtained from subsamples of enamel from a single mammoth tooth from Saskatchewan gravels in Alberta (from Grün *et al.* 1987). Open circles – early uptake model; closed circles – linear uptake model. *(Upper)* Oxygen–isotope record. Other age indications were only that the gravels were interglacial; the ESR ages clearly indicate Stage 5.

dating of the dentine of one of the teeth gave an apparent age of 20,000 years, suggesting delay in the arrival of uranium and hence that the LU model is more appropriate. This confirmation of the great antiquity of the site is particularly convincing because whereas the TL annual dose was dominated by the internal contribution the reverse was the case for the ESR.

An application of ESR to more recent tooth enamel may be noted; this is the work of Ikeya *et al.* (1984) in determination of the radiation dose received by survivors of the Hiroshima atomic bomb – important data in the assessment of cancer risk.

Bone and dentine

These are open-system materials as mentioned above, and earlier in the context of uranium–series dating. Not only is there the uncertainty arising

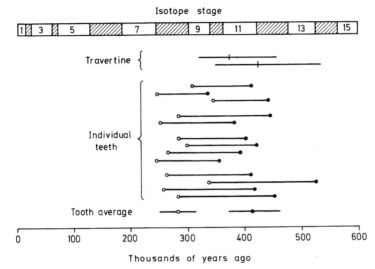

Fig. 7.6 Electron spin resonance ages obtained by Schwarcz *et al.* (1988a) on travertines and rhinoceros tooth enamel from the Lower Palaeolithic site at Bilzingsleben, East Germany. Open circles – early uptake model; closed circles – linear uptake model. Uranium-series dating by the same authors (see section 5.2.5) indicated an age of around 350,000 years or greater. The flora and fauna were consistent with occupation during an interglacial; on the basis of the tooth enamel results this could have been either oxygen–isotope Stage 9 or Stage 11, with the ESR results for the travertine favouring the latter.

from the unknown history of uranium uptake (i.e. EU, LU or other) but there is the continued process of mineralization after death, giving risk that the capability for acquiring ESR is changing during the burial time. Despite these difficulties a substantial amount of work in dating hominid bones has been carried out (e.g. Ikeya and Miki 1980; Ikeya 1985b; Yokoyama *et al.* 1983). The effect of continued mineralization is of course to give an underestimate of age and this has been reported by Grün and Schwarcz, (1987) in respect of dentine, again from the site of Bilzingsleben.

7.4.4 OTHER MATERIALS

Some indication of the possible range of application is given in Fig. 7.7, but except for the materials already discussed there has not yet been substantial involvement in archaeology (but see Goede and Hitchman 1987); no doubt there will be in the future. In Quaternary geology there has been extensive application to corals and mollusc shells. Quartz is becoming of increasing interest; one of its signals can be set to zero by grinding such as occurs in a deep tectonic fault and this has been used to date the last movement of such a fault (see, for instance, Ikeya *et al.* 1982; Miki and Ikeya 1982).

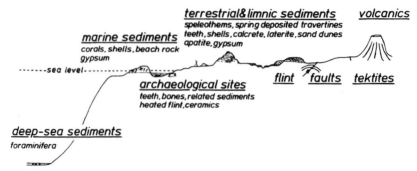

Fig. 7.7 Range of materials on which ESR dating studies have been performed (supplied by R. Grün). As will be evident from the text, it is by no means the case that all these can be successfully dated.

Firing temperature of flint

In many types of flint there are signals which are changed by heating (Robins *et al.* 1978, 1981) otherwise than due to eviction of electrons from traps. Indications about heating in antiquity are obtained by comparing the signal from an archaeologically worked sample with the signal behaviour on laboratory heating of an unworked flint of the same geological origin; the temperature range 300–600 °C can be covered. Thermoluminescence can also be used for this purpose, though perhaps not as decisively.

There is also the prospect of using ESR for the dating of heated flint (Griffiths *et al.* 1983), though it appears in this case that TL is the more practical technique. Another signal in flint, while primarily of use in determining geological age, also shows prospects for unheated flint (Garrison *et al.* 1981).

NOTES

1. Numerically the *g*-value is given by

$$g = \frac{f}{14\,H} \tag{7.2}$$

where f gigahertz (i.e. 10^9 cycles/sec) is the electromagnetic frequency and H tesla is the value of the steady magnetic field at which resonance occurs. Thus for $g = 2$ the magnetic field corresponding to $f = 9$ GHz (X-band) is 0.32 T (3200 gauss); for 35 GHz (Q-band), 1.25 T.

2. According to the Arrhenius equation the lifetime is given by

$$\tau = s^{-1} \exp(E/kT) \tag{7.3}$$

where s is a frequency factor, E electronvolts is the trap depth, k is Boltzmann's constant (at 17 °C, $kT = 0.025$ eV) and T is the absolute temperature. Hence, if the value of τ is measured for a series of elevated temperatures, T, a plot of ($\log \tau$) against ($1/T$) should be a straight line. By extrapolation the value of τ at the burial temperature can be found, but as noted in the text such extrapolation gives only an order of magnitude. A sounder method is to measure the palaeodose of a very old sample that is in steady state. For such a sample

$$\tau = \frac{\text{Palaeodose}}{\text{Annual dose}} \qquad (7.4)$$

The palaeodose reaches 0.95 of this equilibrium value, at an age of about 3τ. The build-up to equilibrium is given by

$$N = N_\infty \{1 - \exp(-t/\tau)\} \qquad (7.5)$$

where t is the age. It follows, for example, that for $t = 0.5\tau$ the apparent age will be 21% lower than the true age; for $t = \tau$, it will be 37% lower.

Note that the lifetime is strongly influenced by burial temperature; for example, a trap having $E = 1.8$ eV and a lifetime at 15 °C of 1 million years, will have a lifetime at 20 °C of only 300,000 years.

REFERENCES

Garrison, E. G., Rowlett, R. M., Cowan, D. L. and Holroyd, L. V. (1981), ESR dating of ancient flints, *Nature* 290, 44–45.

Goede, A. and Hitchman, M. A. (1987) Electron spin resonance analysis of marine gastropods from coastal archaeological sites in Southern Africa, *Archaeometry* 29, 163–174.

Griffiths, D. R., Seeley, N. J., Chandra, H. and Symons, M. C. R. (1983) ESR dating of heated chert, *PACT* 9, 339–409.

Grün, R., 1989, *Die ESR-Altersbestimmungsmethode*, Springer, Heidelberg.

Grün, R. and Invernati, C. (1985) Uranium accumulation in teeth and its effect on ESR dating – a detailed study of a mammoth tooth, *Nuclear Tracks and Radiation Measurements*, 10, 869–78.

Grün, R. and Schwarcz, H. P. (1987) Some remarks on ESR dating of bones, *Ancient TL* 5, (2), 1–9.

Grün, R., Schwarcz, H. P. and Zymela, S. (1987) ESR dating of tooth enamel, *Canadian Journ. Earth Sci.* 24, 1022–37.

Grün, R., Schwarcz, H. P. and Chadam, I (1988a) ESR dating of tooth enamel; coupled corrections for U-uptake and U-series disequilibrium, *Nuclear Tracks* 14, 237–42.

Grün, R., Schwarcz, H. P., Ford, D. C. and Hentzsch, B. (1988b) ESR dating of spring deposited travertines, *Quaternary Science Reviews* 7, 429–32.

Hennig, G. J., Herr, W., Weber, E. and Xirotiris, N. I. (1981) ESR-dating of the fossil hominid cranium from Petralona Cave, Greece, *Nature* 292, 533–6.

Hennig, G. J. and Hours, F. (1982) Dates pour les passages entre l'Acheuleen et le Paléolithique Moyen à El Down (Sytre), *Palaeorient* 8, 81–3.

Hennig, G. J., and Grün, R. (1983) ESR dating in Quaternary Geology, *Quaternary Science Reviews* 2, 157–238.

Hennig, G. J., Grün, R., Brunnacker, K. and Pecsi, M. (1983) $^{230}Th^{234}U$-sowie ESR-Altersbestimmungen einiger Travertine in Ungarn, *Eiszeitalter und Gegenwart* 331, 9–19.

Ikeya, M. (1975) Dating a stalactite by electron paramagnetic resonance, *Nature* 255, 48–50.

Ikeya, M. (1980): ESR dating of carbonates at Petralona Cave, *Anthropos* 7, 143–50.

Ikeya, M., (1985a) Dating methods of Pleistocene deposits and their problems: electron spin resonance, *Geoscience Canada*, Reprint Series 2, 73–87.

Ikeya, M. (1985b) ESR ages of bones in palaeoanthropology: uranium and fluorine accumulation, in Ikeya and Miki (1985), pp. 373–9.

Ikeya, M., (1986) Electron Spin Resonance, in *Dating and Age Determination of Biological Materials* (eds. M. R. Zimmerman and L. Angel), Croom Helm, pp. 59–125.

Ikeya M. and Miki, T. (1980) Electron spin resonance dating of animal and human bones, *Science* 207, 977–9.

Ikeya, M., Miki, T. and Tanaka, K. (1982) Dating of fault by electron spin resonance on intrafault materials, *Science* 215, 1392–3.

Ikeya, M., Miyajima, J., and Okajima, S (1984) ESR dosimetry for atom bomb survivors using shell buttons and tooth enamel, *Japan. Journ. Appl. Phys.* 23, L697–L699.

Ikeya, M. and Miki, T. (eds) (1985) *ESR Dating and Dosimetry (Proc. First International Symposium on ESR Dating)*, Ionics, Tokyo, 538 pp.

McLaughlin, W. L., Scharmann, A. and Regulla, D. (eds) (1989) *Proc. Second International Symposium on ESR Dosimetry and Applications, Journ. Applied Radiation and Isotopes* (in press).

Miki, T. and Ikeya, M. (1982) Physical basis of fault dating with ESR, *Naturwissenschaften* 69, 90–1.

Miki, T. and Ikeya, M. (1985) A plateau method for total dose evaluation with digital processing, *Nuclear Tracks and Radiation Measurements* 10, 913–19.

Molodkov, A. and Hütt, G. (1985) ESR dating of subfossil shells: some refinements, in Ikeya and Miki (1985), pp. 145–55.

Nambi, K. S. V. (1985) Scope of ESR studies in thermally stimulated luminescence studies and chronological applications, *Nuclear Tracks and Radiation Measurements* 10, 113–31.

Poulianos, A. N., Liritzis, Y., Ikeya, M., Hennig, G. J., Herr, W., Weber, E. and Xirotiris, N. I. (1982) Petralona cave dating controversy, *Nature* 229, 280–2.

Robins, G. V., Seeley, N. J., McNeil, D. A. C., and Symons, M. C. R. (1978) Identification of ancient heat treatment in flint artefacts by ESR spectroscopy, *Nature* 276, 703–4.

Robins, G. V., Seeley, N. J., McNeill, D. A. C., and Symons, M. C. R. (1981) Manganese (II) as an indicator of ancient heat treatment in flint, *Archaeometry* 23, 103–7.

Schwarcz, H. P., Grün, R., Latham, A. G., Mania, D. and Brunnacker, K. (1988a) New evidence for the age of the Bilzingsleben archaeological site, *Archaeometry* 30, 5–18.

Schwarcz, H. P., Grün, R., Vandermeerch, B., Bar-Yosef, O., Valladas, H. and Tchernov, E. (1988b) ESR dates from the hominid burial site of Qafzeh in Israel, *Journ. Human Evolution* 17, 733–7.

Smith, B. W., Smart, P. L., Symons, M. C. R. and Andrews, J. N. (1985) ESR dating of detritally contaminated calcites, in Ikeya and Miki (1985) pp. 49–59.

Yokoyama, Y., Quagebeur, J.-P., Bibron, R., Leger, C., Chappaz, N., Michelot, C., Shen, G.-J. and Nguyen, H.-V. (1983) ESR dating of stalagmites of the Caune de l'Arago, the Grotte du Lazaret, the Grotte du Vallonnet and the Abri Pie Lombard: a comparison with the U-Th method, *PACT* 9, 381–9.

Zymela, S., Schwarcz, H. P., Grün, R., Stalker, A. M. and Churcher, C. S. (1988) ESR dating of Pleistocene fossil teeth from Alberta and Saskatchewan, *Canadian Journal of Earth Sciences* 25, 235–45.

Xirotiris, N. J., Henke, W. and Hennig, G. J. (1982) Die phylogenetische Stellung des Petralona Schadels auf Grund computertomographischer Analysen und der absoluten Datierung mit der ESR-Methode, *Humanbiologia Budapestinensis* 9, 89–94.

8 Amino acid racemization; obsidian hydration; other chemical methods

8.1 AMINO ACID DATING

8.1.1 INTRODUCTION

Amino acids are the building blocks of the protein molecules which constitute most of the organic part of living organisms – primarily bone, teeth and shell in the context of dating. At formation each type of amino acid is present in its L form; thereafter slow conversion to the D form commences and continues until an equilibrium mixture of the two forms is reached, usually 50 : 50. Hence dating is based on measurement of the (D/L) ratio, as illustrated[1] in Fig. 8.1.

The form of Fig. 8.1 is similar to that of Fig. 5.3 which showed the build-up of thorium-230 in uranium-series dating. However, whereas the

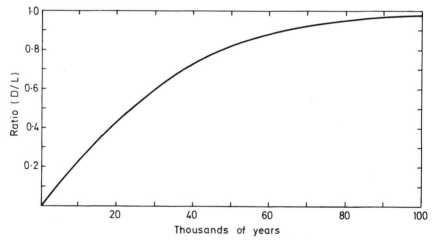

Fig. 8.1 Ratio of D–aspartic acid to L–aspartic acid versus age, for a sample in conditions such that the 'half-life' is 15,000 years. In practice the usable age range for bone is liable to be limited by contaminating intrusive amino acids; this is evidenced by ratios of less than unity for bones old enough for the equilibrium level to have been reached.

latter has a time-scale based on the immutable rate at which radioactive decay proceeds, racemization, being a molecular process, has a time-scale that is strongly dependent on temperature, as well as on some other circumstances. Table 8.1 gives the half-lives for the amino acids principally relevant to dating and it will be seen that at 25 °C the half-life is about 100 times shorter than at 0 °C. Hence in order to obtain reliable dates it is essential to use a procedure that deals satisfactorily with this temperature dependence.

Some terminology

The two forms of an amino acid are almost identical in their chemical behaviour, differing only in the asymmetry of their structural arrangement. Depending on the type of asymmetry one of the following terms is employed: *enantiomers, stereoisomers, optical isomers,* etc. The involvement of 'optical' arises because the D-enantiomer rotates plane-polarized light in the opposite direction to the L-enantiomer. This *optical activity* occurs only with amino acids for which the structural configuration is asymmetric; the configuration is centred on a carbon atom and if the configuration is asymmetric the carbon atom, and the molecule, are referred to as *chiral*; for an amino acid of symmetric configuration, e.g. glycine, the appropriate adjective is *achiral*.

Racemization is the process of conversion from L-enantiomer to D-enantiomer, or vice versa; when equilibrium is reached the D/L ratio equals 1.0 and the mixture is said to be *racemic*. In the process of

Table 8.1 Racemization half-lives and rate constants

	Half-life[a] (thousands of years)		Rate constant[b] (per year)	
	0°C	25°C	0°C	25°C
Aspartic	430	3	0.8×10^{-6}	120×10^{-6}
Alanine	1400	12	0.25×10^{-6}	30×10^{-6}
Isoleucine	⁻6000	⁻50	⁻0.07×10^{-6}	⁻8×10^{-6}

[a] The half-lives are for free amino acids in aqueous solution, pH 7.6, as quoted in Bada (1982). The values given are only a rough guide to order of magnitude and to dependence on temperature; actual half-lives found for amino acids in bone are in general appreciably longer. 'Half-life' does not have the same meaning[1] here as in radioactivity. Particularly in view of its dependence on environmental factors, etc. some authors question whether it is a useful concept in these studies.

[b] The half-life is equal to $(0.693/2k)$, where k is the rate constant; $(0.693/1.75k)$ in the case of isoleucine.

conversion the molecule passes through an intermediate state known as a *carbanion*. In some amino acids there are two chiral carbon atoms instead of the more usual one; the four possible forms are then called *diastereomers* and the conversion process *epimerization*. Conversion of L-isoleucine to D-alloisoleucine is an example of this and the relevant ratio may then be referred to as the (*allo/iso*, or, *aIle/Ile*) ratio. The term 'racemization' is often used in the sense of including epimerization.

A protein molecule comprises a long chain of different amino acids bound together by *peptide* bonds, with a molecular weight greater than 10,000 units; molecules with shorter chains than this are called *polypeptides*. In bone 90% of the protein consists of *collagen* molecules, all having the same sequence of amino acids and hence being recognizable on analysis by their distinctive *amino acid signature*.

Historical

Correlation between the degree of amino acid racemization and age was first noted by Hare and Abelson (1968) based on studies of fossil shells, with application to dating being reported shortly afterwards by Hare and Mitterer (1969) in respect of shells and by Bada *et al.* (1970) in respect of foraminifera from deep-sea sediment. The first archaeological application was to the bones of a goat found in Muleta Cave, Mallorca, for which Bada (1972) reported an age of 26,000 years – in satisfactory agreement with the value of 28,000 years obtained by radiocarbon dating.

These and other dates obtained early in the development of the technique were by means of the 'uncalibrated' method (see below). Subsequently it has been realized that for reliability it is necessary to use the 'calibrated' method and that there are important influences on the effective racemization rate other than temperature – as illustrated by Prior *et al.* (1986) in respect of bone for example (see also Ennis *et al.* 1986). For shell, because of complexity in the form of the build-up curve, the conservative approach of *aminostratigraphy* has usually been preferred; in this, *aminozones* are defined on the basis of (D/L) values, these being measured for the same genus because the racemization rate tends to be species-dependent.

There have also been investigations in respect of wood (e.g. Rutter and Crawford 1984), plant remains and coral. However, the fruitful materials in respect of dating are bone, teeth and shell, the latter being primarily marine molluscs in geological contexts.

Literature

There has been extensive discussion, controversial at times, in learned journals including review articles such as by Hare (1974), Schroeder and Bada (1976), Wehmiller (1982, 1984), Bada (1982, 1985a, 1987), Rutter *et al.* (1985), Miller and Mangerud (1985) and Masters (1986a). Access to research publications (mostly omitted in the following sections) may be obtained by reference to the foregoing; the compendium edited by Hare *et al.* (1980) will give further insight into the complexities of the processes involved; what follows now is a broad overview.

8.1.2 MEASUREMENT

Although there is difference in optical activity between the D and L forms, this property is not now the direct basis of measurement. Instead some form of *gas chromatography* (GC) or *liquid chromatography* (LC) is used, with involvement of ion-exchange techniques. The method of choice is now *high-performance liquid chromatography* (HPLC). This has a remarkable sensitivity – of less than one part *per billion*; also the organic chemistry involved is less complex than in earlier methods and appropriate facilities are likely to be found in most university chemistry laboratories, though purity of reagents needs critical attention. Measurement techniques have been discussed by Engel and Hare (1985), as well as by many others.

8.1.3 SAMPLE SIZE; PRECAUTIONS

Whereas 5–10 g of bone were required in earlier techniques, with HPLC less than 1 g is acceptable. For teeth a few tenths of a gram of purified enamel or dentine are required, and as little as 5 mg of carbonate in the case of shell – though there is then danger of error due to inhomogeneity.

While there are no special procedures for sample packaging there are two obvious precautions: avoidance of organic preservative and avoidance of prolonged heating.

8.1.4 INFLUENCES ON THE CONVERSION RATE

Temperature

As has been indicated in Table 8.1, the conversion rate is strongly dependent on temperature. For aspartic acid a change of 1 °C in the burial temperature causes the rate to change by about 25% and the effect on apparent age will be by at least this percentage. In the 'uncalibrated' method measurements of rate were made at elevated temperatures (such that the conversion proceeded rapidly enough for there to be an appreciable change in ratio) and the rate for any given burial temperature obtained from theory-based calculation. The burial temperature was determined by insertion of temperature capsules into the site; these utilized the hydrolysis of sucrose as temperature indicator. Alternatively, the burial temperature was inferred from air-temperature recordings and knowledge of past climatic variation, the latter of course being relevant with the capsule method too.

Several factors introduce unreliability into the uncalibrated approach, the difficulty of accurate evaluation of the effective burial temperature[2] being the most fundamental. In the 'calibrated' method there is no explicit evaluation of temperature. Instead the effective rate is determined by means of a known-age sample buried in similar conditions to the unknown one. This is discussed further in section 8.1.6.

Degradation
When degradation – *diagenesis* – sets in after death, hydrolysis causes disruption of the peptide bonds and there is break-up into shorter molecules; eventually free amino acids are produced. Racemization (or epimerization) probably takes place during all these phases of break-up; however, the rate appears to be faster when the acid is free than when it is part of a protein or polypeptide molecule, there being some difference too between short and long molecules as well as dependence on position in the chain. Thus the (D/L) ratio found for a given amino acid in a sample will depend on the relative proportions of the various sizes of molecule in which it exists, as well as the rapidity with which the successive stages of breakdown (from long-, to short-, to free-) occurred. A fortunate circumstance in the case of bone and teeth is that free amino acids are not retained, gross effects thereby being avoided; even so, for good reliability the degree of degradation in the known-age sample used for calibration needs to be similar to that in the samples being dated. Another safeguard, requiring more complex procedures, is to restrict analysis to the long-chain molecules.

A further stimulus towards selectivity in analysis is the avoidance of contamination by amino acids that have leached into the sample from ground water or otherwise entered (e.g. by fungal or bacterial growth).

Water and its acidity
Because water is necessary for, or at any rate greatly assists the racemization process, it is to be expected that a sample which has been in a desiccated condition during burial will show an abnormally low (D/L) ratio. However, with bone at any rate, it appears that for the arid conditions encountered in practice, the degree of dryness is rarely sufficient to suppress racemization.[3] As regards degree of acidity, although laboratory experiments at elevated temperature show dependence on pH-value the effect is much less at environmental temperatures; for the range of acidities found naturally the effect is unimportant (see Masters 1986a).

The above refers to the direct effect of water and its acidity. Since hydrolysis is the mechanism responsible for the breakdown of the protein molecules there will be an effect on the observed (D/L) ratio through the rapidity with which degradation has occurred in the sample.

8.1.5 AGE RANGE
As will be seen from Table 8.1 the age range is dependent on burial temperature and on type of acid used. In principle isoleucine can reach

back to millions of years in cold climes; in practice, however, particularly for bone and aspartic acid, there is limitation because with degradation there is little of the primary material left and greater likelihood of contamination. A guide to the upper limits accessible can be obtained from listings of published dates; these suggest around 50,000–100,000 years for aspartic acid from bone and the order of several million years for isoleucine from teeth; using the latter acid an age of 9 million years has been obtained for a shark bone stored on the sea bottom at 3 °C (Bada 1972). For shell, aminostratigraphy using isoleucine extends throughout the last million years.

The limitation in obtaining recent dates is determined by the accuracy with which the (D/L) ratio can be measured, and hence the limiting age continues to decrease as technique improvement continues; a number of aspartic acid dates of the order of 1000 years have been reported.

Error limits
The uncertainty in determination of the (D/L) ratio is around ±5% to ±10%, but it has not usually been considered realistic to translate this into uncertainty in age because of the unquantifiable uncertainties introduced in the process of calibration. However, a comprehensive system for evaluation of precision for calibrated dates of shell has now been developed (McCoy 1987).

8.1.6 APPLICATION TO BONE AND TEETH

Reliability
As has been indicated above the (D/L) ratio observed in the aspartic acid from a sample depends not only on age and temperature but also on the extent to which there has been degradation of the protein material: for two samples of the same age that have been at the same temperature the (D/L) ratio will be lower for the one in which the degradation is least. A concurrent source of unreliability in highly degraded samples is that any contaminating amino acids that have entered the sample from ground water will be a greater proportion of the whole.

One response to these difficulties is to date only those samples which are in a good state of preservation – as judged either by the percentage of protein remaining or by whether the signature given by the relative proportions of different amino acids corresponds to that for collagen (which constitutes 90% of bone protein). However, inevitably there is archaeological incentive to tackle poorly preserved bone and the key to better reliability is through selectivity. One aspect is that the calibration sample should be selected from burial conditions similar to those of the sample being dated and be in a similar state of preservation. With continued advances in technique greater selectivity in analysis becomes feasible and this somewhat relaxes the latter requirement; thus use of the long-chain (high-molecular-weight) fraction both avoids the uncertainty in rate introduced by degradation and guards against interference by contamination; ideally hydroxyproline is used, an amino acid specific to bone and teeth – as indeed is also the case with accelerator-based radiocarbon dating.

Another aspect of selectivity is in the use of tooth enamel rather than dentine or bone; because of its compact nature tooth enamel is less susceptible to degradation and to contamination – it will be recalled from section 7.4.3 that enamel is good material for ESR dating too.

Most of the foregoing applies to the use of aspartic acid, applicable to the last 50,000–100,000 years in round terms. Further back in time the isoleucine to alloisoleucine conversion is used, and because this acid is hydrophobic there is likely to be less tendency for degradation to occur; also, in carbonate-rich soils, such as those in the Olduvai region of East Africa for instance, hydrophobic amino acids are likely to be less abundant than acidic ones such as aspartic and the likelihood of contamination is less. Even so tooth enamel is better than bone. Evidence of the greater reliability of isoleucine in tooth enamel is provided by the observation of an (allo/iso) ratio close to the equilibrium value[1] of 1.3 for 3.5-million-year-old tooth enamel from close to Olduvai. This is in contrast to the situation for aspartic acid in bone; the equilibrium (D/L) value of unity for this acid is not observed in samples old enough for equilibrium to have been reached; presumably this is due to contamination by 'younger' amino acid from the groundwater (see Bada 1985a).

Calibration

Although the 'uncalibrated' method, in which the racemization rate constant for the site, *k*, is deduced from the laboratory measurements at elevated temperature has the advantage of being absolute in the sense that it does not involve other dating techniques, dependencies of rate on the factors discussed inevitably conspire to make it unreliable. In the calibrated method the appropriate value of *k* is determined by measurement of a sample for which the age is known by other means; hence interferences are avoided to a degree that depends on the similarity of the calibration sample to the sample being dated. The stringency with which similarity must be judged becomes less severe with greater selectivity in analysis – though of course the requirement of comparable temperature histories always remains. The most straightforward experimental step towards selectivity in the case of aspartic acid is to measure separately the acid-insoluble and the acid-soluble fractions (see, e.g. Matsu'ura and Ueta 1980; Ennis *et al.* 1986). However, the comments below assume that the (D/L) ratio is obtained through measurement of the total content of the amino acid concerned, as has been the case in many applications.

At one end of the reliability scale is the situation where both come from the same archaeological layer and are of similar type; obviously with such a stringent approach the scope of the technique is severely reduced, almost to the role of detection of intrusive material. At the other end of the scale the calibration sample may be from a similar site in the same[4] or a similar locality. The middle circumstance would be when the calibration sample is from the same site but of different age. In all cases comparability of state of preservation remains an important consideration, particularly if aspartic acid is being used, but the question of comparability of temperature histories is dominant – we may recall that a difference of only 1 °C causes the rate constant to change by 25%. Reference should be made here to the climatic record provided by oxygen–isotope variations (see e.g. Figs 2.7 and 2.8); obviously it is not acceptable to base dates for samples of the last glacial period or beyond on calibration by a known-age sample from the last 10,000 years. Note that it is not the temperature at sample formation that is relevant but the effective average[2] over the whole burial period.

Obviously any error in the date used for the calibration sample is reflected into the dates evaluated for the unknowns. A dramatic illustration of these was provided by the amino acid ages initially evaluated for some Californian skeletons (from Del Mar and Sunnyvale). These lay in the range 40,000–60,000 years and seemed to provide direct evidence for migration of human beings into the Americas long in advance of the previously accepted time of about 13,000 years ago. The skeleton used for calibration – from Laguna Beach, California – was dated to around 17,000 years ago by radiocarbon using conventional beta-decay counting. With the advent of the accelerator-based radiocarbon technique (AMS) the amino acid extract from the Laguna skeleton was dated and the age obtained was substantially lower – around 5000 years ago (Bada *et al.* 1984; Bada 1985b), thereby reducing the amino acid dates by the same factor; use of a rate constant appropriate to a better-preserved sample had also contributed to the erroneously high age.

BURNING AND BOILING

In dating animal bones there is the risk that they may have been cooked, thereby increasing the (D/L) ratio and giving an erroneously high age; there will be a similar effect in bones that have been cremated, but here the evidence of charring usually allows such bones to be avoided. Intrinsic evidence of heating is provided by the disappearance of the amino acid components *serine* and *threonine* and in the dating of bones from Italian caves, for instance, it was noted that anomalously high (D/L) values were obtained from bones for which the serine and threonine content was abnormally low (Belluomini 1981); however, there is the possibility of some enhancement of the (D/L) ratio before the degree of destruction of these two amino acids becomes sufficient to be noticeable.

Comparative (D/L) measurements on coeval material may be put to use in determining thermal histories. A novel example of this is the use of the aspartic ratio to establish that the corpse of the German Emperor Lothar I was boiled before burial. This emperor died, in AD 1137, some 500 km from his castle, where in keeping with tradition he had to be buried. Medieval historians hypothesize that in such situations, where there would be a delay of several weeks before burial, the corpse was defleshed, probably by boiling, in order to avoid problems of post-mortem putrification. Comparative (D/L) evaluations (Bada *et al.* 1989) on this emperor's bones and those of relatives known to have died close to the castle indeed showed a clearly enhanced ratio, consistent with about 6 hours' boiling; this estimate was based on an experimental study using deer (Skelton 1983) in which a growth of the (D/L) ratio by about 0.01 per hour of boiling was observed.

Living and recently deceased mammals

At body heat (37 °C) the racemization rate of aspartic acid is sufficient for a measurable conversion to the D form to occur within the life span of a human being; hence the technique can be used for determination of age at death (to within ±10%) – as long as the amount of racemization occurring during burial is not dominant. Since the racemization rate at burial temperature is more than 100 times slower than at body heat this kind of study can be extended back to about 1000 years – and much further in the case of Eskimos! A review of this aspect has been given by Masters (1986b); besides archaeological application there has also been use in forensic investigations and in wildlife studies.

It is necessary to use tooth enamel or dentine since there the proteins are metabolically stable, i.e. after formation they are not subsequently broken down and replaced as is the case for most other protein in the body – each time the protein is renewed the (D/L) ratio starts from zero again. The ocular lens is another organ in which the protein is metabolically stable. This has been used in the case of baleen whales, which are toothless.

Another aspect is the possibility that racemization has a causative role in the ageing process.

8.1.7 APPLICATION TO SHELL

In contrast to bone, shell has an impermeable structure and there is substantial retention of the free amino acids produced by break-up of the protein molecules; hence even more so than in bone the effective rate constant is a combination of the individual ones corresponding to bound and free amino acid and the growth of the (D/L) ratio is complex[5] except during the early stages. An advantageous consequence of the impermeable structure is the exclusion of secondary, contaminating material. Another difference between bone and shell is that the latter is species-specific.

The discussion below is in respect of marine molluscs from geological contexts; as far as possible only layers deeper than 1 m are sampled, in order to minimize temperature fluctuations. Attempts to date shell middens have not so far been successful (see Masters 1986a) and terrestrial molluscs have received only limited attention.

Aminozones

Although age evaluation on the basis of calibrated samples is undertaken (e.g. Wehmiller 1982, 1984; McCoy 1987), the more conservative approach is that of *aminostratigraphy*. Paraphrasing Miller and Hare (1980) this refers to the direct use, in a region of uniform palaeotemperature variation, of amino acid ratios as stratigraphic correlation tools, not only allowing linkage between disjunct strata but also development of regional chronostratigraphies, the subdivisions being termed aminozones (alternative terminologies: stages, groups, events). To a limited extent the proportions of different amino acids are used but the zones are essentially based on (D/L) ratios in a given species, usually for the epimerization of isoleucine to alloisoleucine; it will be recalled[1] that for this reaction the equilibrium (D/L) ratio is close to 1.3.

A review of Quaternary applications has been given by Wehmiller (1982); for examples of the way in which regional aminostratigraphies are developed the reader may refer to Miller and Mangerud (1985), Bowen and Sykes (1988) or Bowen *et al.* (1985), among others. The latter authors use statistical techniques to establish grouping of the (D/L) ratios obtained for various raised beaches (representing high-sea-level events) in south-west Britain. Several species are used, but from sites where two or more species occur relative epimerization rates are determined, normalization then being possible. From a review of these and other data Bowen and Sykes (1988) propose correlation of aminozones for high-sea-level events on the north-east Atlantic margin with warm stages of the oxygen-isotope time-scale (see section 2.3) thereby obtaining dating of the zones as indicated in Fig. 8.2.

Palaeotemperatures

Because the L–D conversion is strongly dependent on temperature, estimates of effective palaeotemperature can be made (for discussion of precision, see McCoy, 1987). This can be done most effectively when (D/L) ratios are available for the same species in two dated levels which bracket a climatic period (e.g. a glacial stage); in this way it has been estimated that in Scotland during the last glaciation the average temperature was depressed by more than 9 °C below Holocene temperatures (Miller *et al.* 1987).

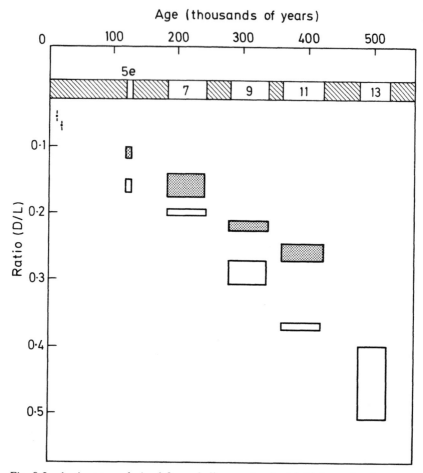

Fig. 8.2   Aminozones derived from shells associated with high-sea-level events on the north-east Atlantic margin plotted on the basis that each zone correlates with an interglacial – as indicated by odd-numbered oxygen–isotope stages (shown below the age scale at the top); hence an age is obtained for each zone. The (D/L) ratios are for the isoleucine–alloisoleucine conversion (epimerization) and the height of each rectangle indicates ± one standard deviation in the scatter of results about the average for the zone; shaded rectangles are date for *Littorina Littorea* and unshaded for *Macoma-Arctica*. (From Bowen and Sykes 1988.)

8.2 OBSIDIAN DATING

Obsidian is a form of volcanic glass widely used for prehistoric tools, and dating is based on the thickness of the hydration layer that develops on it. The technique has been used over a wide age range. As with amino acid racemization there is strong dependence on burial temperature.

There is a compendium edited by Taylor (1976) and review articles by Ericson (1975), by Friedman and Long (1976) and by Michels (1986), among others. The method was first developed in the late 1950s by Friedman and Smith (1960).

8.2.1 HYDRATION RIMS

A freshly chipped surface of obsidian slowly acquires a hydration rim by diffusion into it of water; depending on age, burial temperature and type of obsidian the thickness of the layer found on an excavated obsidian tool is likely to lie in the range 0.001–0.05 mm and to be measurable by optical microscopy. Together with data on the rate of hydration at the burial temperature concerned, this measurement allows evaluation of the time that has elapsed since the surface was freshly exposed, i.e. the archaeological event.

Because the growth of the layer is due to diffusion inwards from the exposed surface the rate of growth progressively decreases as the thickness increases – as illustrated in Fig. 8.3. Although in principle the rate might be expected to depend on the humidity of the environment, in practice this is not a significant factor; the actual amount of water taken up is very slight.

8.2.2 MEASUREMENT

A thin section, about 0.1 mm thick, is prepared from a small wedge removed from the artefact and observed in transmitted light with an

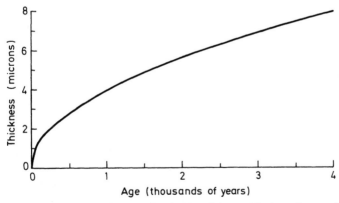

Fig. 8.3 Growth of hydrated obsidian layer with time for an obsidian having a rate constant of 16 μm^2 per 1000 years at the burial temperature concerned. The curve is parabolic because hydration is a diffusion process; hence the thickness is proportional to the square root of the age. The rate constant increases by about 10% for each 1 °C increase in temperature; 1000 μm = 1 mm.

optical microscope (magnification between ×100 and ×1000 according to the type of obsidian being studied). The boundary of the hydration layer is indicated by a diffusion front of less than 0.1 μm and considerable experience is necessary for reliable, accurate measurement. A precision of ±0.1 μm can be achieved using cross–polarized light and an image-shearing eyepiece.

For some regions, e.g. New Zealand, the growth of the hydration layer is rather slow and for artefacts that were chipped only a few hundred years ago the layer thickness may be less than 1 μm. A new technique, *sputter-induced optical spectrometry* (SIPS), may be useful here, having prospect of measurement precision approaching ±0.02 μm (Leach and Hamel 1984). Utilization of nuclear resonance reactions has also been tried, but no significant improvement in precision over optical microscopy has so far been reported (Leach and Naylor 1981).

8.2.3 ABSOLUTE AGE DETERMINATION

Until the late 1970s the favoured approach was by regional calibration using known-age samples. Since then the emphasis has been on obtaining absolute ages independent of other techniques or archaeological chronology. This requires two major evaluations (in addition to measurement of the hydration rim itself): (1) The effective burial temperature, and (2) the rate constant[6] for the obsidian concerned at that temperature.

Laboratory evaluation of the rate constant is achieved through experiments at elevated temperatures (and pressure) in which measurable hydration rims are induced within a few days (e.g. Michels *et al.* 1983a; Stevenson *et al.* 1989). The rate constant appropriate to the burial temperature is calculated using the Arrhenius equation[6], rates at a series of elevated temperatures having been measured. This experimentation needs to be done for each type of obsidian that is dated; however, once obsidian dating has been established in a region a corpus of data becomes available which obviates the need for repetition of rate constant evaluation on each individual specimen. In this context 'type' means source and it is a matter of identifying the source of a specimen by means of chemical analysis of minor impurities (using atomic absorption spectroscopy, XRF, or other routinely available techniques). Rate constant data has now been established for a range of sources throughout the world.

The approach described is equivalent to the uncalibrated technique initially used for amino acid dating instead of the calibrated approach now favoured; in fact the initial work in obsidian dating used an equivalent of the latter. However, besides the intrinsic attractiveness of absolute dating, the necessity for detailed evaluation of burial temperatures became evident, as well as for differentiation between obsidian from different sources. Sites to which obsidian dating is applied tend to be nearer the surface and therefore subject to greater temperature variation than the deeper-lying palaeolithic levels with which amino acid dating is concerned (though obsidian dating has been applied to such levels also – see Michels *et al.* 1983b).

8.2.4 BURIAL TEMPERATURE

As with amino acid dating it is not satisfactory to use the average temperature because, on account of the exponential dependence[6] on temperature, the increase in hydration rate due to a given elevation in temperature does not equal the decrease due to a depression in temperature by the same amount. As a consequence it is necessary to evaluate the *effective hydration temperature* (EHT) taking the exponential dependence into account.

In one approach the temperature and temperature variation at the relevant depth are calculated from soil engineering formulae, based on heat-flow models, using as input data meteorological records of air temperature (e.g. Stevenson *et al.* 1989). This approach is difficult to apply on sites with irregular stratigraphy, and direct measurement of EHT by means of the specially designed *Ambrose cell* (Ambrose, 1976), preferred in any case, is then more reliable. This cell, which is based on a diffusion process, is buried in the relevant layer for a year and then retrieved for measurement; the precision attainable is somewhat better than ±0.5 °C.

A comprehensive evaluation of performance of the cell on sites in New Zealand has been made by Leach and Hamel (1984). As these authors remark, however precisely the EHT is measured it is not necessarily an accurate evaluation relevant to the whole of the burial period. Variations in site aspect, vegetational cover and overburden being among the interfering influences; therefore the relevance of the EHT measurement and hence the reliability of the date obtained is much higher on sites for which there is evidence that these influences have stayed constant. Of course the same applies to the soil engineering approach.

A longer-term interfering influence, as with amino acid dating, is climatic change. Although present-day measurements of EHT may give sufficiently reliable estimates for the last few millennia, growing uncertainty is introduced further back in time; there will be a serious underestimate of age if the burial period has encompassed an appreciable portion of the last glacial period unless allowance is made for palaeotemperature variation (as by Suzuki 1974, for instance).

8.2.5 AGE RANGE

Dates have been reported in the age range from 200 to 100,000 years ago. The limitation for recent ages is the experimental imprecision in measuring the width of the hydration rim (see section 8.2.2); the comparatively rapid hydration rates in tropical countries allow more recent dating than in Arctic regions where it may take a couple of millennia to reach a thickness of only 1 μm; of course there is wide variation between different types too.

The maximum age that can be reached is limited for some types of obsidian by the onset of chemical corrosion; this may seriously damage the hydration rim though in some weathered artefacts it is possible to find areas where the rim is intact. Otherwise the question arises as to whether the law[6] of parabolic growth with time is obeyed indefinitely.

Error limits

Quoted limits are usually based only on the experimental uncertainty in measurement of layer width. On account of the parabolic law a given percentage uncertainty in width leads to a percentage uncertainty in age that is twice as great. Thus for an obsidian of about 2000 years old and a layer thickness of 2 ± 0.1 μm the age error limits will be ± 200 years. However, there is also the uncertainty in EHT and this is liable to be more serious, as well as having the same effect on all samples from a given location (and therefore not discernible through enhanced scatter of individual ages). An uncertainty of $\pm 1°C$ in EHT leads to an uncertainty of about $\pm 10\%$ in age, i.e. to error limits of ± 200 years in a 2000-year-old sample. Although the effect of measurement uncertainty can be reduced by averaging ages from a number of samples, the error limits due to EHT uncertainty are undiminished. In many locations it cannot be assumed that the EHT uncertainty is as little as $\pm 1°C$.

8.3 OTHER CHEMICAL METHODS

8.3.1 GLASS LAYER COUNTING

Following on from obsidian dating it is appropriate to mention the weathering crusts that develop on man-made glass. Some ancient glass exhibits iridescence due to diffraction effects associated with layers within these crusts, and during study of some well-dated specimens Brill and Hood (1961) noted that the number of layers was equal to the age. At one time it was thought that 'layer counting' would be a powerful method of dating, but subsequent investigations (see Newton 1971) showed that the layers could be produced in the absence of environmental variations; this was through accelerated weathering experiments and also by examining glass from natural locations subject to negligible annual variation, such as obtains on the bed of the sea. It was concluded that the layers are produced at a fairly constant rate which is generally rather less than one per year and that examples of apparently annual layers occur when the rate happens to be faster than usual.

The crusts are quite thick; for glasses of poor corrosion resistance which have been buried in moist conditions they may reach several millimetres. The layers lie in the range 0.5–20 μm.

8.3.2 FLUORINE, URANIUM AND NITROGEN CONTENT OF BONE (FUN DATING)
The difficulties caused by the progressive degradation of buried bone
have been discussed already in connection with radiocarbon, uranium
series, ESR and amino acid. The fluorine and nitrogen contents increase
because of incorporation of these elements in the phosphatic mineral
(hydroxyapatite) of which bones are mainly composed; on the other
hand, the nitrogen content decreases due to disappearance of protein
(collagen). Although there is strong dependence on the burial environment
these changes can be used for relative dating of bones found in the same
deposit (e.g. as by Haddy and Hanson 1982). They are also useful in
checking contemporaneity when selecting samples for radiocarbon, less
than 0.1 g being required.

The techniques have had an important role in detecting recent intrusions
in Lower Palaeolithic deposits, an example being the demonstration that
the Piltdown Man was a hoax. Further information may be found in
Oakley (1969); see also Eisenbarth and Hille (1977) and Demetsopoulos
et al. (1983).

Fluorine profiles
Using a nuclear microprobe it is possible to obtain a profile of the
fluorine concentration across a section of a bone. In old enough bone
the profile is flat whereas in young bone the concentration falls steeply
with increasing distance into the bone (see Fig. 8.4). Thus the shape of
the profile is age-dependent, giving an approximate dating tool (see, for
example, Coote and Sparks 1981; Coote *et al.* 1982; Coote and Nelson
1987; Coote and Dennison 1988). The burial soil needs to be moist,
but since the evaluation is based only on the shape of the profile the
concentration of fluorine in the soil is unimportant (as long as it is

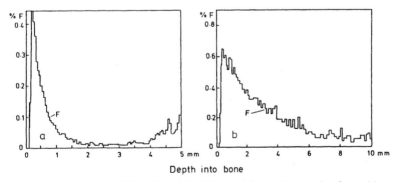

Depth into bone

Fig. 8.4 Fluorine profiles obtained with a nuclear microprobe from (a) a
700-year-old bone, and (b) a 16,000-year-old bone. The horizontal scale shows
the depth into the bone. Dating is based on comparison with theoretical diffusion
profiles calculated for different ages. (From Coote and Nelson 1987.)

sufficient to give a profile). From experience of application in New Zealand, Coote and Dennison suggest it is a useful technique:

(a) for rapid survey of a site as a guide to selection of samples for radiocarbon;
(b) as a substitute for radiocarbon on sites of the last few hundred years (during which the radiocarbon calibration curve is flat – see section 4.4.4);
(c) for surveying museum collections.

Fluorine profiles can also be observed in teeth (e.g. Coote and Nelson 1987; Coote and Molleson 1988) though the situation is complicated by heterogeneity.

NOTES

1. The form of the growth of the (D/L) ratio with age is determined by the kinetic equation for a first-order reversible reaction (see Bada 1985a, for instance):

$$\ln \left\{ \frac{1 + (D/L)}{1 - K(D/L)} \right\} - \ln \left\{ \frac{1 + (D/L)}{1 - K(D/L)} \right\}_{t=0} = (1 + K)\, kt \qquad (8.1)$$

where k is the racemization rate constant and t is time. The constant K is equal to unity for aspartic and other acids which have only one chiral carbon atom, but for isoleucine with two chiral atoms K is about 0.75, and hence the equilibrium (D/L) ratio as t tends to infinity is close to 1.3, instead of unity in the case of $K = 1$.

For $K = 1$ and taking (D/L) $= 0$ at $t = 0$, the equation reduces to

$$\text{(D/L)} = \tanh(kt) \qquad (8.2)$$

and this has been used for Fig. 8.1. The half-life, defined in terms of equation (8.1), is equal to $(0.693/2k)$; hence (D/L) $= 0.33$ when the age is equal to the half-life; the corresponding ratio in the case of $K = 0.75$ is 0.4, again assuming (D/L) $= 0$ at $t = 0$. For radioactive grow-in, such as shown in Fig. 5.3 for thorium-230, the activity ratio is 0.5 at an age equal to the relevant half-life.

The $t = 0$ term in equation (8.1) serves to deal with the case when the initial (D/L) ratio is not zero; in age determination this ratio effectively starts at zero unless severe burning has occurred. However, the term can also be used to make allowance for the racemization that occurs during hydrolysis in sample treatment; some published values of the (D/L) ratio include the effect of such hydrolysis, with a note indicating the (D/L) value appropriate for insertion in the $t = 0$ term.

2. Because the rate of conversion is exponentially dependent on temperature the effective temperature is not the same as the average

temperature; a period during which the temperature is higher than usual has a much greater influence on the average rate than one during which it is lower than usual.

3. However, the remarkably low ratios found in the La Brea tar pits (McMenamin *et al.* 1982) may be an example of the effect of water exclusion.

4. The aspartic acid racemization rate constants for bones from eight caves in southern-central Italy, measured by Belluomini (1981), spread between 2.4×10^{-6} and 5.3×10^{-6} per year. Thus if the rate constant derived from a known-age sample in only one cave had been used for dating of samples in the others, age errors by up to a factor of two might have occurred. In fact Belluomini used a separate rate constant for each individual cave.

5. The growth in (D/L) ratio in bone during laboratory experiments at elevated temperature follows linear kinetics as appropriate to a first-order reversible reaction – equation (8.1). With shell this is not the case, there being an initial period of relatively rapid racemization followed by a period for which the effective rate constant is lower, i.e. non-linear kinetics, which complicates use of the 'calibrated' approach if extrapolation beyond the linear region is attempted (see Wehmiller 1982, 1984). On the other hand the rate of growth in bone increases during burial once the degree of degradation has become appreciable.

6. As proposed by Friedman and Smith (1960), the thickness, x, is related to the burial time, t, according to

$$x^2 = kt \tag{8.3}$$

with the temperature dependence of k, the rate constant, being given by the Arrhenius equation,

$$k = A \exp(-E/RT) \tag{8.4}$$

where A is a constant for a given obsidian, E is the activation energy, R is the universal gas constant (8.3 J/mol per degree K) and T is the absolute temperature in degrees K.

Typical values of E are around 80,000 J/mol; this predicts that at 17 °C the rate constant will increase by 11% for a 1 °C increase in temperature.

REFERENCES

Ambrose, W. R. (1976) Intrinsic hydration rate dating of obsidian, in *Advances in Obsidian Glass Studies* (ed. R. E. Taylor), Noyes Press, Park Ridge, New Jersey, pp. 81–105.

Bada, J. L. (1972) The dating of fossil bones using the racemization of isoleucine, *Earth Planet. Sci. Lett.* **15**, 223–31.

Bada, J. L. (1982) Racemization of amino acids in nature, *Interdisciplinary Science Reviews* **7**, 30–460.

Bada, J. L. (1985a) Amino acid racemization dating of fossil bones, *Ann. rev. Earth Planet. Sci.* **13**, 241–68.

Bada, J. L. (1985b) Aspartic acid racemization ages of California palaeoindian skeletons, *American Antiquity* **50**, 645–7.

Bada, J. L. (1987) Palaeoanthropological applications of amino acid racemization of fossil bones and teeth, *Anthrop. Anz.* **45**, 1–8.

Bada, J. L., Luyendyk, B. P. and Maynard, J. B. (1970) Marine sediments: dating by racemization of amino acids, *Science* **170**, 730–2.

Bada, J. L., Gillespie, R., Gowlett, J. A. J., and Hedges, R.E.M. (1984) Accelerator mass spectrometry radiocarbon ages of amino acid extracts from Californian palaeoindian skeletons, *Nature* **312**, 442–4.

Bada, J. L., Herrmann, B. and Man, E. H. (1989) Amino acid racemization and the boiling of the German Emperor Lothar I, *Applied Geochemistry* **4** (no. 3), in press.

Belluomini, G. (1981) Direct aspartic acid dating of human fossil bones from archaeological sites of central southern Italy, *Archaeometry* **23**, 125–38.

Bowen, D. Q., Sykes, G. A., Reeves, A., Miller, G. H., Andrews, G. T., Brew, J. S. and Hare, P. E. (1985) Amino acid geochronology of raised beaches in south west Britain, *Quat. Sci. Rev.* **4**, 279–318.

Bowen, D. Q. and Sykes, G. A. (1988) Correlation of marine events and glaciations on the northeast Atlantic margin, *Phil. Trans. Roy. Soc. Lond.* **B318**, 619–35.

Brill, R. H. and Hood, H. P. (1961) A new method for dating ancient glass, *Nature* **189**, 12–14.

Coote, G. E. and Sparks, R. J. (1981) Fluorine concentration profiles in archaeological bones, *New Zealand Journal of Archaeology* **3**, 21–32.

Coote, G. E., Sparks, R. J. and Blattner, P. (1982) Nuclear microprobe measurement of fluorine concentration profiles, with application in archaeology and geology, *Nuclear Instruments and Methods* **197**, 213–21.

Coote, G. E. and Nelson, P. (1987) Diffusion profiles of fluorine in archaeological bones and teeth: their measurement and application in *Archaeology at ANZAAS* (ed. G. K. Ward), Canberra Archaeological Society, c/o Australian National University, Canberra, pp. 22–7.

Coote, G. C. and Dennison, K. J. (1988) Fluorine diffusion profiles in archaeological bones: applications in New Zealand and two Pacific Islands, in *Archaeometry: Australian Studies 1988*, (ed. J. R. Prescott), Department of Physics, University of Adelaide, Adelaide, pp. 157–63.

Coote, G. E. and Molleson, T. (1988) Fluorine diffusion profiles in archaeological human teeth: a method for relative dating of burials?, in *Archaeometry: Australian Studies 1988* (ed. J. R. Prescott), Department of Physics, University of Adelaide, Adelaide, pp. 99–104.

Demetsopoulos, J. C., Burleigh, R. and Oakley, K. P. (1983) Relative and absolute dating of the human skeleton from Galley Hill, Kent, *Journ. Archaeol. Sci.* **10**, 129–34.

Eisenbarth P. and Hille, P. (1977) A non–destructive method for age determination of fossil bone, *Journ. Radioanalytical Chem.* **40**, 203–11.

Engel, M. H. and Hare, P. E. (1985) Gas–liquid chromatographic separation of amino acids and their derivatives, in *Chemistry and Biochemistry of the Amino Acids* (ed. G. C. Barrett), Chapman & Hall, London, pp. 462–79.

Ennis, P., Noltmann, E. A., Hare, P. E., Slota, P. J., Payen, L. A., Prior, C. A. and Taylor, R. D. (1986) Use of AMS[14]C analysis in the study of problems in aspartic acid racemization-deduced age estimates on bone, *Radiocarbon* **28**, 539–46.

Ericson, J. E. (1975) New results in obsidian hydration dating, *World Archaeology* **7** (2), 151–9.

Friedman, I. and Smith, R. L. (1960) *Am. Antiq.* **25**, 476.

Friedman, I. and Long, W. (1976) *Science* **191**, 347.

Haddy, A. and Hanson, A. (1982) Nitrogen and fluorine dating of Moundville skeletal samples, *Archaeometry* **24**, 37–44.

Hare, P. E. and Abelson, P. H. (1968) Racemization of amino acids in fossil shells: *Carnegie Institution of Washington Yearbook,* vol. 66, pp. 516–28.

Hare, P. E. (1974) Amino acid dating – a history and an evaluation, *MASCA Newsletter* **10**, 4–7.

Hare, P. E. and Mitterer, R. M. (1969) Laboratory simulation of amino acid diagenesis in fossils: *Carnegie Institution of Washington Yearbook,* vol. 67, pp. 205–8.

Hare, P. E., Hoering, T. C. and King, K. (eds) (1980) *Biogeochemistry of Amino Acids,* Wiley, New York.

Leach, B. F. and Naylor, H. (1981) Dating New Zealand obsidians by resonant nuclear reactions. *New Zealand Journal of Archaeology* **3**, 33–49.

Leach, B. F. and Hamel, G. E. (1984) The influence of archaeological soil temperatures on obsidian dating in New Zealand, *New Zealand Journal of Science* **27**, 399–408.

McCoy, W. D. (1987) The precision of amino acid geochronology and paleothermometry, *Quat. Sci. Rev.* **6**, 43–54.

McMenamin, M. A. S., Blunt, D., Kvenvolden, K. A., Miller, S. E. and Marcus, L. F. (1982) Amino acid geochemistry of fossil bones from Rancho La Brea asphalt deposits, California, *Quat. Res.* **18**, 174–83.

Masters, P. M. (1986a) Amino acid racemization dating – a review, in *Dating and Age Determination of Biological Materials,* (eds M. R. Zimmerman and J. L. Angel), Croom Helm, London, pp. 39–58.

Masters, P. M. (1986b) Age determination of living mammals using aspartic acid racemization in structural proteins, *Dating and Age Determination of Biological Materials,* (eds M. R. Zimmerman and J. L. Angel), Croom Helm, London, pp. 270–83.

Matsu'ura, S. and Ueta, N. (1980) Fraction dependent variation of aspartic acid racemization age of fossil bone, *Nature* **286**, 883–4.

Michels, J. W. (1986) Obsidian hydration dating, *Endeavour* (New Series) **10**, 97–100.

Michels, J. W., Tsong, I. S. T. and Smith, G. A. (1983a) Experimentally derived hydration rates in obsidian dating, *Archaeometry* **25**, 107–17.

Michels, J. W., Tsong, I. S. T. and Nelson, C. M. (1983b) Obsidian dating and East African archaeology, *Science* **219**, 361–6.

Miller, G. H. and Hare, P. E. (1980) Amino acid geochronology: integrity of the carbonate matrix and potential of molluscan fossils, in *Biogeochemistry of Amino Acids* (eds P. E. Hare, T. C. Hoering and K. King Jr), Wiley, New York, pp. 415–44.

Miller, G. H. and Mangerud, J. (1985) Aminostratigraphy of European marine interglacial deposits, *Quat. Sci. Rev.* **4**, 215–78.

Miller, G. H., Jull, A. J. T., Linick, T., Sutherland, D., Sejrup, H. P., Brigham, J. K., Bowen, D. Q. and Mangerud, J. (1987) Racemization-derived late Devensian temperature reduction in Scotland, *Nature* **326**, 593–5.

Newton, R. G. (1971) The enigma of the layered crusts on some weathered glasses, a chronological account of the investigations, *Archaeometry* **13**, 1–9.

Oakley, K. P. (1969) Analytical methods of dating bones, in *Science and Archaeology* (eds D. Brothwell and E. Higgs), Thames & Hudson, London, pp. 35–45.

Prior, C. A., Ennis, P. J., Noltmann, E. A., Hare, P. E. and Taylor, R. D. (1986) Variations in D/L aspartic acid ratios in bones of similar age and temperature history, in *Proceedings of the 24th International Archaeometry Symposium* (eds J. S. Olin and M. J. Blackman), Smithsonian Institution, Washington DC, pp. 487–98.

Rutter, N. W. and Crawford, R. J. (1984) Utilizing wood in amino acid dating, *Quaternary Dating Methods* (ed. W. C. Mahany), Elsevier, Amsterdam, pp. 171–93.

Rutter, N. W., Crawford, R. J. and Hamilton, R. D. (1985) Amino acid racemization dating, in *Dating methods of Pleistocene Deposits and their Problems* (ed. N. W. Rutter), Geoscience Canada, Reprint Series 2, pp. 23–30.

Schroeder, R. A. and Bada, J. L. (1976) A review of the geochemical applications of the amino acid racemization reaction, *Earth Science Reviews*, **12**, 347–91.

Skelton, R. R. (1983) Amino acid racemization dating: a test of its reliability for North American archaeology, Ph.D. thesis, Univ. of Calif., Davis, 343pp.

Stevenson, C. M., Carpenter, J. and Scheetz, B. E. (1989) Obsidian dating: recent advances in the experimental determination and application of hydration rates, *Archaeometry* **31**, 193–206.

Suzuki, M. (1974) Chronology of prehistoric human activity in Kanto, Japan, *Journal of the Faculty of Science, University of Tokyo* **4** (4), 395–469.

Taylor, R. E. (ed.) (1976) *Advances in Obsidian Glass Studies*, Noyes Press, Park Ridge, New Jersey, 360 pp.

Wehmiller, J. F. (1982) A review of amino acid racemization studies in Quaternary molluscs: stratigraphic and chronologic applications in coastal and interglacial sites: Pacific and Atlantic coast, United States, United Kingdom, Baffin Island and tropical islands, *Quat. Sci. Rev.* **1**, 83–120.

Wehmiller, J. F. (1984) Relative and absolute dating of Quaternary molluscs with amino acid racemization: evaluation, applications and questions, *Quaternary Dating Methods* (ed. W. C. Mahany), Elsevier, Amsterdam, pp. 171–93.

9 Magnetic dating and magnetostratigraphy

9.1 INTRODUCTION

Pervading the space in which we live is the earth's magnetic field, its presence manifesting itself most obviously by its effect on the magnetized needle of a compass. As is well known, *Magnetic North* is not the same as *True (or Geographic) North* and the angle between the two does not stay the same; from year to year the change is barely perceptible but over a century it may be as much as 10 °. Relevance to archaeology arises because of a subtle recording mechanism intrinsic to the iron oxides that are usually present as minor impurities in clay; when clay cools down from firing it acquires a weak but permanent magnetization. Hence the floor and walls of a pottery kiln retain a memory of the earth's field direction at the time when the kiln was last used. Evaluation of date requires there to be a reference curve for the region concerned showing what the direction has been during past centuries; this is usually based on similar measurements made on kilns (or hearths, etc.) for which the date is known by other means. Thus it is essentially a matter of transferring chronology rather than making independent evaluation; also, the extent of the region within which transfer can be made is somewhat limited – to an overall span of around 1000 km; a further limitation is the occasional repetition of direction – see Fig. 9.1. On the other hand, the precision that can be achieved in some periods and regions surpasses that of other techniques. Bricks and tiles can also be utilized though only in respect of inclination.

Magnetic involvement of archaeological material is usually referred to as *archaeomagnetism*, primarily relevant to the last three or four millennia. It has a long history, early measurements having been made in Italy by Gheradi (1862) and Folgheraiter (1899). Following Mercanton (1918) comprehensive study began in the late 1930s with the pioneer work of Emile and Odette Thellier in Paris. Archaeomagnetism merges into the much wider field of *palaeomagnetism* – involvement of geological material. The record acquired by volcanic lava as it cooled was the primary subject

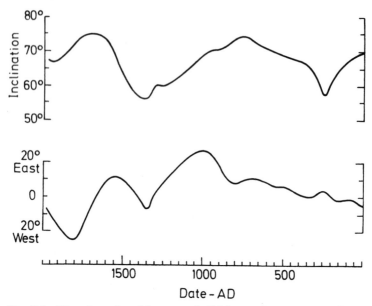

Fig. 9.1 Direction of earth's magnetic field over the past two millennia according to archaeomagnetic measurements, and, from AD 1576, observations recorded by scientists. *Declination* (*D*) is the angle between Magnetic North (as indicated by a compass needle) and True (Geographic) North. *Inclination* (*I*), or *angle of dip*, is the angle between the direction of the lines of force and the horizontal; if a magnetized needle is suspended exactly at its centre of gravity its north-seeking end dips below the horizontal by the angle *I*.

of study, but there is also the more widespread record carried by unburnt sediment – acquired during deposition or fairly soon after. Both of these materials are important for their recording of *polarity changes* in which there was reversal of direction, i.e. during a period of reversed polarity the 'north' end of a present-day compass would have pointed towards the Antarctic instead of the Arctic. There are seven or eight of these within the last 2 million years and the *reversal stratigraphy* derived from them has a vital role in the establishment of Palaeolithic time-scales – already discussed in Chapter 2. As with magnetic dating of kilns it allows transference of chronology, based on potassium–argon dating in this case, rather than independent evaluation but with the important difference of being world-wide rather than regional.

Thus there is dating involvement of the earth's magnetic field both in recent millennia and in distant millennia. The next three sections are relevant to both; the following section deals with the distant millennia and then the subsequent sections with the various aspects of recent millennia. Palaeomagnetic research covers a much wider field than dating; it is a geological tool in elucidating structural features of the earth's crust as well as providing important data for geophysicists concerned with the earth's core, as does archaeomagnetism also. For archaeologists there is more in magnetism than dating; its role in site surveying is well established but also it is increasingly used in environmental studies. The text by Thompson and Oldfield (1986) deals with this aspect as well as giving a concise account of theory and practice relevant to the present chapter.

9.2 THE EARTH'S MAGNETIC FIELD

9.2.1 MAIN FEATURES

Deep within the earth, some 3000 km below the surface and about half-way to the centre, there is the boundary between the solid mantle and the fluid part of the core (which is solid at the centre). In the fluid part there is a dynamo mechanism and the associated electric currents are the source of the earth's magnetism. The magnetic field that we experience at the surface – which controls the direction of a compass needle for instance – is due to these deep internal currents, only a very minor contribution arising externally from currents in the ionosphere, etc.

The main current in the fluid core produces a field which has the same spatial pattern of lines of force as a bar magnet at the centre of the earth (see Fig. 9.2); this main field is known as the *dipole* component. Near the core–mantle boundary there are irregularities in the flow of current and these give rise to *non-dipole* components. These are 'localized' in the sense that they affect restricted regions of the earth's surface several thousand kilometres across. The non-dipole components vary on a time-scale of a few hundred years whereas variation of the dipole is slower. Both components change in strength as well as direction; 'dipole wobble' refers to the tendency for the axis of the dipole field to precess around the earth's axis of rotation, and for the angle between the two, at present 11.5°, to change. The *secular variation* of the direction of the field, as shown in Fig. 9.1 and elsewhere, represents the effect of dipole wobble combined with the effects of growth and of drifting of the non-dipole components; the latter have been compared to atmospheric depressions as they move across the Atlantic and though on a time-scale of centuries the irregularity of their behaviour is no less.

9.2.2 SECULAR VARIATION

Historically minded archaeologists will find interest in the classic paper by Bauer (1899) in which he collates past values of *D* and *I* that earlier scientists derived from observations made on magnetized needles. For London, Paris and Rome these extend over the past four centuries – see Fig. 9.3 – but of course they begin more recently in most other parts of the world, e.g.

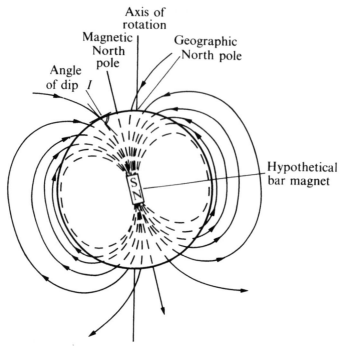

Fig. 9.2 Bar magnet representation of the main part of the earth's magnetic field
– the dipole component. The *lines of force* represent, at any point, the direction in
which a small magnetized needle tries to point. The concentration of these lines
is a measure of the *field strength* or *field intensity*. (From Aitken 1974.)

in 1780 for Boston, USA. Apart from its historical interest Bauer's paper
is useful in illustrating some characteristics of the secular variation. From
Fig. 9.3 we may note that whereas the form of the variation is similar for
the three cities located in Europe within a region of 1400 km across, it
is altogether different for Boston some 6000 km away from the region.
Also, although the pattern for the three European cities is similar, it is
not exactly the same and use of the London curve as it stands would not
yield accurate magnetic dates for sites even as near as Paris, only 350 km
away; more discussion on the extent of the region over which a reference
curve can be expected to be reliably applicable is given in section 9.6.2.
Some of the difference in *I* is due to the dependence on latitude[1] for the
dipole component of the field (see Fig. 9.4), the latitudes of London, Paris
and Rome being 51.5 °, 49 ° and 42 ° respectively. However, the recorded
differences in *I* between these cities change with time – indicative of the
influence of a non–dipole disturbance (or of wobbling of the dipole).

The curves of Fig. 9.3 suggest that the secular variation has a
regular periodicity of 400–500 years and this idea was still current

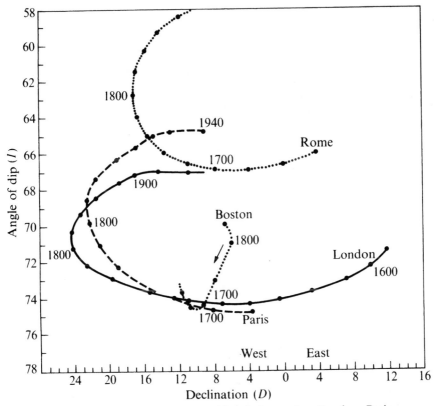

Fig. 9.3 Secular variation according to historical records – London, Paris,
Rome and Boston. The time-scale is indicated by dots at 20-year intervals.
Prior to AD 1900 the curves shown are those obtained by Bauer (1899) using
recorded observations to determine an empirical formula for the change. (From
Aitken 1974.)

during the first half of the twentieth century. However, when the
record is extended over a longer time (see Fig. 9.1) it is evident that
there is no question of a well-defined periodicity; that the curves of Fig.
9.3 appear to be regular is due to the fact that Bauer fitted the data to
an empirical formula – and it happened that for the centuries concerned
the curves approximate to ellipses.

With more data available it is evident that variation on a time-scale of
a few hundred years has occurred during all millennia studied, but that if
there is a well-defined pattern it is submerged beneath irregularities (see,
however, Kawai and Hirooka 1967; also Creer 1977).

9.2.3 WESTWARD DRIFT; CLOCKWISE MOTION
Excluding local anomalies due to iron-ore deposits in the earth's crust

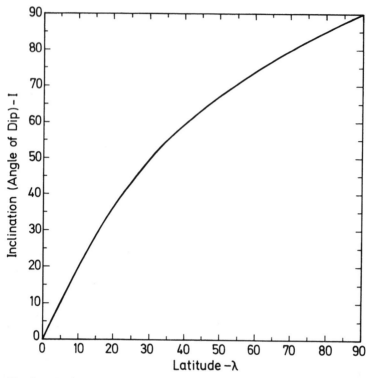

Fig. 9.4 Inclination, *I*, versus latitude, λ, for the dipole component of the field when the dipole is along the axis of the earth's rotation. For this situation the declination, *D*, would be zero everywhere, as long as non–dipole components were absent.

there are, at present, about ten regions where non–dipole components cause strong deviation from the regular pattern of the dipole field, each several thousand kilometres across. At present these regions are drifting westward at the rate of about 20 ° of longitude per century (Bullard *et al.* 1950) and there is evidence that such westward drift has been going on for at least the past four centuries (Skiles 1970).

The geophysical interpretation of this drift is that there is relative motion between the outer part of the core and the mantle (plus crust) – the mantle rotates slightly faster than the core and so magnetic features associated with irregularities in the current pattern in the core appear to an observer on the crust to be drifting westward. Hence it should be possible to derive the past secular variation at a particular station by studying the present-day irregularities observed on looking westward along the line of latitude running through the station. As pointed out by Bauer this is approximately the case for London, Paris and Rome over the past few centuries; however, archaeomagnetic data show that the correlation breaks down in earlier centuries (Aitken and Weaver 1962). This is consistent with the notion that lifetimes of irregularities are no more than a few hundred years; on the other hand there is some evidence (e.g. Latham *et al.* 1986) that lifetimes can be of the order of 1000 years. However, even if it were the general rule that irregularities persist long enough to drift right round the world it is to be expected that some modification of characteristics will occur; hence postdiction of past secular variation from present-day observations is highly unlikely to be of other than academic interest as far as magnetic dating is concerned.

The motion of the curves shown in Fig. 9.2 may be described as *clockwise*. It can be shown (Runcorn 1959, but see Dodson 1979; also Creer and Tucholka 1982) that this is an expected consequence of westward drift, and that eastward drift would result in counter-clockwise motion – as was occurring before about AD 1350 according to the archaeomagnetic data of Fig. 9.11). Obviously such a change in direction of drift would further debar any attempt at postdiction.

9.2.4 POLARITY CHANGES

Much more dramatic than secular variation are occasional world-wide changes of polarity – meaning that in the representation of Fig. 9.2 the direction of all arrows should be reversed. A polarity change is due to the reversal of the dynamo currents producing the main dipole field and the transition is thought to involve the falling to zero of these currents with subsequent regrowth in the opposite direction. The major *chrons* of polarity for the last few million years are illustrated in Fig. 9.5; within these are *subchrons* (see Table 9.1) lasting several hundred thousand years and sometimes much less. The transition time for reversal is the order of a few thousand years.

Reversal does not occur every time the main currents fall to zero, there being a 50 : 50 chance of regrowth in either direction; regrowth in the same direction may be termed an *aborted reversal*. The falling to zero of the main field is not necessarily accompanied by a falling to zero of the non-dipole components; hence the influence of the latter may become dominant during the transitional period of a polarity change, or

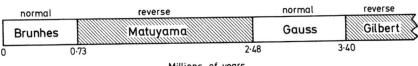

Fig. 9.5   Major polarity chrons of the last 5 million years with ages for transitions based on potassium–argon (see Mankinen and Dalrymple 1979). Alternative terminology is *zone*, formerly *epoch*.

equally during an aborted reversal, thereby leading to much more violent changes in direction than occur during normal secular variation. Similar violent *excursions* of direction may also be due to exceptionally strong non-dipole components in a particular region; sometimes these may be strong enough to cause a localized reversal in direction even though the main dipole field does not change.

9.3 RECORDING MECHANISMS

9.3.1 THERMOREMANENT MAGNETISM (TRM)

Most clay and soil, and some rocks, contain a few per cent of iron oxide, dispersed as fine grains. Usually these are so small that each consists of a single magnetic domain – in which the atomic magnetic moments are all aligned in the same direction (a direction determined by the axes of the crystal structure). The grains are randomly orientated, and in raw clay so too the domains (Fig 9.6); hence the net magnetic effect is very small since on average every domain is balanced by another pointing in the opposite direction. If the temperature is raised to a few hundred degrees centigrade or more, the thermal agitation of the crystal

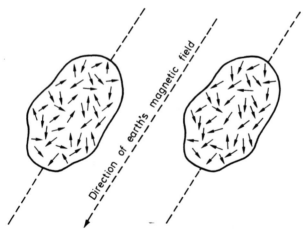

(a) **Before baking**   (b) **After baking**

Fig. 9.6 Domain alignment in baked clay. (a) Unbaked clay: the domains are in random directions and net magnetization is very small. (b) Baked clay: elevated temperature has allowed preferential alignment which subsequently remains 'frozen' at normal temperatures; this gives the clay a net magnetization in the same direction as the earth's magnetic field. In fact, contrary to what is shown, only a small proportion of the domains change; hence the magnetization is rather weak (although permanent).

lattice allows some of the domains to reverse their direction so there is now an excess having a component in the same direction as the earth's field. On cooling, the domain directions are frozen and because of the preferential alignment there is now a weak permanent magnetization in the same direction as the earth's field. The same mechanism pertains in igneous rocks and volcanic lava.

The temperature at which domains can reverse their direction, the *blocking* temperature T_B, depends on the size and shape of the grain and its mineral composition (e.g. whether the iron oxide is in the form of haematite, magnetite, or maghemite). Usually there is such a variety of grains present that there is continuous distribution of blocking temperatures up to around 500–700 °C – see Fig. 9.7. The magnetization carried by grains having blocking temperatures above 200–300 °C is stable over very long periods – hundreds of thousands of years or more – whereas the magnetization carried by grains having lower blocking temperatures will change more rapidly, a new magnetization being acquired corresponding to the new direction of the field (this is termed *viscous* magnetization – see below).

A new magnetization is acquired also by the most stable carriers if there is a second heating in which the temperature reaches their blocking temperature. Hence the remanence found in a sample today

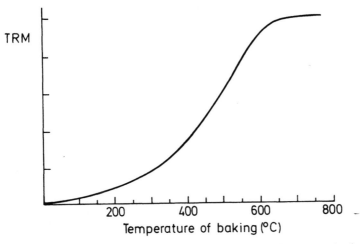

Fig. 9.7 Acquisition of TRM. The curve indicates the magnetization, measured at 20 °C, acquired in cooling down from the temperature indicated, in a magnetic field. If after magnetization by cooling from 750 °C the sample is heated to 300 °C (say) and cooled in zero magnetic field, then those grains which acquired TRM in the temperature interval 300 °C to 20 °C now become demagnetized. The form of the curve is dependent on the mineral composition of the sample; the one shown is typical for baked clay.

is that acquired from the last heating (strictly speaking it is acquired during the last cooling down). If the temperature of the second heating did not exceed that of the first then the remanence will consist of two components (see Fig. 9.8). These can be identified using step-by-step thermal demagnetization during which the sample is heated (and cooled) in zero magnetic field using successively increasing temperatures. When the temperature of the second heating is reached only the remanence of the higher blocking temperature carriers remains. The example of Fig. 9.8 is given to emphasize a remarkable facet of TRM – that the magnetic carriers are specific to a given temperature range – and does not represent a situation normally encountered in the dating of kilns, etc. because the field direction does not change appreciably during the lifetime of the kiln. However, it illustrates one way in which remanent magnetism can be used to elucidate the thermal history of ceramics – and other material, e.g. the temperature of emplacement of ash from the late Minoan eruption of the volcano of Thera in the Aegean (Downey and Tarling 1984).

Another non-dating use is in determining the temperature of the primary heating, provided this is less than the upper limit to the blocking

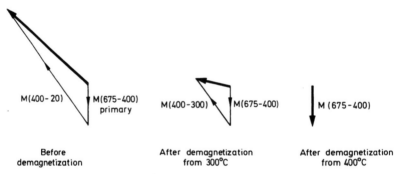

M(400-20) ▼M(675-400) primary   M(400-300) ▼M(675-400)   M (675-400)

| Before demagnetization | After demagnetization from 300°C | After demagnetization from 400°C |

Fig. 9.8 Demagnetization of a two–component remanence. At some time subsequent to its initial cooling from 675 °C the sample was heated again but only to 400 °C and in a different orientation to the earth's magnetic field. Before any demagnetization the composite remanence (indicated by the heavy arrow) consists of a secondary component carried by grains having blocking temperatures in the range 20–400 °C and a primary component carried by grains having blocking temperatures in the range 400–675 °C. If the sample is now heated to successively increasing temperatures, being cooled in zero magnetic field after each heating, the remanence is gradually eroded. Grains are unaffected until their blocking temperature is reached and so the total remanence remaining gradually swings round in direction until after heating to 400 °C only the high-temperature component is left; on heating to higher temperatures there is no further change in direction, only diminution in magnitude. It is assumed in this example that the durations of the heatings for demagnetization are roughly the same as that of the second heating in antiquity; if the former is substantially shorter than the latter the effective temperature of the demagnetization is a little lower than the actual.

temperatures of the carriers. Thus in the example of Fig. 9.8 if the primary heating had only reached 500 °C then the sample's remanence would have disappeared on demagnetization from that temperature. Application in studies of low-fired pottery has not so far had any comprehensive exploitation but various other determinations have been made, e.g. the temperature to which burnt clay found on an early hominid site had been subjected (Gowlett *et al.* 1981); the temperature to which material at Herculaneum had been heated when Vesuvius erupted in AD 79 (Kent *et al.* 1981).

The upper limit to the range of blocking temperatures present in a sample is sometimes lower, sometimes higher than the 650 °C indicated in the example of Fig. 9.7. The upper limit can never exceed the *Curie temperature* of the minerals present – 585 °C for magnetite and 675 °C for haematite. Above the Curie temperature magnetic domains disappear (but form again when the temperature falls).

Viscous remanent magnetism (VRM)

As mentioned above, grains with blocking temperatures below the range 200–300 °C slowly acquire a new magnetization if the field direction is changed. Grains with blocking temperatures below 50 °C do this in a matter of minutes and hours whereas 'harder' grains with higher blocking temperatures take months, years and hundreds of years, etc. A stone or pottery fragment that has remained in the same position for, say, 5000 years will carry a 'harder' VRM than one that has been in position for only a few hundred years. The hardness of the VRM can be evaluated by an appropriate laboratory technique, and can be used as a rough method of dating – *viscosity dating* (Heller and Markert 1973).

Effect of lightning

The strong magnetic field associated with the current in a flash of lightning may cause magnetization of material in close proximity. The remanence is of two types: isothermal (IRM) and anhysteritic (ARM). The former is acquired from a strong steady magnetic field and the latter from a weak steady field (such as the earth's field) in the presence of a strong alternating field. Both types can be distinguished from TRM by appropriate laboratory analysis.

Self-reversal

Although extremely rare in natural rocks, acquisition of TRM in the opposite direction to the applied field has been demonstrated for some rather special types of magnetic mineral. When rocks of reverse polarity were first being investigated it was hypothesized by some that this was the result of a self-reversal mechanism rather than a reversal of the field; subsequently the evidence in favour of the latter became overwhelming – because of the world-wide synchroneity of the potassium–argon ages obtained for polarity changes. However, the possibility of natural self-reversal exists and indeed has been suggested in respect of the Laschamp–Olby event some 30,000–40,000 years ago (Heller 1980).

9.3.2 SEDIMENTS (DRM, PDRM, CRM)

The remanent magnetization of unburnt sediment is an order of magnitude weaker than TRM but no less permanent. As a result there is a magnetic record in a wide variety of sediment types – on the deep-ocean floor, in glacial varves and on the bottom of freshwater lakes, in estuarine mud and in the thick wind-blown deposits on land known as loess; at archaeological sites there may be a reliable record in the silt of a ditch, of a pond or a well, in cave sediment or in archaeologically related river and marine alluvium.

A number of processes can contribute:

1. Detrital magnetic particles (e.g. of iron oxide) having a previously acquired permanent magnetization (e.g. through being derived from a volcanic rock which acquired a TRM while cooling) are aligned with the earth's magnetic field if they fall through calm water; the deposited sediment then has a *detrital remanent magnetization* (DRM).

2. Another form of DRM is acquired subsequent to deposition (and hence called *post-depositional remanent magnetization* (PDRM)) due to alignment of particles while the sediment is still in the form of a slurry. The magnetization is locked in as the sediment consolidates and whereas in some cases this takes only a few days, in some slowly deposited sediments it may take tens of thousands of years.

3. 'Chemical' remanence (CRM), also after deposition, can be acquired through formation of a new magnetic mineral (e.g. the reducing environment engendered by organic matter can cause the reduction of haematite to magnetite); alignment of the magnetic moment of domains occurs as the new material forms. Also, CRM can occur through growth of existing magnetic material or deposition from solution of fresh.

4. There are forms of bacteria that can synthesize magnetite and as with CRM there is alignment during formation. This process can occur not only in surficial aerobic conditions but also in long-term anaerobic sediments (see Bazylinski *et al.* 1988).

Through laboratory experiments it has been found that process (1) can lead to a shallowing of inclination (due to rolling of both spherical and non-spherical particles as they settle); distortion of declination by bottom currents is liable to occur also. Hence it is fortunate that the post-depositional processes are the dominant mechanisms in most types of sediment; in any case if bioturbation occurs in the surface layer any immediately formed magnetization will be destroyed.

The drawback of dominance by post-depositional processes is that there may be substantial lag of the magnetic record behind the date of deposition. Also, because the recording is not instantaneous, there is smoothing-out of strong deviations in direction that do not last very long; it is even possible for a short polarity event to be missing altogether. The completeness of the record also depends on the rapidity of deposition; obviously for a rate of only 1 or 2 mm per thousand years, such as in some deep-sea sediments, events that last only a few thousand years will not be discernible – hence the advantage of deposits such as loess in which the rate may be fifty times greater.

Post-depositional processes can give rise to *overprinting* of the initially recorded direction by a later one. Thus a sediment that has acquired an initial direction through drying and consolidation may acquire a secondary magnetization if it is rewetted; the primary magnetization may be retrievable by laboratory 'cleaning' (partial demagnetization using thermal or alternating-field procedures – see section 9.4.2 and Fig. 9.9). In the context of reversal stratigraphy it should be noted that overprinting during normal polarity may obliterate the primary magnetization of a sediment deposited during an earlier period of reversed polarity.

In considering what features on archaeological sites are likely to yield reliable directions the emphasis is on sediments that are likely to have remained substantially dry and sterile, such as those in ditches on a sandstone bedrock and cave sediments. Next preferred after sediments that have remained continuously dry are those that have remained continuously wet; sediments that have been subject to a rising and falling water-table, or other post-depositional changes, are prone to overprinting. As in non-archaeological sediments bioturbation is a major cause of disturbance, not least by the feet of ancient man – for further discusion see Clark (1988).

Stalagmites

Within stalagmites there is usually some detrital material and this carries a stable remanent magnetization acquired at deposition or soon after. Measurements on a stalagmite from Mexico (by Latham *et al.* 1986) have shown acceptable agreement with the archaeomagnetic record. The main difficulty is in dating; the uranium-series method requires clean, sediment-free calcite for reliability and for such material the magnetic signal tends to be too weak.

9.3.3 SEDIMENTS: SUSCEPTIBILITY AS A CLIMATIC INDICATOR

The low-field magnetic susceptibility (χ) of a sediment is a measure of the temporary magnetization that is acquired in a weak magnetic field; its value depends on the concentration of magnetic constituents present and also on grain-size and chemical state – for a given percentage of iron oxide the susceptibility is nearly 100 times higher if it is in the form of magnetite (Fe_3O_4) than if it is in the form of haematite (α - Fe_2O_3). As illustrated in Fig. 2.4 there is considerable variation of susceptibility in a loess profile (as also in lake and deep-ocean profiles) and high susceptibility correlates with warm climatic phases, at least in general. Although in some cases this is due to chemical change (e.g. conversion of haematite to magnetite), for Fig. 2.4 the presently accepted explanation is in terms of greater dilution by non-magnetic sediment (loess) during cold periods, the deposition rate of the magnetic component remaining constant; this is consistent with the assumption that a given thickness of high susceptibility ('warm') sediment represents a longer time interval than the same thickness of low susceptibility ('cold') sediment – an assumption necessary for good correlation with the oxygen–isotope record (see also Heller and Liu 1986).

There is also variation of the as-found 'natural' remanent magnetization and other magnetic parameters. The advantage of using susceptibility is that it can be conveniently measured on a loess profile without taking samples. A small detector coil is placed against the cleaned section and the susceptibility is indicated by a lightweight electronic pack.

9.3.4 SUNBAKED BRICKS

In ancient Egypt, and elsewhere, bricks were made by throwing clay forcibly into a mould, prior to hardening in the sun. The same practice is current today in some parts of the world and study of these shows the bricks carry a remanent magnetization acquired at the time of moulding (and that it is not altered by sunbaking). It is termed *shear,* or *shock,* remanent magnetization (SRM) and it has been used for evaluation of ancient field intensity (Games 1977). A similar magnetization process occurs when clay is tamped around a post or in a floor that is hardened in a similar manner.

Though permanent, this type of magnetization is rather weak, of similar strength to VRM. However, the latter being comparatively 'soft', can be separated by laboratory analysis.

9.3.5 REMANENCE IN METALS

Iron objects themselves are not of interest because the direction of remanence is dictated by the shape of the object and because of lack of magnetic stability. Struck coins with a slight iron impurity (~0.1%) carry a stable remanence acquired at the time of striking, but unfortunately its direction is predominantly vertical and does not relate to the direction of the earth's magnetic field; cast coins can be distinguished from struck coins by magnetic analysis and other details of production technique found too (Tarling 1982; Hoye 1983; Goulpeau *et al.* 1987).

9.4 SAMPLING AND MEASUREMENT

9.4.1 KILNS AND HEARTHS, ETC.

Two essential requirements are that the material has remained undisturbed since cooling down from its last firing, and that this event is the event of archaeological interest. Structures that are underlain by pits and soft occupation deposits, rather than baked on firm subsoil or bedrock, should be avoided. The degree of heating should be sufficient for the material (primarily clay) to have lost all plasticity when wet. The purpose served is the next consideration: there are some periods when the change in direction was so slow that the significance of the result, either for dating or for geophysics, does not justify the substantial effort involved in sampling and measurement.

For the sampling itself it is vital that the exact orientation is 'attached' to the sample before disturbance. The traditional technique is by encasing an isolated stump of material in gypsum plaster, an exactly horizontal surface being formed on which the azimuthal direction is marked. To do this a miniature 'ditch' is dug, using a knife or otherwise, so that a stump is left in the middle, the stump being a few centimetres across. A separate frame (*not* of iron) is placed in the ditch and levelled. Plaster is then poured in and the top surface smoothed flush with the top of the frame. When the plaster has set, a line is sighted from a nearby theodolite and marked on the surface. The theodolite orientation datum is found by shooting the sun at a known time and using astronomical tables. In some climates it is practical to use a sun compass instead of a theodolite; in this the direction of the shadow from an exactly vertical wire is marked, at a known time on the horizontal surface. A magnetic compass is sometimes used but this is far from ideal because the direction indicated may be distorted by the magnetization of the clay; this effect can be reduced, except for strongly magnetic structures, by using a block to raise the compass about 10 cm above the sample.

A less damaging method is to use small plastic reference discs that are fixed to the structure using epoxy glue; the discs are levelled and then marked, as above, before being removed with a small piece of baked clay (about 1 cm across) attached.

Whichever method is used it is preferable for the sampling to be done by laboratory staff. This also allows proper assessment of the number of samples required. Six are a minimum but for kilns a dozen or more, well distributed, are necessary in order to obtain a reliable average value of the ancient direction. This is because of distortion of the field direction at the time of cooling by the magnetism of the structure itself.

Measurement

In some samples the viscous component, i.e. that due to carriers having a blocking temperature not exceeding 200–300 °C, is sufficiently strong that the total magnetization has a direction which is significantly different from the direction recorded by the more stable carriers; this is most likely to be the case with clay that is poorly fired. The situation is similar to that illustrated in Fig. 9.9 and removal of the viscous component can be most effectively achieved by thermal demagnetization – the sample is heated to around 300 °C using an oven in which the magnetic field has been annulled (by means of large current-carrying coils around it or by means of Mumetal shielding); removal can also be achieved by application of a strong alternating magnetic field to the shielded sample (*af cleaning*).

The measurement itself is usually by means of a *spinner magnetometer* in which the sample is rotated rapidly inside pick-up coils; alternatively fluxgate detectors may be used. The equipment is essentially the same as that required for palaeomagnetic work (see Collinson 1983).

9.4.2 SEDIMENT

On an archaeological site the sediment is usually available in an exposed section, and if soft a short 5 cm plastic cylinder or cube can be pushed into it, appropriate orientation marks being made; otherwise a stump can

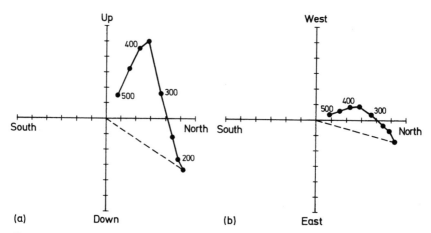

Fig. 9.9 Removal of overprint by thermal demagnetization (the As–Zijderveld diagram). The sample is allowed to cool to room temperature from successively increasing temperatures (150 °C, 200 °C, 250 °C . . .) in zero magnetic field. The magnetization remaining after each step is plotted in (a) as the vertical and horizontal components in a north–south plane, and in (b) as the north–south and east–west components in the horizontal plane. In the example illustrated the overprint was acquired during a period of normal polarity, whereas the initial magnetization was during a period of reversed polarity. The direction of the NRM, indicated by a dashed line, suggests a reversed polarity for the sample, whereas after demagnetization to 400 °C the primary magnetization is revealed – the latter sometimes being termed the 'characteristic' magnetization (ChRM).

be isolated and encased in plaster, as in the technique for kilns. Sediment at the bottom of a lake or the sea is sampled by means of long coring tubes (3 m long or more), driven in pneumatically or by gravity. Though advantageous in rapidity there is the possibility that the tube twists as it is forced in; recovery of declination information then requires removal of the trend due to this twisting; warping may also occur.

Measurement (NRM; ChRM)
Basically the same equipment as for burnt material is used except that at least an order of magnitude better sensitivity is required – hence the advantage of ultrasensitive cryogenic magnetometers. Also, overprinting is more common and use of thermal or af cleaning is essential; the direction of the natural remanence (NRM) may be quite different from that of the *characteristic remanent magnetization* (ChRM) remaining after removal of the overprint. Indication that the cleaning has been sufficiently stringent is obtained by successively increasing demagnetization steps – as indicated in Fig. 9.9; when the ChRM is reached there is no further change in direction.

For sediments collected in core tubes initial measurement can be made while the material remains undisturbed in the core liner; it is then cut into small samples for detailed analysis.

9.5 THE MAGNETIC POLARITY TIME-SCALE
(reversal stratigraphy)

As indicated in section 2.3, the transition from reversed to normal polarity in deep-sea cores provided an important time mark for oxygen-isotope stratigraphy – the occurrence of the transition in sequences of volcanic lavas having been dated by potassium–argon. More direct application to Palaeolithic sites is sometimes possible through measurement of the polarity recorded in the sediments at such sites, though the recording of subchrons – short periods of polarity opposite to that for most of the chron (see Table 9.1) – complicates interpretation even if eventually providing a basis for more detailed dating; the usual difficulty on a site is the incompleteness of the record. However, these subchrons are particularly valuable in confirming the accuracy of other techniques. Thus in the Koobi Fora region of Kenya hominid fossils, including *Homo erectus*, were found in levels stratigraphically related to one which was normally magnetized, with sediment of reverse polarity above it; the potassium–argon age for this level was 1.64 ± 0.03 million years, consistent with deposition during the Olduvai subchron (McDougall *et al.* 1985). (The name of the latter subchron derives from levels associated with the Olduvai Man.)

Another example of application has been the dating of early tool-making in Asia at about 2 million years ago. At Riwat in Pakistan a lithic assemblage

Table 9.1 Some polarity subchrons of the last 2.5 million years

(a)	*Within the Brunhes normal polarity chron (0–730,000 years ago)*			
	Ages (thousands of years)			
	Gothenburg	*c.* 12	Lake Mungo	*c.* 30
	Lake Biwa	*c.* 18	**Blake**	104–117
	Lake Mono	*c.* 25	Biwa I	*c.* 180
	Laschamp–Olby	30–45	Biwa II	*c.* 295

(b)	*Within the Matuyama reversed polarity chron (0.73–2.48 million years ago)*			
	Ages (millions of years)			
	Jaramillo	0.90–0.97	**Olduvai**	1.67–1.87
	Cobb Mountain	*c.* 1.12	**Réunion I**	2.01–2.04
	Gilsa	*c.* 1.58	**Réunion II**	2.12–2.14
			'X'	*c.* 2.31

Note: Only those shown in **bold** are generally accepted as worldwide events; for some of the others, e.g. the Gothenburg, even the status as a localized event is in dispute because of ambiguity in interpretation of the evidence. Besides those listed a number of others have been proposed (see Tarling 1983). For the Matuyama chron the dating is from the review by Mankinen and Dalrymple (1979).

with evidence of hominid flaking was found near the bottom of a 70 m section in which the sediment was reversely magnetized (Rendell *et al.* 1987; Dennell *et al.* 1988), suggesting an age early in the Matuyama reverse polarity chron. Geological evidence, based on a fission track age of 1.6 ± 0.18 million years and the tectonic context, indicates a minimum age for the assemblage of 1.9 million years. A horizon of normal magnetization a few metres below the assemblage is interpreted as probably representing the Réunion I subchron at 2.01 million years thereby giving a tentative maximum age. Thus the artefacts are far older than any others found outside Africa, implying either that *Homo habilis* lived in Asia as well or that *Homo erectus* lived in Asia while *Homo habilis* was still living in Africa.

Rapidity of deposition allows good recording of subchrons in Chinese loess (e.g. Rolph *et al.* 1989) and together with the use of susceptibility stratigraphy (see section 9.3.3) this facilitates comprehensive correlation of climate with the deep-sea isotope record.

9.6 ARCHAEOMAGNETISM

9.6.1 REFERENCE CURVES

No dating is possible until a reference curve has been established for the region concerned. In general, an archaeological chronology is necessary for this, if possible based either on historical records or on dendrochronology; hence the role of archaeomagnetism lies in the interpolation and embellishment of existing chronologies. Radiocarbon and TL can also be used in deriving the reference curve, but the dating uncertainty introduced then limits the accuracy obtainable from archaeomagnetism.

Figure 9.10 shows an example of a reference curve and it will be seen from this that to obtain the necessary detail reliable data are needed from an average of at least five well-dated structures (i.e. kilns, ovens, fireplaces or hearths) per century; in any planning of resources provision should be made for ten per century since not all structures yield a reliable direction. Not only is this a very substantial task in terms of time and effort but there is also the question of whether sufficient well-dated structures are available in the region.

However, reference curves are now available for various parts of the world; among the more comprehensive, in most cases extending over the last two or three millennia, are those for the American South-west (Dubois and others: see Sternberg 1983; Eighmy *et al.* 1980; Sternberg and McGuire 1990a), Arkansas (Wolfman 1990a), Britain (Aitken 1970; Clark *et al.* 1988), Bulgaria (Kovacheva 1983), China (Wei *et al.* 1983), France (Thellier 1981; Langouet *et al.* 1983; Bucur 1986), Japan (see Hirooka 1983), meso-America (Wolfman 1990b) and the USSR (see Burlatskaya 1983). Other regions where work has been done or is in progress include Australia (Barbetti 1983), Egypt (Hassan 1983), Greece (Evans and Mareschal 1988a), Iran (Kawai *et al.* 1972; Hesse 1975), Italy (Tanguy *et al.* 1985; Evans and Mareschal 1988b), Peru (by D. Wolfman), Thailand (Barbetti and Hein), Turkey (Becker 1979). As additional well-dated structures become available, reference curves are revised and extended; hence archaeologists with interest in a particular region are advised to make contact with the relevant investigator.

Early practice in construction of reference curves was to draw a free-hand line through or near the data points giving intuitive weighting to the more reliable. Various statistical approaches have now been developed; that of Sternberg and McGuire (1990a, b) for the American South-west employs a moving window of 50 or 100 years according to the density of data, and takes account also of the error limits of the reference dates;

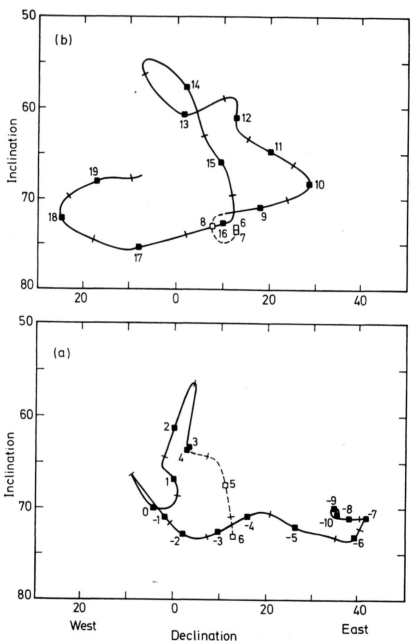

Fig. 9.10 Reference curves for Britain, normalized to 52.4 °N, 1.6 °W (redrawn from Clark *et al.* 1988): (a) 1000 BC–AD 600, (b) AD 600–1975. Figures on the curves indicate date in hundreds of years (negative for BC); transverse ticks are half-century points. Data used are from dated archaeological features, from lake sediments and from direct recording after 1576.

of course the reference curve is really a band of finite width representative of uncertainty rather than a line, and these authors estimate that for their present data the half-width of this band varies between 1° and 5°.

Lake sediments

A much quicker way of discovering the secular variation for a region is by measurement of the remanent magnetization of lake sediments, with dating by radiocarbon or luminescence. As mentioned earlier there is a tendency for rapid swings of direction to be smoothed out and sometimes delayed, but comparison of Fig. 9.11 for Britain with an earlier reference curve (Aitken 1970) which was based only on kilns, etc. suggests that such

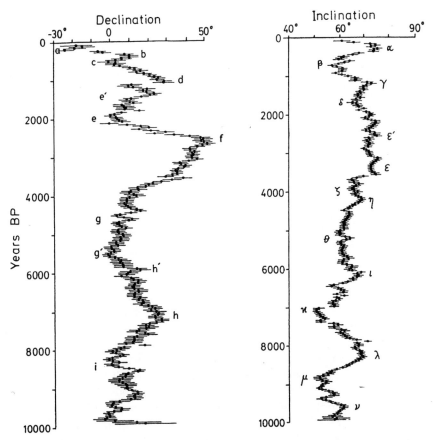

Fig. 9.11 Composite lake sediment record for Britain derived by Turner and Thompson (1982) from ten cores of sediment. The letters mark the extremities of the swings of direction and facilitate comparison with other records: thus 'd' corresponds to the easterly declination seen in the archaeomagnetic record *c.* AD 1000, and 'β' to the shallow inclination from AD 1200 to 1400.

effects are barely significant in this case at any rate. The lake sediment data have been incorporated in the curve of Fig. 9.10.

Of particular interest in Figs. 9.10 and 9.11 is the big swing in declination between letters f (at 600 BC) and e (50 BC); the rate of change is about 10 ° per century. This covers a period of time when radiocarbon dating is not at all accurate, due to the vagaries of the calibration curve (see Ch. 4). Hence whenever fireplaces or hearths of the British Iron Age are available in good condition it is highly worth while to apply archaeomagnetism. Unfortunately the lake sediment records from Geneva indicate that the corresponding swing seen in that region is substantially attenuated, so that the same is less true for Iron Age sites on the European continent.

For reviews of the lake sediment record in other regions see Creer (1982) and Creer and Tucholka (1982).

Volcanic lava

As with baked clay, igneous rocks are magnetized as they cool down; hence the successive lava flows from a volcano carry a record of the secular variation. Unfortunately there is usually difficulty over dating. Thus although the multitudinous flows of Mount Etna, Sicily, would seem to be an attractive source of data for a reference curve, those of the last millennia being dated by mention in historical documents, careful investigation has led to the conclusion that many of the historical dates may be erroneous (Tanguy *et al.* 1985). This suggests that, in general, historical dates for lava flows should be treated with reserve.

Sometimes lava flows can be dated by radiocarbon, using fragments of burnt wood and other organic material embedded in the lava (e.g. Champion 1980, for the western USA).

VGP plots

An alternative way of expressing an ancient direction is to calculate[2] the angular position of a dipole placed at the centre of the earth which would produce, at the measuring station, the observed values of *D* and *I*; this position is known as the equivalent *virtual geomagnetic pole* (VGP), and is expressed as the latitude and longitude of the point at which a line through the dipole strikes the earth's surface. Figure 9.12 shows part of a reference curve for the American South-west presented in this way.

The advantage of this form of representation is that it facilitates comparison between regions. If the secular variation had been due entirely to dipole wobble then all regions around the world would have the same VGP curve; hence disagreement is indicative of the influence of non-dipole disturbances. Also, the representation automatically makes first-order correction for site-to-site differences in direction that are due to difference in geographic position – further discussed shortly.

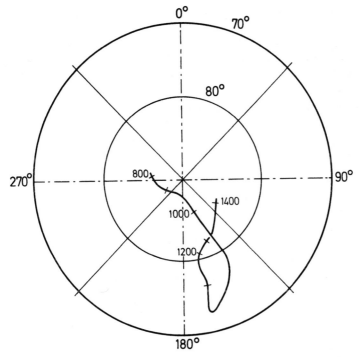

Fig. 9.12 VGP path for American South-west (based on Sternberg and McGuire 1990a). The centre of the diagram represents the geographic North Pole and the concentric circles are lines of latitude; the VGP is the position of the virtual dipole that would produce the observed values of declination and inclination at the site concerned. Transverse marks indicate 100-year intervals; dates are in years AD. The path shown is obtained from weighted averages within a moving window; other versions for this region (see Sternberg 1983) show substantially more variation.

9.6.2 PRECISION AND ACCURACY

The Fisher index and α_{95}

With a scalar quantity (i.e. a magnitude) the scatter of individual measurements about the mean value is described by the standard deviation, σ; if the experimental errors causing the scatter are random (and some other conditions are fulfilled too), then the error limits on the mean value are given by the standard error $\sigma/n^{1/2}$, where n is the number of measurements. There is a 68% probability that the true value lies within 1 standard error of the mean value, and a 95% probability that it lies within 2 standard errors. For a direction it is appropriate to use the parameter α_{95} derived from the Fisher index;[3] there is a 95% probability that the true direction lies within α_{95} of the mean direction.

Because direction is a vector quantity it has to be envisaged using an imaginary sphere, as indicated in Fig. 9.13. The angle α_{95} defines a *circle of confidence* on the surface of the sphere and there is a 95% probability that the vector representing the true direction will strike the sphere within this circle. The true value of I will lie (at a level of probability a little higher[4] than 95%) within $\pm\alpha_{95}$ of the average value; the true value of D will lie within $\pm\alpha_{95}/\cos I$) of the average value. Thus the precision in D gets rather poor for high values of I.

When the circle of confidence for a remanent direction is transformed into VGP representation it becomes[5] an 'oval of confidence'.

Systematic errors; magnetic distortion
One obvious source of systematic error would be a mistake in determining the azimuth datum of the theodolite; this would not increase the scatter of results from the individual samples and so would not be reflected in α_{95} – but the value for D would be in error. Another is tilting of the structures as a whole, at some time between cooling-down and sampling. Another is distortion of the local field (i.e. that 'seen' by the samples as they cool) by iron objects or by iron slag.

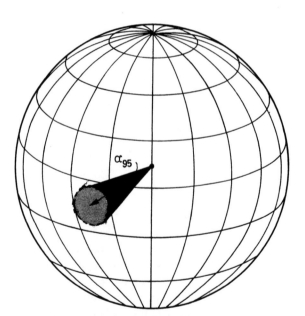

Fig. 9.13 The arrow represents the average of the individual directions measured for a feature. Assuming the scatter is due to random experimental error there is a 95% probability that the true direction lies within a cone of semi-angle α_{95}, calculated from the scatter. The *circle of confidence* is formed by intersection of the cone with the sphere.

Less expected is the distortion of the local field due to the magnetism of the baked clay itself – often referred to as magnetic refraction. Samples from the floor of a pottery kiln tend to give a remanent inclination which is one or two degrees shallower than that given by samples from the wall; also, some parts of the circumference of the wall give values of *D* which are too easterly, whereas for other parts *D* is too westerly and for strongly magnetized clay the extremes of *D* may differ by as much as 10 °. Thus to get a reliable average value for *D* it is necessary to obtain upwards of a dozen samples well distributed around the circumference, and to get a reliable average for *I* a proportion of floor samples needs to be included too (since some parts of the wall give a value for *I* which is too steep).

As long as the samples are well distributed there will be a degree of extra scatter in the individual directions due to magnetic distortion (if present) and hence a widened circle of confidence. Since the average direction is less reliable when there is appreciable distortion, this is appropriate. In general one does not expect significant distortion in weakly magnetized structures; however, quite often the observed distortion pattern does not have a straightforward explanation in terms of magnetic refraction. The phenomenon is not well understood.[6]

Geographic correction

We now consider the question of the acceptable size of an archaeomagnetic region, i.e. the area over which a single reference curve is applicable; related to this is the technique for transferring the direction found in one part of a region to a part that is distant. We have already noted (see Fig. 9.3) that although the secular variation curves for London, Paris and Rome are similar in shape the amounts by which *D* and *I* have to be shifted to get from one curve to another changes with time; more specifically it is evident that use of the London curve for dating the kilns even as near as Paris, only 350 km away, would involve significant error[7] – unless a satisfactory 'transfer correction' can be made.

Although non-dipole components have a substantial influence on the secular variation it has been found (e.g. Shuey *et al.* 1970) that correction on the basis of the VGP substantially extends the region over which a given reference curve can be used without introduction of significant error. This correction is automatically incorporated if VGP presentation is being used; if not then it is a matter of calculating[2] first the VGP corresponding to the measured remanent direction found for a kiln and then the *D* and *I* values that this VGP would produce at the central reference site chosen for the region. The conclusions of Shuey *et al.* based on present-day field gradients, indicate[8] that a region can be about 1000 km across before the error introduced becomes significant. There is of course no question of direct use of the present-day field to make correction – it can only be used as a guide as to what the ancient field may have been like.

9.6.3 APPLICATION

Whether the reference curve is expressed in terms of separate D and I plots as in Fig. 9.1, a combined D and I plot as in Fig. 9.10 or as a VGP path as in Fig. 9.12, the use of it in converting the direction obtained from an archaeological feature into a date has complications – as illustrated in Fig. 9.14. A statistical procedure for this conversion has been developed (Sternberg and McGuire 1990b) in which the feature direction is compared with successive segments of the reference curve and the probability that

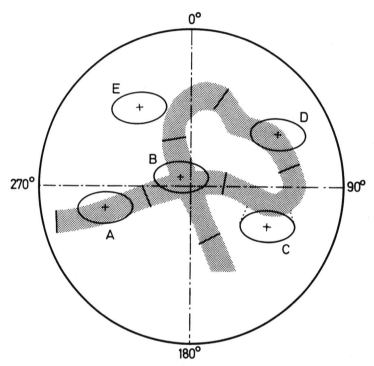

Fig. 9.14 Conversion of remanent direction to date: various circumstances (based on Sternberg and McGuire 1990b). The shaded band represents the reference curve and its confidence limits, in terms of the VGP path, with transverse markers every 100 years. The ellipses represent the 95% confidence limits for the VGPs corresponding to specific archaeological features (of different date). *Case A* is straightforward and the date span is that corresponding to the intersection of the ellipse with the band. *Case B* gives two alternate date spans; sometimes one of these can be rejected on archaeological grounds. *Case C* implies rather a short date span, though wider on a more conservative interpretation. *Case D* gives a date span that is asymmetrical about the midpoint. In *Case E* there is no basis for giving a date; perhaps the feature belongs to an earlier or later part of the reference band not shown in the diagram; of course the same could be true for the other features and archaeological evidence is needed in order to rule out that possibility.

they are not significantly different, having regard to the error limits, is evaluated; in this way date spans for the feature corresponding to the chosen level of confidence (usually 95%) can be obtained. In broad terms the date spans correspond to segments for which the circle of confidence for the feature overlaps the circle of confidence for the reference curve. The authors concerned suggest that for the American South-west (Fig. 9.12), spans corresponding to between ±50 and ±100 years are typical, with reduction to ±25 years *c*. AD 1050.

Other authors have claimed much better precision for the method. This is usually on the basis of assuming a fairly rapid change of direction, say by 10 ° per century, and a rather small circle of confidence for the feature, such as an α_{95} value of 1 °; these values lead to a span corresponding to ±10 years if imprecision in the reference curve is neglected.

From the foregoing it is evident that the precision obtainable is highly dependent on century and region; hence in considering the significance of a quoted magnetic date it is prudent to look at the detail of the reference curve used and judge whether the date span quoted seems justified; this presupposes that the direction and α_{95} for the kiln or hearth concerned are given along with the date span. Similarly, in publication of a reference curve the archaeological features utilized should be indicated; this allows reassessment to be made in the event that the basic chronological framework for the region is modified.

Cave sediments

Where a long sequence of undisturbed sediment is available dating can be attempted by sampling the whole sequence and matching the swings of declination and inclination with those from a dated reference sequence such as given in Fig. 9.11. The latter was derived by combining several cores from different lakes in order to average out 'noise'; an individual record is subject to irregularities and has poorer definition of the swings. In addition, in cave sediments, there is risk of interference by undetected periods of hiatus and erosion. Some examples of long cave sequences have been reviewed by Papamarinopoulos and Creer (1983).

Inclination only: bricks, tiles and pots

As first demonstrated by Thellier (1938) the ancient inclination can be obtained from bricks and tiles despite movement since baking. This is because of the regular way in which they were stacked while being baked. Tiles are always stacked on edge and consequently there are only two possibilities; normally one of these can be ruled out. The same applies to many types of ancient brick. Extensive dating use of such 'displaced material' is being made by the group at Rennes in France (see, for instance, Langouet and Goulpeau 1984).

It is also possible to deduce the ancient value of inclination from measurements on a pot – as first demonstrated by Folgheraiter (1899)

– but only when the ornamentation or glazing dictates that it must have been baked standing upright on a horizontal surface. This is not the case for most archaeological pottery (see, e.g. Clarke and Connah 1962) but there are some exceptions, for example good results have been reported for Chinese Yueh ware (Aitken 1958); of course, a special large-scale magnetometer is required and with the current emphasis on measuring small cylinders, not more than a few centimetres across, it is doubtful whether a suitable facility now exists (except in the Science Museum, London).

9.6.4 ANCIENT INTENSITY

Whereas the direction of remanent magnetization in a sample is the same as the direction of the ancient field, the intensity (or strength) of the remanent magnetization is not the same as the intensity (or strength), *F*, of the ancient field, but it is proportional to it. Because of this proportionality *F* can be determined – by comparing the sample's as-found magnetization with the TRM it acquires after heating and cooling in a known laboratory field.

The basic notion of intensity dating is the same as for directional dating – establishment of a reference curve of past variation and comparison with that curve of the intensity evaluated from the sample. As in the case of direction there are contributions to the variation from transient non-dipole disturbances and from changes in angle of tilt of the main dipole field; in addition there is contribution from changes in the magnitude of the dipole field. The attraction of ancient intensity as a dating tool is that it does not require *in situ* samples, nor does it require that the sample position during baking can be inferred (as for bricks and tiles). Hence pottery fragments can be used, thereby giving vastly increased scope; furthermore if a highly sensitive cryogenic magnetometer[9] is used measurements can be made on 3 × 3 mm cylinders extracted from the fragment with a coring tool. Because there is negligible deterioration in appearance this means that museum-quality specimens can be used.

Figure 9.15 shows the reference curve so far obtained for Greece. However, it will be seen that only in the second millennium BC, and possibly the first, is the variation strong enough for useful dating – given that the accuracy obtainable from a sample is about ±5%; for the second millennium this gives a dating accuracy of about ±80 years. As with directional dating there is repetition of values and it is necessary to have other evidence that the fragment lies somewhere within the second millennium. On the other hand, the high values of 1000–500 BC are not repeated in other periods (the indications for millennia earlier than 2000 BC are that the intensity ratio was within 20% of unity) and consequently a fragment yielding a high value can be reliably placed in that date range.

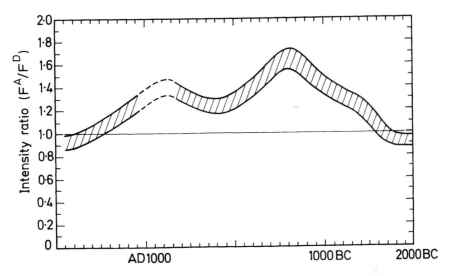

Fig. 9.15 Ancient magnetic field intensity, F^A, expressed relative to the present-day intensity, F^D (based on Aitken *et al.* 1989.)

Another aspect of using intensity values is in respect of testing authenticity – applicable to ceramics of any period in which the intensity ratio is substantially different from unity.

In addition to limitations in general applicability, there is the drawback that the measurements themselves are difficult and time-consuming – much more so than for direction. For reliable results either the Thellier technique or the Shaw technique needs to be used (for summaries of these, refer to Aitken *et al.* 1986, 1988). The complexity of the techniques arises from the tendency of samples to undergo mineral alteration during the laboratory reheating; hence there is a change in the sensitivity of the sample, i.e. in its TRM capacity; one of the main causes of alteration is probably dehydration during laboratory heating of iron hydroxides which have formed, during burial in wet conditions, from the iron oxides present in the clay at the time of the ancient firing. Because the results are unreliable when such changes occur there is a high rejection rate – almost always greater than 50%. For some regions, particularly those in which firing conditions were primitive, or in which the burial environment has been humid, the rejection rate may be so high that no worthwhile results can be obtained. At the time of writing comprehensive data have been published for various regions including Japan (Sakai and Hirooka 1986), China (Wei *et al.* 1987), western Asia, Egypt and Greece (Aitken *et al.* 1989; Hassan 1983), Bulgaria (Kovacheva 1983), France and North Africa (Thellier 1977), south-western USA (Sternberg and Butler 1978; Champion 1980) and various parts of the USSR (see Burlatskaya 1983).

9.7 OTHER ARCHAEOLOGICAL INVOLVEMENTS OF MAGNETISM

There is about 1 ton of baked clay in a pottery kiln and the magnetic field from its TRM is detectable at ground level (as long as the depth of burial is not more than a few metres). The distortion of the normal earth's field is only slight, but portable magnetometers of sufficient sensitivity have been available since the late 1950s; from then on *magnetic prospection* has been a highly effective tool for exploration of many types of archaeological site. Besides burnt features pits, ditches and walls can be found, though the detection depth is less than for kilns, particularly in the case of walls; obviously iron objects are also detectable – though this is a drawback because of the tendency for any site near present-day habitation to contain a scatter of iron litter. Pits, ditches and walls are detectable on account of having different magnetic susceptibility to the adjacent soil. The principal instruments in use are the *proton magnetometer* and the *fluxgate magnetometer*. An outline of magnetic prospection and of other geophysical prospection techniques used in archaeology, has been given by Aitken (1974, 1978).

Magnetic properties can also be used for provenance determination of obsidian (McDougall and Tarling 1983), as a rapid non-destructive alternative to chemical analysis. There is also potential in respect of technological investigations, as has been discussed by Tarling (1983). Earlier in this chapter (section 9.2.4) it was mentioned that the remanence in struck coins was not useful for dating; however, the investigations did clearly indicate that Roman coins were always struck with the emperor's head facing downwards. Firing temperature of pottery is another technological application, either using remanence or other magnetic properties (Coey *et al.* 1979); no doubt there are more to come.

NOTES

1. When the dipole is along the axis of the earth's rotation the dipole component of the field at latitude λ_s has an inclination given by

$$I = \tan^{-1}(2 \tan\lambda_s) \tag{9.1}$$

The value of I so defined (and illustrated in Fig. 9.4) is known as the 'axial dipole value' of the inclination at a site.

If the dipole is tilted away from the axis then λ_s is replaced by the *geomagnetic latitude* λ_m, defined with respect to the dipole axis in the same way as λ_s is defined with respect to the axis of rotation. The *geomagnetic colatitude* is $(90° - \lambda_m)$.

2. The latitude, λ, and the longitude, ϕ, of the VGP corresponding to declination D and inclination I, for a site having latitude λ_s and longitude ϕ_s, are given by

$$\sin\lambda = \sin\lambda_s \sin x + \cos\lambda_s \cos x \cos D \qquad (9.2)$$

and

$$\phi = \phi_s + \sin^{-1}(\cos x \sin D/\cos\lambda_s) \qquad (9.3)$$

where

$$\tan x = \tfrac{1}{2}\tan I \qquad (9.4)$$

3. The Fisher index, k, is an estimate of the scatter of a set of directions about the true direction, and as long as the latter is not too large

$$k = \left(\frac{S}{81}\right)^2 \qquad (9.5)$$

where S is the angular standard deviation, given by

$$S^2 = \frac{1}{N-1}\sum_{i=1}^{N}\theta_i^2 \qquad (9.6)$$

where ϕ_i is the angular deviation of the ith direction from the average; about 63% of the directions will lie within an angle S of the average.

A measure of the precision of the average is given by

$$\alpha_{95} \approx \frac{140}{(kN)^{\frac{1}{2}}} \qquad (9.7)$$

and there is a 95% probability that the true direction lies within an angle α_{95} of the average.

An approximation to the value of α_{95} is given by

$$\alpha_{95} = 1.4(\sigma_I + \sigma_D \cos I) \qquad (9.8)$$

where σ_I and σ_D are the standard deviations derived from the scatter in the individual values of I and D respectively.

4. Referring to Fig. 9.13 there can be some vectors lying outside the circle of confidence which nevertheless lie within the limits $\pm \alpha_{95}$ for I and $\pm (\alpha_{95}/\cos I)$ for D; hence the qualification 'a little higher'. The $\cos I$ term arises because the limits for D are obtained by projecting the circle of confidence on to a horizontal plane.

5. It can be shown (see, for example, Tarling 1983, or Merrill and McElhinny 1983) that the 'radius' parameters of the oval are given by

$$\alpha_{95} \ (\cos\lambda \ /\cos I) \ \text{and} \ \tfrac{1}{2}\alpha_{95} \ (1 + 3 \cos^2\lambda) \qquad (9.9)$$

where λ is the latitude of the VGP, as in note 1.

6. For further discussion of distortion effects, see Aitken (1974: 159–60); see also Harold (1960), Weaver (1962), Aitken and Hawley (1971), Schurr et al. (1984).

7. 'Significant error' is taken to be a deviation of about 1.5 ° from the correct angle since this is the typical value of α_{95} found for a 'good' kiln, etc. This corresponds to a deviation of not more than 1.5 ° in I and not more than $(1.5/\cos I)$ ° in D, i.e. 3 ° for midlatitudes where $\cos I$ is around 0.5.

8. Shuey et al. (1970) used the world magnetic chart for 1965 to compute the standard error coefficient when the VGP correction is applied to the direction at site A in order to predict the direction at site B. Their results represent an average over the region between latitudes 50 °S and 50 °N (for higher latitudes the errors become larger). Averaging all around the world within this region, for sites separated by 100 km the α_{95} would be 0.36 ° for sites at the same latitude and 0.53 ° for sites at the same longitude, the value for intermediate relative orientations lying in between. Hence if an acceptable archaeomagnetic region is taken to be such that the scatter of errors in correcting from sites on the periphery to the central reference station corresponds to an α_{95} of 2° one obtains an oval region about 800 km across in the north–south direction and 1100 km across in the east–west direction.

   Of course there is no guarantee that the spatial variations in the present-day field are quantitatively representative of those in the ancient field (at the time concerned) – only very extensive archaeomagnetic research can answer that question.

9. Often known by the acronym SQUID (superconducting quantum interference device), which refers to its detecting element; this has to be immersed in liquid helium (at −269 °C). For discussion of archaeomagnetic use refer to Walton (1977) and Aitken et al. (1986, 1988).

REFERENCES

Aitken, M. J. (1958) Magnetic dating, *Archaeometry* 1, 16–20.

Aitken, M. J. (1970) Dating by archaeomagnetic and thermoluminescent methods, *Phil. Trans. R. Soc. Lond.* A269, 77–88.

Aitken, M. J. (1974) *Physics and Archaeology* (2nd edn), Clarendon Press, Oxford, 291pp.

Aitken, M. J. (1978) Archaeological involvements of physics, *Physics Reports* 40C, 277–351.

Aitken, M. J. and Weaver, G. H. (1962) Magnetic dating: some archaeomagnetic measurements in Britain, *Archaeometry* 5, 4–22.

Aitken, M. J. and Hawley, H. N. (1971) Archaeomagnetism: evidence for magnetic refraction in kiln structures, *Archaeometry*, 13, 83–5.

Aitken, M. J., Allsop, A. L., Bussell, G. D. and Winter, M. B. (1986) Paleointensity determination using the Thellier technique: reliability criteria, *J. Geomag. Geoelectr.* 38, 1353–63.

Aitken, M. J., Allsop, A. L., Bussell, G. D. and Winter, M. B. (1987) Archaeomagnetic intensity determination: a nineteenth century pottery kiln near Jordan, Ontario, *Canadian J. Earth Science* 24, 2392–5.

Aitken, M. J., Allsop, A. L., Bussell, G. D., Winter, M. B. (1988) Determination of the intensity of the earth's magnetic field during archaeological times: reliability of the Thellier technique, *Reviews of Geophysics* 26, 3–12.

Aitken, M. J., Allsop, A. L., Bussell, G. D. and Winter, M. B. (1989) Geomagnetic intensity variations during the last 4000 years, *Physics Earth Planet. Int.* 56, 49–58.

Barbetti, M. (1983) Archaeomagnetic results from Australia, in *Geomagnetism of Baked Clays and Recent Sediments* (eds K. M. Creer, P. Tucholka and C. E. Barton), Elsevier, Amsterdam, Oxford, New York, Tokyo, pp. 173–5.

Barbetti, M. and Hein, D. (1989) Palaeomagnetism and high-resolution dating of ceramics in Thailand: a progress report, *World Archaeology* 21, 51–70.

Bauer, L. A. (1899) On the secular variation of a free magnetic needle, *Phys. Rev.* 3, 34–8.

Bazylinski, D. A., Frankel, R. B. and Jannasch, H. W. (1988) Anaerobic magnetite production by a marine, magnetotactic bacterium, *Nature* 334, 518–19.

Becker, H. (1979) Archaeomagnetic investigations in Anatolia from prehistoric and Hittite sites, *Archaeophysica* 10, 382–7.

Bucur, I. (1986) Fourteenth century archaeomagnetic field directions from widely distributed sites in France, *Proc. 24th International Archaeometry Symposium, Washington DC*, Smithsonian Institution, pp. 449–58.

Bullard, E. C., Freeman, C., Gellman, H., and Nixon, J. (1950) The westward drift of the earth's magnetic field, *Phil. Trans. Roy. Soc. Lond.* 243, 67–92.

Burlatskaya, S. P. (1983) Archaeomagnetic investigations in the USSR, in *Geomagnetism of Baked Clays and Recent Sediments* (eds K. M. Creer, P. Tucholka, and C. E. Barton), Elsevier, Amsterdam, Oxford, New York, Tokyo, pp. 127–37.

Champion, D. E. (1980) *Holocene Geomagnetic Secular Variation in the Western United States: Implications for the Global Geomagnetic Field*, US Dept. of Interior Geological Survey, Open-file Report 800–824.

Clark, A. (1988) *Scientific Dating Techniques*, Institute of Field Archaeologists, London, technical paper.

Clark, A. J., Tarling, D. H. and Noel, M. (1988) Developments in archaeomagnetic dating in Britain, *Journ. Archaeological Science* 15, 645–668.

Clarke, D. L. and Connah, G. (1962) Remanent magnetism and beaker chronology, *Antiquity*, **36**, 206–9.

Coey, J. M. D., Bouchez, R. and Dang, N. V. (1979) Ancient techniques, *Journ. Appl. Phys* **50**, 7772–7.

Collinson, D. W. (1983) *Methods in Rock Magnetism and Paleomagnetism,* Chapman & Hall, London.

Creer, K. M. (1977) Geomagnetic secular variations during the last 25,000 years; and interpretation of data obtained from rapidly deposited sediments, *Geophys. J. R. Astron. Soc.* **48**, 91–109.

Creer, K. M. (1982) Lake sediments as recorders of geomagnetic field variations – applications to dating post-glacial sediments, *Hydrobiologia* **92**, 587–96.

Creer, K. M. and Tucholka, P. (1982) Secular variation as recorded in lake sediments: a discussion of North American and European results, *Phil. Trans. Roy. Soc. Lond.* **A306**, 87–102.

Dennell, R. W., Rendell, H. and Hailwood, E. (1988) Early tool-making in Asia: two-million-year-old artefacts in Pakistan, *Antiquity* **62**, 98–106.

Dodson, R. E. (1979) Counterclockwise precession of the geomagnetic field vector and westward drift of the non-dipole field, *J. Geophys. Res.* **84**, 637–44.

Downey, W. S. and Tarling, D. H. (1984) Archaeomagnetic dating of Santorini volcanic eruptions and fired destruction levels of late Minoan civilization, *Nature* **309**, 519–23.

Eighmy, J. L., Sternberg, R. S. and Butler, R. F. (1980) Archaeomagnetic dating in the American Southwest, *American Antiquity* **45**, 507–17.

Evans, M. E. and Mareschal, M. (1988a) Secular variation and magnetic dating of fired structures in Greece, *Proc. 26th International Archaeometry Symposium,* Toronto, 75–79.

Evans, M. E. and Mareschal, M. (1988b) Secular variation and magnetic dating of fired structures in Southern Italy and North Africa, *Proc. 25th International Archaeometry Symposium,* Athens, in press.

Folgheraiter, G. (1899), Sur les variations séculaires de l'inclinaison magnétique dans l'antiquité, *Archs. Sci. phys. nat.* **8**, 5–16.

Games, K. P. (1977) The magnitude of the paleomagnetic field: a new non-thermal, non-detrital method using sun-dried bricks, *Geophys. J. R. Astron. Soc.* **48**, 315–29.

Gheradi, S. (1862) Sul magnetismo polare de palazzi ed altri edifizi in Torino, *Il Nuovo Cimento* **16**, 384–404.

Goulpeau, L. P. Lanos, P. and Langouet, L. (1987) The remanent magnetization of ancient struck coins, *Archaeometry* **29**, 175–86.

Gowlett, J. A. J., Harris, J. W. K., Walton, D. and Wood B. A. (1981) Early archaeological sites, hominid remains and trace of fire from Chesowanja, Kenya, *Nature* **294**, 125–9.

Harold, M. R., (1960) Magnetic dating: Kiln wall fall-out, *Archaeometry* **3**, 47–50.

Hassan, A. G. (1983) Archaeomagnetic investigations in Egypt: inclination and field intensity determinations, *J. Geophys.* **53**, 131–40.

Heller, F. (1980) Self-reversal of natural remanent magnetization in the Olby–Laschamp lavas, *Nature* **284**, 334–5.

Heller, F. and Markert, H. (1973) The age of viscous remanent magnetization of Hadrian's Wall, *Geophys. J. R. Astr. Soc.* **31**, 395–406.

Heller, F. and Petersen, N. (1982) The Laschamp excursion, *Phil. Trans. R. Soc. Lond.* **A306**, 169–77.

Heller, F. and Liu T–S, (1986) Palaeoclimatic and sedimentary history from magnetic susceptibility of loess in China, *Geophys. Res. Lett.* **13**, 1169–72.

Hesse, A. (1975) Contribution de la géophysique à la connaissance de l'archéologie Iranienne, *Proc. 3rd Annual Symposium on Archaeological Research in Iran*, Iranian Centre for Archaeological Research, Tehran, pp. 301–10.

Hirooka, K. (1983) Results from Japan, in *Geomagnetism of Baked Clays and Recent Sediments* (eds K. M. Creer, P. Tucholka, and C. E. Barton), Elsevier, Amsterdam, Oxford, New York, Tokyo, pp. 150–67.

Hoye, G. S. (1983) Magnetic properties of ancient coins, *Journ. of Archaeological Science* 10, 441–52.

Kawai, N. and Hirooka, K. J. (1967) Wobbling motion of the geomagnetic dipole field in historic time during these 2000 years, *J. Geomagn. Geoelect.* 19, 217–27.

Kawai, N, Hirooka, K., Nakajima, I., Tokieda, K. and Tosi, M. (1972) Archaeomagnetism in Iran, *Nature* 236, 223–4.

Kent, D. V., Ninkovich, D., Pescatore, T. and Sparks, R. J. (1981) Paleomagnetic determination of emplacement temperature of Vesuvius AD 79 pyroclastic deposits, *Nature* 290, 393–6.

Kovacheva, M. (1983) Archaeomagnetic data from Bulgaria and south eastern Yugoslavia, in *Geomagnetism of Baked Clays and Recent Sediments* (eds. K. M. Creer, P. Tucholka, and C. E. Barton), Elsevier, Amsterdam, Oxford, New York, Tokyo, pp. 106–110.

Langouet, L., Bucur, I. and Goulpeau, L. (1983) Les problèmes de l'allure de la courbe de variation séculaire du champ magnétique terrestre en France, *Revue d'Archéometrie* 7, 37–44.

Langouet, L. and Goulpeau L. (1984) La datation archéomagnétique du temple du Haut-Becherel à Corseul, *Rev. archéol. Ouest* 1, 85–8.

Latham, A. G., Schwarcz, H. P. and Ford, D. C. (1986) The paleomagnetism and U-Th dating of Mexican stalagmite, DAS2, *Earth Planet. Sci. Lett.* 79, 195–207.

Levi, S. and Merrill, R. T. (1976) A comparison of ARM and TRM in magnetite, *Earth Planet. Sci. Lett.* 32, 171–84.

Lingenfelter, R. E. (1963) Production of carbon-14 by cosmic-ray neutrons, *J. Geophys. Res.* 78, 5902–3.

Mankinen, E. A. and Dalrymple, G. P. (1979) Revised geomagnetic polarity timescale for the interval 0–5 m.y. B.P., *J. Geophys. Res.* 84, (B2), 615–26.

McDougall, I. and Tarling, D. H. (1983) The magnetic sourcing of obsidian samples from Mediterranean and Near Eastern sources, *J. Archaeological Science,* 10, 441–52.

McDougall, I., Davies, T., Maier, R. and Rudowski, R. (1985) Age of the Okote Tuff Complex at Koobi Fora, Kenya, *Nature* 316, 793–4.

Mercanton, P. (1918) Etat magnétique de quelques terres cuites préhistoriques, *C. R. Acad. Sci. Paris,* 166, 681–5.

Merrill, R. T. and McElhinny, M. W., (1983) *The Earth's Magnetic Field,* Academic Press, London, 401pp.

Néel, L. (1955) Some theoretical aspects of rock-magnetism, *Advances in Physics* 4, 191–243.

Papamarinopoulos, S. and Creer, K. M. (1983) The palaeomagnetism of cave sediments, in *Geomagnetism of Baked Clays and Recent Sediments* (eds. K. M. Creer, P. Tucholka, and C. E. Barton) Elsevier, Amsterdam, Oxford, New York, Tokyo, pp. 243–9.

Rendell, H. M., Hailwood, E. A. and Dennell, R. W. (1987) Magnetic polarity stratigraphy of Upper Siwalk Sub-Group, Soan Valley, Pakistan: implications for early human occupation of Asia, *Earth Planet. Sci. Lett.* 85, 488–96.

Rolph, T. C. and Shaw, J. (1985) A new method of palaeofield magnitude correction for thermally altered samples and its application to Lower Carboniferous lavas, *Geophys. J. R. Astron. Soc.* **80**, 773–81.

Rolph, T. C., Shaw, J., Derbyshire, E. and Wang, J. (1989) A new basal age for the loess of Lanzhou, Northern China, *Physics Earth Planet. Int. 56*, 151–164.

Runcorn, S. K. (1959) On the theory of the geomagnetic secular variation, *Ann. Geophys.* **15**, 87–92.

Sakai, H. and Hirooka, K. (1986) Archaeointensity determinations from Western Japan, *Journ. Geomag. Geoelectr.* **38**, 1323–9.

Schurr, K., Becker, H. and Soffel, H. C. (1984) Archaeomagnetic study of medieval fireplaces and ovens and the problem of magnetic refraction, *J. Geophys.* **56**, 1–8.

Shaw, J. (1974) A new method of determining the magnitude of the paleomagnetic field, *Geophys. J. R. Astron. Soc.* **39**, 133–41.

Shuey, R. T., Cole, E. R. and Mikulich, M. J. (1970) Geographic correction of archaeomagnetic data, *J. Geomagn. Geoelectr.* **22**, 485–9.

Skiles, D. D. (1970) A method of inferring the direction of drift of the geomagnetic field from paleomagnetic data, *J. Geomagn. Geoelect.* **22**, 441–62.

Sternberg, R. (1983) Archaeomagnetism in the southwest of North America, in *Geomagnetism of Baked Clays and Recent Sediments* (eds K. M. Creer, P. Tucholka, and C. E. Barton), Elsevier, Amsterdam, Oxford, New York, Tokyo, pp. 158–67.

Sternberg, R. S. and Butler, R. F. (1978) An archaeomagnetic paleointensity study of some Hohokam potsherds from Snaketown, Arizona, *Geophys. Res. Lett.* **5**, 101–4.

Sternberg, R. S. and McGuire, R. H. (1990a) Archaeomagnetic secular variation in the American Southwest, AD 700–1450, in *Archaeomagnetic Dating* (eds J. L. Eighmy and R. S. Sternberg), University of Arizona Press (in press).

Sternberg, R. S. and McGuire, R. H. (1990b) Techniques for constructing secular variation curves and for interpreting archaeomagnetic dates, *Archaeomagnetic Dating* (eds J. L. Eighmy and R. S. Sternberg), University of Arizona Press (in press).

Tanguy, J. C. (1970) An archaeomagnetic study of Mount Etna, *Archaeometry* **12**, 115–28.

Tanguy, J. C., Bucur, I. and Thompson, J. F. C. (1985) Geomagnetic secular variation in Sicily, *Nature* **318**, 453–5.

Tarling, D. H. (1982) Archaeomagnetic properties of coins, *Archaeometry* **24**, 76–9.

Tarling, D. H. (1983) *Palaeomagnetism*, Chapman & Hall, London and New York, 379pp.

Thellier, E. (1938) Sur l'aimantation de l'intensité du champ magnétique terrestre dans le passé, *Ann. Inst. Phys. Globe, Paris* **15**, 179–84.

Thellier, E. (1977) Early research on the intensity of the ancient geomagnetic field, *Phys. Earth Planet. Inter.* **13**, 241–4.

Thellier, E. (1981) Sur la direction du champ magnétique terrestre, en France, durant les deux derniers millénaires, *Phys. Earth Planet. Inter.* **24**, 89–132.

Thompson, R. and Oldfield, F. (1986) *Environmental Magnetism*, Allen & Unwin, London, 227pp.

Turner, G. M. and Thompson, R. (1981) Lake sediment record of the geomagnetic secular variation in Britain during Holocene times, *Geophys. J. R. Astron. Soc.* **65**, 703–25.

Turner, G. M. and Thompson, R. (1982) Detransformation of the British geomagnetic secular variation record for Holocene times, *Geophys. J. R. Astron. Soc.* **70**, 789–92.

Walton, D. (1977) Archaeomagnetic intensity measurements using a SQUID magnetometer, *Archaeometry* **19**, 192–200.

Weaver, G. H., (1962) Archaeomagnetic measurements on the second Boston experimental kiln, *Archaeometry* **5**, 93–107.

Wei, Q. Y., Li, T. C., Chao, G. Y., Chang, W. S., Wang, S. P. and Wei, S. F. (1983) Results from China, in *Geomagnetism of Baked Clays and Recent Sediments* (eds K. M. Creer, P. Tucholka, and C. E. Barton) Elsevier, Amsterdam, Oxford, New York, Tokyo, pp. 127–37.

Wei, Q. Y., Zhang, W. X., Li, D. J., Aitken, M. J., Bussell, G. D. and Winter, M. (1987) Geomagnetic intensity as evaluated from ancient Chinese pottery, *Nature* **328**, 330–3.

Wolfman, D. (1990a) Archaeomagnetic dating in Arkansas and the border area of adjacent states, in *Archaeomagnetic Dating* (eds. J. L. Eighmy and R. S. Sternberg), University of Arizona Press, (in press).

Wolfman, D. (1990b) Mesoamerican chronology and archaeomagnetic dating: AD 1–1200, in *Archaeomagnetic Dating* (eds J. L. Eighmy and R. S. Sternberg), University of Arizona Press, (in press).

Appendix: Radioactivity data

A.1 RADIOCARBON

The nuclear reaction by which thermal neutrons produce radiocarbon in the atmosphere is

$$^{14}N + n \rightarrow {}^{14}C + {}^{1}H \tag{A.1}$$

The cross-section is about 1.7×10^{24} cm^2. It is the dominant way in which neutrons interact with nitrogen; for oxygen the cross-section is lower by a factor of 1000. The neutrons concerned are secondary particles produced by the incidence of the primary cosmic ray flux on the atmosphere. Although they may have high energy on formation, the neutrons rapidly become thermalized by collision and because of the dominance of reaction (A.1) the effective fate of each neutron is to produce an atom of ^{14}C. It is known from high-altitude balloon measurements that the average neutron production rate is about 2/sec per cm^2 of the earth's surface; this yields a global production rate of 7.5 kg of ^{14}C per year.

Radioactive decay of ^{14}C is accompanied by the emission of a weak beta particle (maximum energy, 160 keV) according to

$$^{14}C \rightarrow {}^{14}N + \beta \tag{A.2}$$

The presently accepted value for the half-life is 5730 ± 40 years (see section 3.1.1).

A.2 POTASSIUM-40

The decay of ^{40}K is characterized by a half-life of 1250 million years, but only 10.5% of the decays lead to the formation of ^{40}Ar, the remaining 89.5% leading to ^{40}Ca; formation of ^{40}Ar is accompanied by the emission of a 1.46 MeV gamma ray and the formation of ^{40}Ca by a beta particle (maximum energy, 1.36 MeV); both ^{40}Ar and ^{40}Ca are stable.

Uranium - 238 series

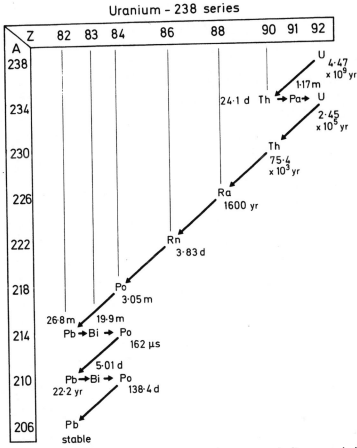

Fig. A.1 The major uranium series. A long arrow indicates emission of an alpha particle and a short one emission of a beta particle. Branching is shown except when less than 1%.

Rubidium-87
In evaluating annual dose for luminescence and ESR dating it is relevant to note that potassium is usually accompanied by rubidium and ^{87}Rb is a weak beta emitter (maximum energy 0.274 MeV) with a half-life of 49,000 million years. The potassium/rubidium ratio is typically in the region of 200 : 1; the ratio of beta doses is then about 100 : 3.

A.3 URANIUM SERIES
The major and minor series are given in Figs A.1 and A.2 respectively. The atomic abundances in natural uranium are 99.28% for ^{238}U and 0.72% for ^{235}U. Because the half-lifes are 4470 and 700 million years respectively, the activity ratio between the two series is 95.6/4.4.

Uranium - 235

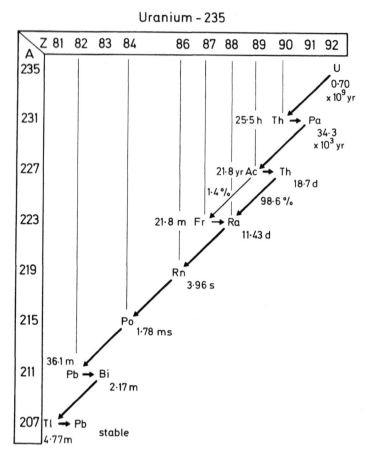

Fig. A.2 The minor uranium series. Comment as for Fig. A.1.

Annual dose; disequilibrium

Of particular interest for luminescence and ESR dating is the gas radon (^{222}Rn) which occurs half-way down the ^{238}U series. If there is complete escape of this gas from the sample then the alpha and beta contributions to the annual dose are reduced to about 45% of the no-escape value; if there is complete escape from the soil the gamma contribution is reduced to only 5% of the no-escape value. Hence if the annual dose is derived from the parent concentration (e.g. by neutron activation) it is necessary to estimate whether there has been escape of radon during burial, and if so, to what degree. This can be done by measuring either the ^{210}Pb or the ^{210}Po activity, by high-resolution gamma or alpha spectrometry respectively. Because the radioelements between ^{210}Pb and ^{222}Rn are short-lived the former stays in equilibrium with the latter and its activity is equal to the

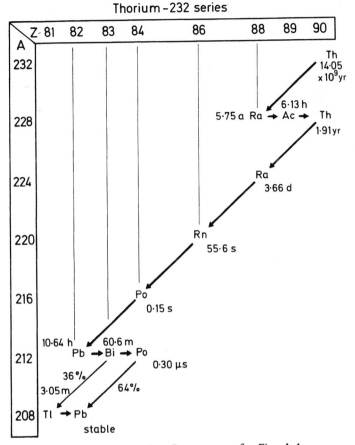

Fig. A.3 The thorium series. Comment as for Fig. A.1.

^{222}Rn activity during burial – because of the 22-year half-life its activity does not change much in the first year or two after excavation even though increased escape of radon may occur.

Some allowance for radon escape also needs to be made when the annual dose is derived by radioactivity measurements, but it is not then so critical. Ideally high-resolution spectrometry is used but it is not usually available. It has the advantage also that it checks for other types of disequilibrium such as arise from radiochemical leaching.

Gas escape in the ^{235}U series is not important because it is inhibited by the short half-life (4 sec) of the radioisotope concerned.

A.4 THORIUM SERIES

Annual dose

With this series (see Fig. A.3) complete escape of gas (^{220}Rn) causes reduction to about 40% of the no-escape value irrespective of type of radiation; although the half-life (56 s) is shorter than for ^{222}Rn substantial escape certainly occurs for some types of pottery and soil. Hence evaluation of the possible effect needs to be made and the error limits widened appropriately; unfortunately a 'memory' radioisotope is not available in this series.

Index

Page numbers in bold type indicate main entries.